"Meeting"
Anne Frank

OTHER PUBLISHED WORKS BY THE AUTHORS

Anne Talvaz

Poetry Collections

> *Le rouge-gorge américain* (1997)
> *Imagines* (2002)
> *Entre deux mers* (2003)
> *Panaches de mer, lithophytes et coquilles* (2006)
> *Confessions d'une Joconde [and] Pourquoi le Minotaure est triste* (2010)

Prose

> *Ce que nous sommes* (2008–2010)
> *Un départ annoncé, trois années en Chine* (2010)

Cara Wilson-Granat

Strength from Tragedy: Anne Frank's Father Shares His Wisdom with an American Teen (2015)

Strength from Nature: Simple Lessons of Life Taught by the Most Unlikely Masters: The Nature Teachers (2018)

Federica Pannocchia

Quando dal cielo cadevano le stelle (2016)

Joop van Wijk-Voskuijl

Bep Voskuijl, het zwijgen voorbij: een biografie van de jongste helpster van het achterhuis (republished Dutch edition, 2018)

Anne Frank the Untold Story: The Hidden Truth about Elli Vossen, the Youngest Helper of the Secret Annex (English edition, 2018)

Ryan Cooper

We Never Said Goodbye: Memories of Otto Frank (2021)

Sondra Learn

Written and Directed Plays (*award winning)

Sweet Memories (1998; *Burlington, Ontario; *Flint, Michigan)
Secrets (1999; *Leamington, Ontario; *Salem, Massachusetts)
Attics (2010)
A Harmless Game (2011)
Broken Butterfly (2012)
M. I. F. (2014) (My Invisible Friend)*
Sunshine Steps: A Story of Autism (2016)*
A Completely Different Show (2020; Zoom performance)
Rose in a Bottle (2020; Zoom performance)

Written and Directed Full-length Plays (*award winning)

Slow Down and Look (2001)*
Memory Shadows (2006)
Watching through the Window (2008)

Directed Plays

The Miracle Worker (2011)
The Diary of Anne Frank (2014)

Tim Whittome (as Simon Cambridge)

Denied! Failing Cordelia: Parental Love and Parental-State Theft in Los Angeles Juvenile Dependency Court (series)

Book One: The Cankered Rose and Esther's Revenge (2014)
Book Two: Pride and Legal Prejudice (2016)
Book Three: Climbing the Broken Judicial Ladder (2019)

"Meeting" Anne Frank

An Anthology

Edited by Tim Whittome

Foreword by Joop van Wijk-Voskuijl

Library of Congress Control Number:		2020923921
ISBN:	Hardcover	978-1-6641-4557-3
	Softcover	978-1-6641-4556-6
	eBook	978-1-6641-4555-9

Diary references to *Anne Frank: The Diary of a Young Girl* © Anne Frank-Fonds, Basel (1991 and 2002), Otto H. Frank, Mirjam Pressler, and Susan Massotty; *Definitive Edition* published by Doubleday (1995 and 2001), Puffin Books (1997), and Puffin Modern Classics (2002; reissued, 2007); online © Anchor Books by arrangement with Doubleday (2006).

Print information available on the last page.

Rev. date: 03/05/2021

To order additional copies of this book, contact:
Xlibris
844-714-8691
www.Xlibris.com
Orders@Xlibris.com
806296

We would like to dedicate this anthology to Anne and Margot Frank and to their father, Otto, who did so much after the Second World War to keep the memory of his beloved daughters alive.

*   *   *

To the memories of Johan Voskuijl and his daughter Bep Voskuijl, Miep and her husband Jan Gies, Johannes Kleiman, and Victor Kugler.

*   *   *

Thank you to Hannah ("Hanneli") Pick-Goslar, Jacqueline (Jacque) van Maarsen, Nanette ("Nanny") Blitz-Konig, and Susanne ("Sanne") Ledermann for being Anne's friends.

*   *   *

We also dedicate this anthology to the 102,000 Dutch and other Jews who never came home from Auschwitz-Birkenau and other concentration camps in occupied Europe.

*   *   *

A special thank you to Savanna Shaw who loves Anne Frank and to her father, Mat, who has inspired me to believe that Otto's love and understanding for his vibrant daughter has lived on in another compelling family. Mat and Savanna's wonderful father-daughter musical duets have helped many of us through the pain of COVID-19.

The cast, crew, and production team of the Indiana Repertory Theater and Seattle Children's Theatre production of The Diary of Anne Frank (2019).
—Miranda Antoinette Troutt

CONTENTS

Part I "Meeting" Anne Frank An Anthology

Part II Getting to Know Anne

Part III   Playing Anne: An Interview with Melina Zaccaria

Part IV   Walking with Anne

Part V   Playing Anne: An Interview with Miranda Antoinette Troutt

Part VI   Words from Cara

Part VII Endnotes and Diary References

Part VIII Bibliography, Website Resources, and Index

So let me happily say, as an Anne Frank collector, that I am a child of Anne Frank! We who have succeeded Anne in her physical demise—as her fans and followers—are her offspring and heirs.

—Pine Delgado

I do not actually recall not *knowing about Anne Frank. It seems strange to say that, but for as long as I can remember, I have known about Anne.*

—Sondra Learn

Your diary was indeed a gift to the world, but I would gladly give up that gift if only you had been able to survive the war.

—Yvonne Leslie

I truly felt like Anne was my dearest friend and talking to me from the past.

—Kirsi Lehtola

I turned the last page of Anne's diary. It had been an intense read, but I felt such a connection to her, feeling as I did as if she had written those words to me.

—Colleen Snyman

But it was not until the end of 2018 that I finally started to write my own letters to Anne . . . I tell her my feelings, my life, and my problems. I tell her everything and I feel—as Anne did with Kitty—that Anne has become my own best friend.

—Amanda Tomkins

Today, a large portrait of Otto Frank hangs in my library. It used to hang in Otto's home after his death. Fritzi would look at it and remember the man whom she loved. I look at it, and I, too, remember the man whom I was blessed to have known—the father of Anne Frank.

—Ryan Cooper

Anne taught me some of the most important life lessons, she showed me the way to writing, and she taught me to laugh.

—Anne Talvaz

FOREWORD BY JOOP VAN WIJK-VOSKUIJL

During the hiding period, Bep [Voskuijl] developed the habit of usually having lunch in the Annex. She was always welcome, especially to Anne, who demanded that Bep sit with her at the table. Apparently, Anne considered her to be a permanent fixture at the afternoon table. When she discussed the goings-on during lunch in her diary, she described Bep [Elli Vossen in Anne's diary] as well as the eight hiders [August 9, 1943]: "No. 9 is not an Annex family member, but certainly a house and table companion. Elli has a healthy appetite. Doesn't leave anything on her plate, is not picky. One can please her with anything and that pleases us. Happy and cheerful, willing and good-natured, those are her traits."
—Joop van Wijk-Voskuijl and Jeroen De Bruyn, *Anne Frank, the Untold Story*

THIS IS A quote from the biography of Bep Voskuijl, which I wrote being her youngest son, together with my coauthor Jeroen De Bruyn.[1] My grandfather, Johan Voskuijl, is the creator of the legendary revolving bookcase, and my mother was the closest friend of Anne during the twenty-five months that she was in hiding.[2]

My mother was intensely involved with, amongst others, the whole Frank family before, during, and after the Second World War. Of course, I met Otto Frank and Miep and Jan Gies many times at my parental home; and via the stories of my mother, I "met" Anne on different levels.

In fact, I am—via the new social media—still "meeting" Anne every day; I am not the only one.

"Meeting" Anne—that is what this book is all about.

All the authors are strongly connected with Anne and her ideas, and some statements in this book include

> *"Her words and her ideals were within me all the time."* (Federica Pannocchia)

> *"I saw Anne Frank as a friend I never had the chance to meet."* (Joy Gafa')

> *"I have come to view Anne more as an understanding spirit during various interesting and challenging times in my own life."* (Tim Whittome)

One of the contributors is the director of the play *The Diary of Anne Frank*.[3]

Another one was so inspired that she set up an "Anne organization," of which the highest ambition is to fight anti-Semitism.[4]

After all, the Holocaust did not take place so long ago, now did it?

Again, others looked for and found a few main characters like Miep Gies, Otto Frank, and others who *actually* knew Anne; a few were even allowed to see Anne's original diary.[5]

And last but not least, there is a priest, and he declares that "Anne Frank is still very much with us and she is, indeed, one of those great lights who can lead us out of the darkness."[6]

I experience all the contributions in this book as being sincere and genuine; partly, because I recognize the feelings and words that belong to the same.

I have a great respect for the contributors. They are not only inspired and dedicated but vulnerable at the same time—a vulnerability that, in times as insane now as they were during Anne's time, is of the utmost importance if we are to be able to meet each other in moments of depth.

Out of sincere meetings originate dear friendships, and out of these arises a loyalty to each human being.

This anthology invites you to do the same!

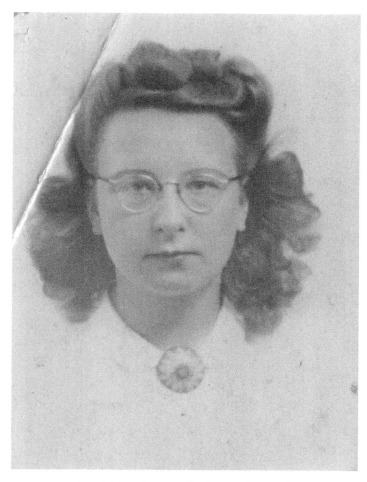

Bep Voskuijl, 1937 © Van Wijk Family

*Joop van Wijk-Voskuijl in 2014 near the famous bookcase designed and
built by his grandfather Johan Voskuijl © Joop van Wijk-Voskuijl*

Johan Voskuijl and his daughter Bep (alias Elli Vossen in the earliest editions of Anne's diary) in 1938/1939 © Van Wijk Family

*Miep Gies and Bep Voskuijl in 1945 © Anne
Frank Huis and Museum Collection*

Otto Frank and Bep Voskuijl, 1978 © Van Wijk Family

MY FRIEND, ANNE FRANK
BY AFTON COCHRAN

I first "met" Anne Frank in Mrs. Boatman's seventh-grade English lit class at Carmichael Junior High School, in Richland, Washington, in the mid-eighties. We were assigned *The Diary of a Young Girl*, and to this day, I vividly remember hanging on every word that Mrs. Boatman said about the Franks, the van Daans, Dr. Dussel, the helpers, and the Secret Annex. I read the black-and-white Penguin paperback copy of the diary from cover to cover many times until it fell apart, memorized passages from it, and even had conversations with Anne when I felt low and sad.

I remember going through the school library, desperately searching through books looking for the real names of everyone involved, as the pseudonyms were still being used and the real names not widely publicized. Anne's diary gave me strength and courage—not only through my teenage years but as an adult during my darkest times. Her words sustained me through a suicide attempt, the cancer of a child, a divorce, and being locked down during the COVID-19 epidemic of 2020, just to name a very few.

I had the wonderful opportunity of visiting the Anne Frank Huis in 1995, when it all became real to me. I stood in the rooms where she and the others lived for over two years, looked at the pasted photos on the wall of the tiny room where my dear friend Anne lived and wrote during some of her darkest times. I wept for the friend that I had lost before we could meet.

Anne Frank, my dear friend, lives on, even after her death in 1945. She lives on in my heart and the hearts of those lives whom she touched through the little checkered book.

ACKNOWLEDGMENTS

Unfortunately, there is no delete button for the mind. I would like to be able to erase everything I have lived and seen, especially all the suffering. And the suffering was not only inside me—it was outside as well. I could breathe in that suffering; it was part of my world. But then I stop and think, what good would it do to forget it all? What could I have to gain? Peace of mind? Perhaps, but it would have been a fake peace, a blind peace, because I know that forgetting is allowing others to experience the worst of your nightmares. I remember so I can stay alive, because forgetting means dying and losing my family forever.

—Nanette Blitz-Konig, *Holocaust Memoirs of a Bergen-Belsen Survivor* (2018)

[Anne] has left only a faint trail behind her. She was gracious, capricious at times, and full of ideas. She had a tender, but also a critical spirit; a special gift for feeling deeply and for fear, but also her own special kind of courage. She had intelligence, but also many blind spots; a great deal of precocity alongside extraordinary childishness; and a sound and infrangible moral sense even in the most hopeless misery. All in all, she seems to have been what the Greeks would have called a good and beautiful person.

—Ernst Schnabel, *The Footsteps of Anne Frank* (2014)

FIRST, AND MOST importantly, I would like to acknowledge the support of all my enthusiastic contributors to *"Meeting"* *Anne Frank*. Everyone has worked hard and displayed considerable heart, devotion, and patience throughout challenging times to bring this anthology before the public. The COVID-19 coronavirus, which dramatically affected the preproduction and production stages of this work, stretched everyone's personal stamina to the limit. I truly appreciate the fact that so many of my coauthors were also willing to help me by proofreading the work of others involved in the project. I assigned each of them the task of reading one other essay in addition to their own. They came through magnificently, which helped me enormously in my task of supplementing the professional editing work done by our publisher.

I am especially grateful to Joop van Wijk-Voskuijl for agreeing to write a *foreword* to this book and for his support and suggestions as to how to make the book better. Joop is also the son of Bep Voskuijl, who was one of the key helpers to Anne Frank, her family, and friends after they were forced to hide in the "Secret Annex" of her father's office at Prinsengracht 263 in Amsterdam.

Joop has written his own biography of his mother, which he referred to earlier in his foreword. Just as importantly, we must acknowledge that Joop is also the grandson of Johan Voskuijl; it was Mr. Voskuijl who designed and built the famous bookcase that helped to conceal the entrance to the Secret Annex.

I would also like to thank Cara Wilson-Granat for writing an *afterword* to this work. Cara has written and published her own book documenting her years of correspondence with Otto Frank and then of meeting him in Basel just before he died. Cara has been an enthusiastic and kind supporter of this project and has lent me invaluable support in countless ways.

In a similar vein, I would like to express my appreciation to Fr. John Neiman and to Ryan Cooper for being willing to share so many of their experiences of also meeting Otto and Fritzi Frank in Basel. Their support for this project has allowed me to understand the full importance of Otto's life and mission to keep Anne's name and ideals alive after his liberation from Auschwitz-Birkenau in January 1945. I truly envy the fact that Joop, Cara, Father John, and Ryan were each able to meet Otto and learn more about his two daughters.

Helaine Sawilowsky's wonderful artistic portraits of Anne adorn the cover of this work and I invite readers to go to her website https://HelaineSawilowsky.com to learn more. I am grateful to Helaine for patiently helping me to design the overall cover art.

My gratitude must be extended to the two "Annes" who played the young teenager in two different versions of *The Diary of Anne Frank*. I was only able to see the version with Miranda Antoinette Trout in Seattle but, sadly, not the equally well-received production with Melina Zaccaria in Hamilton, Canada. I thank them both for sharing their thoughts on how they approached such an iconic and complex role. With regard to Melina's portrayal of Anne, I must also extend my gratitude to Sondra Learn, who not only directed Melina in the role, but has written her own account of "meeting" Anne for this anthology.

* * *

No book however long, short, complex, or simple publishes itself; thus, I would also like to acknowledge the role of our publishing consultant Monique Gomez at Xlibris and our submissions representative Iris Johannsen. I have worked with Monique for many years now, and this is my fourth self-published work with Xlibris.[7]

I would also like to thank Emman Villaran and Andy Ferrer from the Xlibris copyediting team for their work on the editing and indexing stages of this book. Similarly, I must acknowledge our patient production coordinator Sheila Legaspi for her help during the all-important galley stage of production.

Self-publishing is *not* an easy endeavor, and many steps must be taken in close coordination and precise follow-up. Diligent and sometimes ponderous self-checking and the need for critical self-approval at all points along the way are the essential keys to the success of any self-published work. The reward is that of a work that has been shaped more by the author or authors involved than one where the final content and scope have been shaped by the publisher.

While this can work both for and against the author's best interests, I have always been confident that Xlibris broadly knows what is needed.

After many years of vigilant practice, I am now much more experienced in how best to navigate the various stages of preparing and approving manuscripts. Given how much is involved in scrutinizing the results prior to final publication and marketing, I have asked my fellow contributors to be as zealous in this regard as I have needed to be. I am grateful to them that they have each understood this need for vigorous self-checking.

Self-publishing is also expensive because all publishing costs must be met by the author or authors involved. This *collaborative* anthology is no different in this regard to each of my other *self*-published works. The need for marketing this anthology will reflect the fact I have largely financed the venture myself *and* that I have been unable to pay my fellow writers in advance for their contributions. I am enormously grateful to them for not even asking me about this, let alone wondering about any future royalties. This is testimony not just to their support for me but also to their love for Anne Frank and her family. None of us here wishes to commercialize Anne's legacy beyond what is reasonable given the hard work that has been involved in bringing this anthology to a public that has long been fascinated with her life. I also know that this is a strong area of concern not just to Anne's one-time "best friend" Jacqueline van Maarsen but also to the Anne Frank Huis and Museum in Amsterdam and to the Anne Frank-Fonds (Foundation) in Basel.[8]

*   *   *

Given that this work should be published in 2020, I should mention that COVID-19 became an uninvited and unwanted guest just as I was about to send our manuscript for initial content evaluation and copyediting. In line with the extensive shutdown process that has affected most of the world's economy, Xlibris was forced to severely limit the number of staff available to help their authors. This necessarily delayed the final publishing of our book, and again, I must thank both Xlibris and my fellow authors for their patience in this regard.

On the positive side, it *did* allow me to add both Anne Talvaz and Afton Cochran to our book from France and the United Kingdom, respectively. They have both made it known to me that they are very excited to see this work in print. Elsewhere, Joy Gafa' now has a whole group of eager school friends, school staff, and relatives hoping for a signed copy at her school on the Mediterranean island of Malta. Her school assistant principal is very excited, and I hope that we will have not let any of her school down with our final effort.

*   *   *

Lastly, much love as always must go to my beloved mother, who died during the final editing stages of this book from the tragedy of Alzheimer's. It crashed into me like a hurtling train leaving its rails, and it hurts me that she will never be aware that I have edited and contributed to this special project. I firmly believe that she would have loved what we have come up with here. She will one day run to greet me in heaven as she would so often run up the arrival escalator at SeaTac Airport when she first saw me on the occasion of her yearly visits to Seattle.

FORMATTING OF DUTCH NAMES

B Y WAY OF an apology to Dutch readers of our anthology, please forgive any remaining errors of Dutch capitalization or names in this work. Many of these concerns also apply to the formatting of German names.

I have done my best to be as accurate and faithful as possible to the Dutch language, but English editions of Anne Frank's diary and works about her life and times in the Netherlands are notoriously inconsistent in terms of how they refer to Dutch names. Speaking as someone who sits on the fussier end of the autism spectrum, this level of inconsistency became a big problem for me. Notwithstanding, I hope that our readers will agree with me that the following locations and words sound much nicer and more respectful in their proper Dutch!

Thus, I have seen both the "*van* Pels family" in use and the "*Van* Pels family"; I have seen "Mr. *Van* Pels" and "Mr. *van* Pels." My understanding based on asking others more familiar with Dutch is that the *van* is always lowercased unless it starts a sentence. In this work, I have chosen to use "Mr. van Pels" or his full name of "Hermann van Pels" to refer to the character whom Anne Frank refers to as "Mr. van Daan" in her diary. In English and following the current publishing guidelines of the latest edition of the *Chicago Manual of Style*, this will probably look confusing as we usually capitalize the first letter of the first word after a period.

As far as the names of Anne's friends are concerned, I have used their "proper" names only when referring to their published memoirs or autobiographies. Hanneli Goslar published her memoirs under her proper name of "Hannah." Because she would have been known to Anne as "Hanneli" (or "Hanne"), I have elected to use her nickname to refer to her in non-publishing contexts. The same with Susanne Ledermann. Susanne didn't get the chance to publish any memoirs as she was killed in Auschwitz in November 1943, but while she lived, Anne would have known her as "Sanne."

Turning to the formal names of Anne and Margot's schools in Amsterdam, I have seen references to Anne attending the "6th Montessori School" (English) and the "6e Montessorischool" (Dutch). I decided to go with the lovely Dutch variant. With respect to Margot's different primary school, I have elected to use the Dutch "Jekerschool" in place of the English "Jeker School."

Margot then attended the "Gemeentelijk Lyceum voor Meisjes" (the Municipal Lyceum for Girls in English). I have decided to retain the full Dutch name as shown. I have also not lowercased the word *Meisjes* as the word seems to be part of the formal name for the school and is shown on photographs from the time as such.

After the Germans decreed in 1941 that all Jewish children could only attend Jewish schools, both Anne and Margot were forced to attend the Jewish Lyceum on Voormalige Stadstimmertuinen. Unfortunately, I have also seen the name of this school referenced in lowercase as in "the Jewish lyceum." Since Anne and Margot both went to *the* Jewish Lyceum—which suggests that it was a formal name for the school— and not *a* Jewish lyceum, I have decided to retain the capitalization as shown. Although this is how the school appears in many reliable sources, Melissa Müller chose to use the lowercase version in her equally reliable biography of Anne and her family. Readers may respond as they deem appropriate to this issue. I am sure that it is a pedantic point!

To complicate things further, the Jewish Lyceum is attributed in most of my sources as being on "Voormalige Stadstimmertuinen" in Amsterdam, while Google Earth refers to the street as "Voormalige Stadstimmertuin" with no final *en*. Although a Dutch street sign for the road shows the name as "Voormalige Stadstimmertuin," it is possible that this could be an updated spelling. As other streets in Amsterdam have been renamed since the war after Dutch resistance heroes such as Gerrit van der Veenstraat and allied leaders such as Roosevelt and Churchill, why not this one?

With respect to the formal Dutch name of the "Anne Frank Stichting" in Amsterdam, I decided to mix Dutch and English and use the phrase "Anne Frank Huis and Museum" as opposed to any purer English reference to the "Anne Frank House and Museum." Informally, the former office location of the Secret Annex (Prinsengracht 263) is known simply as the "Anne Frank House." Technically, the property managed by the Anne Frank Stichting comprises both the main *huis* as well as the museum.

The Franks' former address of "Merwedeplein 37" is retained in its original and meaningful Dutch and has not been changed (complete with added space) to "Merwede Square 37." The house number is usually shown in Dutch *after* the name of the street; thus, I have decided to refer to "Prinsengracht 263" and "Merwedeplein 37" throughout this text and not to their reverse variants. Readers should be aware, though, that both ways of referring to these iconic addresses are in usage across the many sources that I have reviewed.

Where Dutch (and also German) names are used infrequently in the text—such as *Oase* as the name of one of Anne's favorite ice-cream vendors and *Sicherheitsdienst* as the name of the German SS security service—I have used italics as shown. Other frequently used words—such as Opekta as the name of Otto Frank's business—are *not* italicized *except* at the time of their first mention in the main text.

*   *   *

Our goal throughout this anthology has been to support and respect the Dutch language and other phraseology wherever possible. In the following pages you will read about Amanda Tompkins's efforts to learn Dutch so that she can eventually be able to read *Het achterhuis* in its original language. I fully support her in this endeavor.

Finally, this anthology is dedicated in no small measure to the Dutch who suffered so much during the Hunger Winter ("Hongerwinter") of 1944–45, and in the confusion of the immediate aftermath of liberation in May 1945.

SEPTEMBER 2020

EARLIER THIS FEBRUARY and March 2020, many of us in the "Anneverse" paused to reflect on the fact that seventy-five years ago, Anne Frank died in the Bergen-Belsen concentration camp of virulent typhus, with a severe lack of food, medical attention, and clothing having weakened her resistance to the disease plaguing the camp. Anne was still *only* fifteen years old. Her dreams of becoming a journalist or author after the war and a full Dutch citizen would die with her. The exact date of Anne's death is unknown.

Her older sister Margot died just a few days earlier at the age of nineteen, or was she still only eighteen? As Anne had noted in her diary entry for May 8, 1944, Margot had once hoped to be able to "nurse newborns" in Palestine after the war. Future babies and their parents would not get the chance of seeing this bright and talented young lady. The exact date of Margot's death is also unknown.

*   *   *

Ironically, considering how both Anne and Margot died from typhus in 1945, I began my final preparations for this work against a backdrop of COVID-19, another virulent disease that to date (September 2020) has killed over 200,000 people in the United States alone. It has also made many across the world even more attuned to the restrictive circumstances of Anne's life while she and her family and their chosen friends were in hiding for twenty-five months. If *Anne* could manage to survive locked away between July 6, 1942 and August 4, 1944, then so can *we* cope without complaint in our self-isolation, quarantining, and inability to go anywhere. Although no one is currently suggesting that our isolation will also last twenty-five months, it has *not* stopped anyone from feeling frustrated and angry any more than the obviously even more restrictive circumstances stopped Anne from experiencing and exploring similar feelings.

Earlier this April 2020, we were living in a world where our prime ministers, presidents, and governors were issuing advisory notices and incremental restrictions on most business, social, and sporting activity. We were asked to self-isolate and self-quarantine if we felt sick, social distance if we were well, and to work from home if we could and if were not deemed "essential" to be on the "front lines." This would all be for "two weeks," "thirty days," or "six or eight weeks" when I first wrote this. The possible timeline kept changing in line with shifting scientific and medical knowledge.

Schools and public libraries closed; the airlines were forced to fly with mostly empty planes or ones filled with personal protective equipment; regular flight schedules were reduced to a bare skeleton; restaurants, theaters, coffee shops, and bars had to close; sporting events and seasons were suspended; gatherings of two or more households were banned; we were asked to wear masks; stores plunged into a confusing process of implementing evolving restrictive measures to protect their customers and their staff. One of my local favorite stores changed its procedures weekly and my local post office had everything short of sandbags to keep their staff protected from their anxious customers. Disinfectant wipes flew off the shelves and face masks and other coverings flew in.

The closures and the numbers of people impacted changed almost daily, and we were facing a recession of catastrophic proportions. It was decreed that many businesses, theaters, and restaurants would probably never return.

Steeped as I had been in reading about Anne Frank and the incremental nature of the proclamations introduced against the Jewish population of the Netherlands during the Second World War, it was far too easy for me to equate Anne's frustrations with what the coronavirus had reduced us to feeling. Many have asked those complaining to consider that Anne and her family had to endure this level of isolation for twenty-five months with restrictions on their normal activity for several years before that. How is this remotely comparable to the present?

However much our frustrations and anger might *feel* the same, most everything is really very different because we get told how many weeks and months that we will probably need to "hide" or be in self-isolation at any given moment. Anne had *no* idea how long she would need to remain in social isolation, and the occupying German authorities were certainly not likely to tell her or any other Jew. Hence the greater highs of optimistic hopes for eventual freedom (such as after the D-Day landings in June 1944) and the greater lows of entrenched fear and self-critical despair that would gather around Anne like vultures after sharp arguments with her family and others in the Secret Annex.

In my view, the similarities between how Anne coped during her own enforced lockdown and how many of us are coping today stop well short of the presumed union of the respective circumstances. Anne and her family could *never* leave their hidden home. The reasonable rules surrounding brief exercise and access to essentials such as food and medicine that we have in 2020, simply did not apply to Anne because of other prejudicial rules that said that she and other Jews in occupied Amsterdam were undesirable and suitable only for deportation. There is *no* risk in 2020 of anyone dying under deliberate circumstances in extermination camps.

From July 1942, *none* of Anne's friends knew for certain where she was. It was considered far too risky for them to hear about her from those who did continue to see her in hiding. Thanks to a decoy trail left behind at Merwedeplein 37, Anne's friends imagined that she and her family had fled in haste to Switzerland via Belgium, not seemingly pausing to consider the sheer unlikelihood of them being able to get to either country safely or without considerable help.

In 1942, Zoom, Facebook, Messenger, and other text, visual, and IM messaging services obviously did not exist. Anne and her friends were completely isolated from one another. Indeed, during the first few months in hiding, Anne not only wrote a letter *to* her best friend Jacqueline van Maarsen that she could not then post, but she also had to pretend that she had heard back *from* her.

By July 2020, the lockdown restrictions that we had been living with for almost four months began to lift with varying degrees of speed and appropriateness in our respective states and countries. A summer of reasonable optimism that corners had been turned in most states and countries led to hopes of a return to a modified and moderated normality. The United Kingdom introduced an "approved" but always changing list of COVID-successful countries that travelers could visit via government-approved "air bridges." Just as importantly, no one would need to quarantine for two weeks on their return from these "safe" countries. This list did *not* include the United States and countries could be added to or dropped from the approved list on a weekly basis and sometimes with little warning. The news would then be filled with British tourists scrambling to return home *before* the new restrictions would have to make them quarantine on their return.

As of September 2020, COVID-19 looks to be returning to Europe and the United States as part of a punishing "second wave." The United Kingdom has promised not to reimpose a "national lockdown," but rather a localized "whack-a-mole" response. The response here in the United States remains confused and steeped in partisan wrangling and tedious mask wars. The United States remains on the United Kingdom's list of "unapproved" countries and much of Europe (including the Netherlands) has joined us.

Yet we *still* compare ourselves with the privations and isolated experiences of Anne Frank, her family, and her friends for the duration of time that they were able to survive in the occupied Netherlands during the Second World War. In *Much Ado About Nothing* by William Shakespeare, Dogberry misquotes the familiar saying of "comparisons are odious." I think we can leave the subject there.

PART I

"Meeting" Anne Frank
An Anthology

Her story means a lot. It's profound. And hard to articulate or paraphrase, especially in modern culture.

—Bob Dylan on why he included a reference to Anne Frank in his recent song, "I Contain Multitudes"; interview with Douglas Brinkley, *New York Times*, June 12, 2020; updated June 18, 2020: https://www. nytimes.com/2020/06/12/arts/music/bob-dylan-rough-and-rowdy-ways.html

It is correct that she wanted to be a writer. That I remember. It started early with her, very early . . . and I imagine she might very well have become one. She was able to experience more than other children, if you know what I mean. I might almost put it that she heard more, the soundless things too, and sometimes she heard things whose very existence we have almost forgotten. That happens with children, you know.

—Mr. van G[elder]) (Anne's first-grade teacher) in conversation with Ernst Schnabel, *The Footsteps of Anne Frank* (1958; 2014)

EDITOR'S PREFACE

MUCH HAS OBVIOUSLY been written about the life and death in horrific circumstances of *Annelies Marie Frank*, or Anne Frank as she is better known throughout the world. Millions have read *Anne Frank: The Diary of a Young Girl* since its original Dutch edition was published in 1947 as *Het achterhuis: Dagboekbrieven 12 Juni–1 Augustus 1944*. Over the years, it has been published in a myriad of world languages.[9]

As a result, the decision to publish *another* new book, produce and perform *another* play from a *different* perspective, write the script for *another* documentary or film, or write *another* musical about Anne's life when so much exists already in these respective formats, should not be taken lightly. It should also be humbling because Anne is such an iconic historical figure, a protected and valued Dutch treasure, and someone whom so many across the world identify with and claim to "know."

There is also a risk of adding another book that will end up disappointing someone with a preconceived idea of who Anne was, adding little to what we know already, and even of overly hyping her fame without justification. The latter risks leading some of her more ardent followers to further obsess about someone who carries enough burdens already. I have wanted to avoid this in this anthology since my contributors and I have been at some pains to humanize Anne in our stories and pay tribute not just to her, but also to Margot, Otto, Edith, and the other hiders in the Secret Annex, and to their six helpers. By focusing and then dispersing the spotlight, we can both honor Anne's reputation *and* identify ourselves with those around her in healthy and positive ways.

I have had similar issues with another iconic figure who means a lot to me: Bob Dylan. There are *hundreds* of books about Bob Dylan, and he is one of those public figures whom many wish to define in accord with their own sensibilities and then impress with their obvious sincerity and dedication. In many ways, these processes are not dissimilar to how many try to define the memory of Anne Frank and then impress others with their commitment.

In my view, neither Bob Dylan nor Anne Frank *needs* to be impressed by anyone, and there is a huge risk involved in trying to define both beyond their basic humanity and merits. That said, both *do* still deserve most of the accolades that they receive. I don't know whether Anne Frank would have ever won a Nobel Prize for Literature, but Dylan did receive one, and he deserved it for achievements in his literary and musical field. Although it is not *impossible* that Anne might have received a Nobel for literary endeavor, it is more likely that she would have gone down the road of getting prizes for journalism if she had lived, since becoming a journalist was one of her "greatest" wishes.[10] This is overly speculative.

Anne's memory has been preserved not just in the dedicated publishing of her own words, but in autobiographies written by those who knew her from school and elsewhere and in biographies written by scholarly admirers devoted to keeping her life and message alive.

We also have the efforts of museums and conferences dedicated to documenting and reminding us of the horrors of the Holocaust or Shoah from Anne's perspective, to say nothing of the many statues that exist around the world, the plays, the documentaries, and the films made on a regular basis about her brief life and tragic end.

Even saplings from the horse chestnut tree that Anne could see from the attic windows of the Secret Annex have been preserved in cities and parks across the world. Where I live in Seattle has one, and it is a tangible reminder for me, and for others who visit it, of a small part of the world as Anne would have witnessed it while she was in hiding. Seattle's sapling flourishes, as I hope others are doing elsewhere; otherwise, it will feel as if Anne will die a second time if we lose these young and growing trees. I will be talking more about the saplings in my own story for this anthology.

*   *   *

Whether directly or indirectly, anyone who once knew Anne during her years of being a child living freely in the triangular square outside her Amsterdam home on Merwedeplein, of being a trapped teenager trying to keep herself together while in hiding, and of being an arrested Jewish girl desperately trying to survive with her parents and sister in the last seven months of her life, has also become a source of fascination.[11] Only recently, when reading *We All Wore Stars* by Theo Coster, did I realize that many of Anne's surviving school friends have equally fascinating tales to tell about their own lives and survival in hiding in the occupied Netherlands during the Second World War. These friends are rightly interesting in their own right regardless of whether they once knew Anne well or did not have much contact with her.[12]

Of these friends, only Anne, by virtue of tragic historical circumstances and through the love of her surviving father determined to preserve her memory through publishing her diary and speaking to others about her message, has become famous across much of the world. It is no disrespect to Anne to suggest that her current fame has both surprised and *not* surprised those who knew her as both an ordinary schoolgirl and as someone with a clearly precocious talent for broadcasting her many talents and defining her identity. In her diary, Anne writes a lot about her growing self-awareness as a teenager, which is why so many of us (children and adults) now feel as if we *know* her. It is also why so many teenage girls find her story and words so powerful as a way of understanding their own adolescent dreams and desire for self-fulfillment.

From a fictional perspective, Jane Austen succeeded in a comparable way with Miss Elizabeth Bennet's timelessness as a role model in *Pride and Prejudice*. Some voices are *easily* recognizable and timeless, and from a literary perspective, it is fair to say that both Anne Frank and Jane Austen have been able to reach similar audiences with their respective works.

While Jacqueline van Maarsen believes that Anne would have loved and relished her fame because she so enjoyed being the center of attention, Theo Coster makes it clear that we should also view Anne as *one* of the *102,000* Jews and other political prisoners who died during the Holocaust after having passed through the Nazi-run transit camp of Kamp Westerbork. This camp (which was formerly used as a Jewish refugee camp in the Dutch northeast province of Drenthe) would be used by the Nazis during the Second World War as a transfer staging point for Dutch Jews and other prisoners prior to their further selection for further weekly transports to labor and extermination camps in Germany, Poland, and elsewhere.[13]

None of these remarks should be taken as part of any effort to diminish Anne's suffering, of course, or to take anything away from the lasting impact of her story; however, we do need to contextualize it by noting that there *were* many others (children and adults) who died after being rounded up in raids or betrayed while in hiding. I am confident that if Anne had survived, she too would have recognized everything that I have just said.

It is also not too much of a stretch to suggest as well that *We All Wore Stars* could well have been the type of book that Anne Frank *might* have written if she had survived. I can imagine her wanting to rally her surviving friends (as Mr. Coster did) to read them early drafts of just such a book and then of inviting them to tell her their own wartime stories for inclusion!

What This Anthology *Is*

In preparing this project, I needed to get around the fact that books about Anne for all ages and interests are ubiquitous. Some are full of pictures of Anne growing up as the writer places her life in a richly historical and pictorial context; others are scholarly biographies or works that look at Anne's diary as a literary and historical artefact; not a few take her life as background to the suffering that she and millions of others endured during the Second World War. I have read, often loved, and always appreciated each one for what they add to my understanding of Anne's world, the suffering of the Jews in the Netherlands, and the wider suffering of the Jews throughout occupied Europe.[14]

The digital- and social-media age that we now inhabit prompted me to think of a "new" way of approaching Anne's story—through the expressed thoughts and feelings of those who wish they *could* have met her and become her friend. I felt that this hope could just as easily be extended to wanting to walk with Anne's shadowy sister Margot and her suffering mother Edith. Both sister and mother have needed to be led into the light by those who have come to love them as much as they love Anne and her father. Although we will not be ignoring her declared ambivalent feelings, most of us here will be recognizing that Anne was very much *Margot's* sister and *Edith's* daughter and that both are interesting and compelling in their own right.

The Anne Frank who appears in this anthology will come across as someone with whom you might want to share a lavish picnic after a long and chatty stroll among the protecting trees and the colorful wildflowers. Such enlightening walks have been cherished by many a well-loved character in Victorian literature and I believe that it is not stretching the point to argue that many of my fellow writers have imagined themselves doing the same here with regard to walking with Anne.

Deciding to take many walks with Anne, and with her diary acting as our starting point, has allowed us to share stories that either involve her or other members of her family in very personal and imaginative ways. I also think that it is fair to say that no one writing for this anthology has wanted to say goodbye to her, and this is what I hope for from our readers as well. Anne continues to shape our way of looking at the world; in our imagination, there is no setting sun on our regard.

On one level, the decision to write my own contribution and then collate the efforts of others involved in this anthology constituted a departure for me from the core mission of my earlier published *Denied! Failing Cordelia* trilogy. That series had documented my struggles to advocate for my adopted daughter in a world ignorant of her needs and overly willing to discredit my own efforts.

On another level, though, my contributors and I throughout this anthology have chosen to capture similar feelings of needless struggle, painful loss, and callous robbery that can be consequential to actions taken by others absorbed by feelings of irrational hatred and targeted prejudice.

My contributors and I have chosen to explore the overwhelming sense of having been robbed. We have done so by identifying the continuing loss on a daily basis of the insight, humor, and warmth of Anne Frank and others like her following the prejudicial actions taken by Nazi occupying authorities across occupied Europe. I decided to approach my new endeavor in a spirit of acknowledging how the childhood and teenage aspirations of Anne to be a writer and of Margot to be a midwife in Palestine were extinguished by irrational ways of seeing. I also wanted to acknowledge how the parenting achievements and hopes of Otto, Edith, and parents like them were likewise extinguished.

In thinking about presenting Anne and Margot in this way, my intention in my own submission, at least, was to show how my "meeting" Anne and acknowledging the prejudice that surrounded her affected my understanding of what happened to my daughter in Los Angeles. However strange that it might look to others, it was not hard for me linking aspects of Anne's story to my own.

However, this anthology is not just about *my* journey, but about how my fellow contributors "met" Anne Frank and then chose to walk with her and other members of her family in the years since.

It will become abundantly clear as we move forward that many writing for this anthology have recognized in Otto Frank the epitome of the type of father who they may have been lucky to have had in their lives. I am sure that some of our readers will feel the same after reading this work, while others will doubtless be thinking that they *wish* they could have had an "understanding Otto" in their own lives. It wouldn't need to be a *father* necessarily, but one *parent* at least. While Otto loved both his daughters, he *really* understood Anne and she loved him for it.

Sadly, and as already noted, we will only be "meeting" Anne through the words and thoughts of those who never knew her personally. Nevertheless, we *will* be able to get closer to her through the testimony of Joop van Wijk-Voskuijl, Cara Wilson-Granat, Fr. John Neiman, and Ryan Cooper, who were each lucky enough to have met Otto Frank. Priscilla Smits has been lucky enough over the years to have met many of those who knew Anne as their friend as well as Buddy Elias, who was Anne's cousin. Federica Pannocchia was also able to write to Buddy and is still friends with Hanneli Pick-Goslar, who was one of Anne's earliest friends and her nearest neighbor on the Merwedeplein in Amsterdam. Anne's best friend, Jacqueline van Maarsen, and a former classmate, Nanette Blitz-Konig, are both still alive at time of writing and some of my contributors have met both. So, we do have *some* direct connections to Anne. Just as importantly, Eva Schloss is still alive, and she became Anne's posthumous stepsister when her mother married Otto in November 1953.

*   *   *

We obviously now live in a quite different age to Anne Frank. Actual *written* diaries and journals, and *written*, *stamped*, and *mailed* letters were extremely important and highly valued in Anne's time. These, along with the telephone, were the chief means of communicating. Several of Anne's letters have survived, and you can read them in *Anne Frank: The Collected Works*; full publishing details are in our bibliography.

In this age of passionate social media and instant communication via Messenger, text, Facebook, Twitter, and email, it is very easy to convince ourselves and others that our strong feelings on historical figures and events can easily break down any remaining barriers of time and the lack of direct knowledge that may otherwise exist. We all feel as if we *must* have known Anne in some capacity because of the love and energy that she inspires in us.

As a result, it should be very easy for readers to imagine how Anne Frank is viewed by most here and by others elsewhere in the "Anneverse" as the *best friend, girlfriend, sister, daughter, mother,* or *spouse* we may be needing in our own lives. It is also possible that some readers may even relate to the impression given by contemporary observers that Anne may have been viewed as one of the "mean girls" on Merwedeplein.[15] Although no one writing here seriously believes in this side of her, we do acknowledge that Anne was *not* a saint while she was still alive, but, instead, a sentient human being who died in tragic circumstances and with a considerable promise left unfulfilled.

Joop noted some of these complex feelings in his own foreword to this anthology, and I included some aspirational lines as opening epigraphs from some of my other contributors. While these roles may seem like they would be an incredible burden for Anne, I have a feeling that she would not *totally* shy away from welcoming the spirit of any of these expectations had she survived the Holocaust, published her own work, and was still alive to meet my contributors and me.

I know I have personally felt such wish fulfillment with respect to many famous people and events from history and literature. How great it would be if I could go back to the time of Queen Victoria and Prince Albert and tell them that they saved the monarchy after the dissolute reigns of their immediate Hanoverian predecessors! How wonderful it would feel if I could have stopped the assassinations of President Kennedy in 1963 and then his brother Bobby in 1968 and then become friends with both in the process! At university, I was especially passionate about a former Labour Party leader Hugh Gaitskell. I well remember writing to his chief biographer at Oxford University and trying not to be overly gushing. Many of the above were highly flawed in certain areas of their lives, but they were heroes nevertheless and they defined the age they inhabited.

Elsewhere, and in the realm of literature, Anne Brontë, who died in May 1849, is *still* my favorite heroine from the world of literature after first reading her work thirty years ago. Bob Dylan has been my musical hero for forty years now. The best heroes teach, and the most receptive of their followers can learn a lot from them. We weave their inspiration into the tapestry of our daily lives—threads that we unravel each night when we sleep so that we can weave them again the next day into a tapestry that will only finish with the end of our lives.

Anne Frank easily takes a deserved place in my extensive roster of people worthy of love or acknowledgment. As I often do when reading about Senator Robert Kennedy's last campaign in 1968 or when contemplating the early deaths of Emily Brontë in 1848 and Anne Brontë in 1849, each time I read a work about Anne Frank, I keep hoping that her tragic end will somehow end differently. It does not happen, of course, but the longing still makes my heroes live beyond their allotted time and helps to frame their overall standing in my life.

For me, this magical thinking—which may seem almost childish and unrealistic in its naivety—extends to regularly daydreaming about famously fictional heroines. Whether it be Elizabeth Bennet from *Pride and Prejudice*, Maggie Tulliver from *The Mill on the Floss*, Tess from *Tess of the D'Urbervilles*, Anne Shirley from *Anne of Green Gables*, or Hermione Granger from the Harry Potter series, I relate best to figures who are complex, vibrant, imaginative, tragic, courageous, or loving. In her own life, Anne Frank displayed each of these ennobling characteristics, and my fellow scribes will be acknowledging this understanding as part of their own contributions to this anthology.

We need the spirit of Anne more than ever during these uncertain times of COVID-19, political partisanship, and deep social trauma. Does Anne speak to these aspects of modern life, or should she remain as silent and unavailable for comment as the German field under which she and her sister are now buried? We hopefully go some way toward addressing some of these questions in our journeys with her and other members of her family. We do not need to resolve them, though, to connect with Anne and her family since each writer's journey has been their own, and for many of our readers it will be the same. Walking with Anne involves traveling a highway with many lanes, pleasant shortcuts, and interesting detours.

*   *   *

I was inspired to write this work and collate the submissions of my fellow contributors by the obvious fervor surrounding Anne Frank on at least two Facebook groups dedicated to her lasting influence:

https://www.facebook.com/groups/annefrankbookclub/
https://www.facebook.com/groups/RememberingAnneFrank

The first of the above, the "Anne Frank Book Collectors' Club," is managed by Pine Delgado, who will be telling us more about his inspiration for collecting works about Anne in all media later in this work; the second, "Remembering Anne Frank," is dedicated to Anne's memory and inspiration. The group regularly posts iconic pictures of Anne and her family.

Thinking that it might be a good idea to try to capture powerful lightning in a literary bottle, I reached out to two of the groups and then invited my eventual contributors to address how they first "met" Anne and how they have continued to be inspired by her life and words in the years since. I challenged them to talk freely about when they first found and read Anne's diary, and then to talk about how they were subsequently inspired to learn more about her. This would naturally include any efforts that my coauthors might have made to follow in Anne's known footsteps around Amsterdam and elsewhere. Sadly, not all of us have yet had the chance to visit the city; but with respect to those of my coauthors who have, I was interested to hear whether they had visited Merwedeplein 37 in the River District or Quarter (*Rivierenbuurt*) of Amsterdam where Anne lived from 1934 to 1942 as well as the two schools most associated with her—the *6e Montessorischool* (now renamed as the *6e Montessorischool Anne Frank*) and the *Jewish Lyceum*. There will be far more on Anne's life on Merwedeplein and both these schools later.

I am not sure if we can count the location of the famous Secret Annex behind Prinsengracht 263 as a *residence*, but for the purposes of following in Anne's footsteps the term will suffice. It *is* the place that is most associated with her today.

I also challenged my contributors to talk about any wider visits that they might have made to Kamp Westerbork, to Auschwitz-Birkenau, or to Bergen-Belsen where Anne and Margot both died within days of one another from typhus and starvation; however, I did ask that they *only* talk about their visits to these places because of what they read and knew of Anne's tragic journey and not for any other reasons of curiosity about the Holocaust.

At this point, I should pay respectful tribute to Ernst Schnabel, whose early and important pioneering work on tracing Anne's footsteps influenced many of my contributors to follow in their own footsteps through Anne's world.[16]

Many younger readers should appreciate the ardor felt by my contributors for someone whose wider historical context and meaning they will be learning about in their schools and elsewhere. This anthology should help them to recognize how the tragic context and lessons of Anne Frank's life affected my writers' understanding of their own lives and aspirations. Many readers will be aware of some of these lessons already as Anne's idealism and message are telegraphed extremely effectively on lots of social media, through cultural events, in museum displays, and through the work of many organizational platforms. Federica Pannocchia will be explaining more about her own such organization shortly. It does not take much effort to find out *something* about Anne, her diary, or what happened to her. It takes *more* effort, though, to find a greater transformative personal meaning, and this is what my writers and I have done here in this anthology.

While *"Meeting" Anne Frank* clearly centers on Anne's life and her inspirational legacy, I must stress again that we also pay deserving tribute to her forgotten sister Margot, to her maligned mother Edith, and to her much-ridiculed roommate in the Secret Annex, Dr. Fritz Pfeffer. Each has been unfairly ignored and even slighted over the years, with Anne being sadly responsible through some of her more barbed diary commentary for much of the negativity surrounding them.

Although Otto clearly had a special bond with his younger daughter, no one has ever said that he did not love Margot any the less for being easier to manage and less trouble to him as a parent. Margot will glow brighter in this tribute, and our understanding of Anne's world will be the better for it. Margot has all too often resembled an interesting but distant star transmitting her light only to those with powerful telescopes compared to the blazing and easily seen meteor that is Anne. Yet both exist whether we just look up at the night sky for Anne or use high-powered telescopes to find Margot and Edith. After reading this book, I am hopeful that just regular binoculars will be sufficient.

Similarly, and Anne's opinion notwithstanding, no one should take away the impression that Otto found his wife insufferable or unlovable or that she was anything less than interesting and courageous in her own right. Edith Frank will also glow warmly in this book, and her suffering was truly heartbreaking at the end of her life.

Likewise, we must recognize that Dr. Pfeffer was the only occupant of the Secret Annex who did not have *any* family members on hand to confide in. A kinder view of Anne's "Mr. Dussel" would recognize that he was lonely and as much of a romantic in some respects as Anne herself. It seems strange that she would not have recognized this given her own generous and warm nature. As I will be noting later, many have attributed Anne's frustration to the sleeping arrangements of the Secret Annex and to Dr. Pfeffer being invited to share Anne's room in place of Margot.

What This Anthology Is *Not*

I did *not* want *"Meeting" Anne Frank* to become yet another book about the technical and other atrocities of Nazi labor and death camps, given that both have been well documented in films and other works on the Holocaust. I took the view that because Anne Frank managed to survive not just the immediate selection process that took place on her arrival at Auschwitz-Birkenau on September 6, 1944, but also the ultimate horrors, we did not need to dwell on the "technical" side of the nightmare. As it happened, neither Anne nor Margot was at Auschwitz for long as both girls were transported to Bergen-Belsen in late October or early November 1944. There is some speculation that both *could* have survived to liberation if they had remained in Auschwitz and not been forced to another camp.

This anthology is also *not* a work of original scholarly research about Anne and her family and does not pretend to be. I do, though, make copious use of well-received secondary sources and important websites to help us understand more of Anne's world as well as the wider suffering of the Jewish population in the Netherlands. Melissa Müller's biography of Anne and Carol Ann Lee's biography of Otto have been invaluable resources in this regard and readers can find publishing details for both in our bibliography.

What did surprise me, though, as I was working on this project, was the lack of much factual consistency across the sources available. Two of the silliest that I have seen is that Anne died when she was "sixteen," which would have meant that she survived not just the liberation of Bergen-Belsen in April 1945, but also the end of the Second World War itself in May 1945. Anne was only *fifteen* when she died. Another claimed that Otto and Edith were married in "September 1925," which would have meant that Margot would have been conceived out of wedlock, given that she was born the following February 16, 1926. Otto and Edith were married earlier on May 12, 1925. Other factual discrepancies, such as where Margot went to primary school in Amsterdam and what happened to Otto's companies *Opekta* and *Pectacon* during the Second World War, will be noted as they arise. I will be doing my best throughout to present our readers with *only* the most reliable information for readers.

Although this journey with Anne has extended to wanting to learn more about the Dutch who suffered with her in the Netherlands during the Second World War, there is *no* original research on this subject either.

Just as importantly, this anthology chooses *not* to speculate or offer any confirmed opinions as to who *might* have betrayed the eight occupants of the Secret Annex on August 4, 1944. There is enough speculation out there already, and readers who are interested can consult comprehensive works by Melissa Müller, Carol Ann Lee, and our own Joop van Wijk-Voskuijl among others.[17] I will only say on this point that I believe that Otto always knew who betrayed his family and friends but that he decided not to expose the person or persons involved. Nor does Otto appear to have borne any grudges for what happened to him and his family during the Second World War. At time of writing, a new Cold Case Diary forensic effort is underway to try to prove conclusively who might have betrayed the occupants of the Secret Annex. While the findings are not yet published, readers can find further information on this effort in our website resources.

Although I later provide important web links outlining some of the controversy surrounding the authenticity of Anne's diary, my fellow contributors and I believe that the issue has been fully resolved; thus, readers will *not* find any additional research on the topic outside what has been presented by the Anne Frank Huis and Museum in Amsterdam and reference made to the forensic analysis of Anne's work in *The Diary of Anne Frank: The Revised Critical Edition*.[18]

The Structure of *"Meeting" Anne Frank*

At one point, I wanted to add vivid, varied, and loud *epigraphs* to each chapter of this work to show our readers the full range of Anne's self-knowledge, humanity, and idealism as she expressed herself through her diary entries. I wanted to add extracts from Anne's diary that I felt would serve as appropriate and lasting pillars of witness to her evolving perspective on her own feelings and her response to the restricted circumstances of her life in hiding. The concept of "pillars of witness" refers to how another of my favorite writers, Anne Brontë, once referred to the purpose of writing poems for her protagonist in her 1847 novel *Agnes Grey*. While Anne Frank wrote diary entries, expressed herself in self-aware musings, and wrote short stories in place of Agnes Grey writing poetry, I believe that the overall function is comparable since it is the *act* of writing that serves as the midwife to the greater exploration of feelings and the meaning of life.

Unfortunately, none of my epigraphs would end up surviving the licensing and copyright guidelines that all authors must adhere to when extracting the work of other writers that is still under legal copyright.[19]

Hitherto, as an autobiographical writer of instructive legal works, I have always loved the use of *footnotes* as a means of explaining certain topics in a less distracting but still highly visible way.

In this work, though, I have chosen to use less visible *endnotes* in place of the upfront and more visible footnotes that I deployed in my earlier autobiographical works. We decided that readers would find the endnotes to be less intrusive with respect to the flow of the main text.

Each reader would then be able to read or ignore the endnotes in line with his or her own preferences.

I would still advise the reader that the information in the endnotes *does* constitute a valuable exploration through the historical and traumatic landscape of Anne's life and world. I approached most of my endnotes with much the same enthusiasm as a botanist coming across an unusual plant or a bright and stunningly beautiful flower in an otherwise crowded meadow. I love arriving at stunning vistas of unexpected information, and I decided that my readers and I would benefit from further illumination on certain points after having wandered in an unfocused fog of prior ignorance. I learned a lot about Anne and Margot's schooling this way, the principles of a Montessori education, the differences between the Wester*kerk* as a church and the Wester*toren* as the same building's tower and bells, and the incremental hostility of the Nazis toward the Dutch Jewish population. I wanted to know more about Kamp Westerbork, which I had not really heard of before going on my own personal journey with Anne through her world.

The Contributors

One of my contributors, Pine Delgado, did a huge public service for his "hero" and "great wartime diarist" when he decided to put together his Anne Frank Book Collectors' Club Facebook group page and then invite others to join him. Since then we have celebrated Anne's life through the many books, plays, artwork, and films that exist in our personal collections.

When I joined this group as a founding member in 2019, I was amazed at just how many books and other media on Anne Frank many have in their personal collections. I decided to invite some of the more enthusiastic and engaged of the members to join my anthology project. Most of them have nearly everything that has ever been written to date about Anne and her family.

I should point out, though, that *some* of those whom I asked were clearly far too busy eulogizing and collecting everything and anything about Anne to step back and submit their personal stories for my review. While I considered this to be a shame, this just made me even more grateful to those who *did* pause in their busy lives to write something.

Just as importantly, for those who *did* submit their stories (and stunning artistic depictions of Anne in the case of Helaine Sawilowsky), I did not have to reject any as they were just too personal, beautifully written, and relevant to decline. They all managed to focus their work on their personal journeys with Anne and her family. As no one offered me anything ridiculous, extreme, unhealthily obsessive, or plain weird, I believe that readers will learn more about the power of connection across the dividing lines of time and circumstance. We might *not* be united in every aspect of modern political and social life in this anthology, but we *are* united in our love for Anne Frank and her family. This unity is extremely important because it is a transformative feeling worthy of sharing with other readers.

I do need to pay special tribute here to Joy Gafa' as the youngest of my twenty contributors to this anthology. Joy wrote her story when she was only fourteen years old. This was Anne Frank's age on June 12, 1943; she was then in hiding from the Nazis in the Secret Annex. Joy is now fifteen years old and has an engagingly independent spirit that is based on her being able to go to school, to live without fear, and to travel freely. By way of contrast, Anne spent most of her fifteenth year as a terrified prisoner in Nazi-run transit and concentration camps in the Netherlands, Poland, and Germany. Joy has an inspirational personality that Anne would easily recognize, and her love of wanting to learn more about the history of the Second World War extends to taking part in historical (and fashion) reenactments in her native Malta. This is surely rare for one so young, and I feel sure that Anne must have inspired her in this regard along with other members of her own family who served during the war. You will hear more from Joy shortly.

As I also periodically remind Joy, the island of Malta was once of enormous strategic importance to the Allies as they fought the Luftwaffe in the skies above it and tried to disrupt vital Axis supply lines between Italy and North Africa. Although very quiet now, Malta was one of the most-bombed places in Europe between June 1940 and November 1942.[20]

Although some of my contributors might have been born elsewhere, Anne (Talvaz) is now living in France; Afton, Amanda, Colleen, and Simon live in the United Kingdom; Federica lives in Italy; Priscilla and Joop live in the Netherlands; Kirsi lives in Finland; Sondra and Melina live in Canada; Yvonne, Ryan, Father John, Helaine, Miranda, Cara, Pine, and myself live in the United States. As we have just seen, Joy lives on the small island of Malta in the Mediterranean. This has truly been a worldwide effort!

Readers should be aware that I have *not* changed the spirit or unique voice of each author's story or interview. I have only made grammatical and other changes as needed to take account of the fact that some of the original essays were not written by those who normally work with English as their native language. If this work thrives as I hope it will, then maybe it can be translated into other languages as demand and finances dictate. I would like to see Dutch, French, Italian, and Spanish versions at the very least!

Cherishing Anne

My contributors and I are linked to Anne Frank *not* purely by our recognition of her deserved fame, but also by our understanding of what she had to endure during her short life and how she tried to address it through her writing. This is extremely important to grasp since Anne and everyone else in the Secret Annex obviously had no firm idea of what would happen if they ended up in Auschwitz-Birkenau, Bergen-Belsen, or elsewhere. Anne had *no* consciousness of her eventual fame as a writer and poster child for all the children who died during the Holocaust. Her writing shows how she tried to live each day as if her liberation, her swift return to school, and her future claim of Dutch citizenship were each likely to happen and on *her* own terms. The fact that none of these hopes materialized should not distract us from the fact that while we cannot separate Anne from the bleak circumstances that surrounded her and the fame that would be her eventual destiny, she remains interesting as an extraordinary and talented youngster and writer in her own right. More on all this later.

We *all* wish that *no* Jewish family had been forced to make the rushed choices in the German-occupied territories that Otto Frank had to make preemptively on the evening of July 5, 1942, when Margot received her call-up notice to report for labor duty. Such decisions imposed huge stress not just on those in hiding, but also on those helping them in terms of their guarded silence and the need to find clothes, interesting books, and food in a time of ration books, black market profiteering, and general shortages.

One can only imagine how much harder things would have been for both the hiders and the helpers during the last six months of occupation (the Hunger Winter) when the Dutch were forced to eat tulip bulbs and tear up trees for heating. I can only imagine how Anne would have reacted to a diet of tulip bulbs and to the other shortages of the last six months before the country's eventual liberation. I have yet to read of anyone posing this difficult question or of anyone attempting to answer it. In many ways, of course, we do not have to ask or answer it because the hiders in the Secret Annex were all betrayed, arrested, and then deported before the failure of Operation Market Garden in September 1944 led quickly to the Hunger Winter and then to so much subsequent misery for the Dutch.[21]

While we continue to eulogize Anne's words, read her diary, visit places associated with her life, and discuss our favorite pictures of her in many iconic, contemplative, and mischievous moments, we also understand that millions of Annes; Margots; Ediths; Hermann, Auguste, and Peter van Pelses; and Dr. Fritz Pfeffers died during the Holocaust.

We also acknowledge that some of Anne's best friends and classmates were deported, and that some among them were killed, with Susanne ("Sanne") Ledermann and her parents being among those who died at Auschwitz. Nanette ("Nanny") Blitz and Hannah ("Hanneli" or "Hanne") Goslar were among the more fortunate to survive Bergen-Belsen. Anne's declared best friend, Jacqueline van Maarsen, somehow managed to avoid having to hide through the help of her mother intervening with the Nazi authorities and having her daughter declared as non-Jewish.

To say that Anne has had the last laugh over her Nazi captors is only to acknowledge the sheer irony of Karl Josef Silberbauer and his cohorts only looting tangible jewelry and other valuables recognizable to them at the time of her arrest on August 4, 1944; thus, Anne's now priceless diary ended up being left behind for Miep, Bep, and even the suspected warehouse manager, Willem van Maaren, to find over the course of the coming days.[22]

As we look to cherish and honor the memory of Anne Frank with this anthology, I urge our readers to follow the way in which my contributors have woven her story into the journey of their own lives. You will find whatever connections mean the most to you. Anne is *still* alive on many levels as a kindred spirit, and she *is* willing to "meet" everyone. Whatever meaningful role my contributors have assigned her in their own lives, I have every confidence that wherever Anne now is, she will know instinctively *what* my writers have needed her to be.

Much of this might sound like an incredible burden to place on the shoulders of a young girl who died in tragic circumstances at the age of fifteen and even on those of our readers in searching for how best to connect with her. Yet if you read her diary and her stories and then reflect on her known life outside the parameters of her writing, it is not *that* hard to imagine how Anne would have been delighted to have been assigned some of these roles in posterity.

*   *   *

Finally, I feel that Anne Frank and Otto Frank visited us a lot as we prepared our contributions for this anthology and that both were always looking over our shoulders. Out of curiosity, and hopefully interest as well, Margot and Edith have done the same.

I hope that Anne cherishes this tribute and knows how much she is loved. Not *just* Anne, of course, but *also* Margot, Edith, and Otto. Not *just* the Frank family, but *also* Hermann and Auguste van Pels and their son, Peter. Not *just* the van Pels family, but *also* Dr. Fritz Pfeffer, their humble dentist and long-suffering companion. Not *just* the hiders in the Secret Annex, but *also* the six trustworthy and committed helpers—Johan and Bep Voskuijl, Miep and Jan Gies, Johannes Kleiman and Victor Kugler. Not *just* the helpers, but *also* Anne's many school friends. Not *just* her school friends, but *also* Jewish children everywhere who suffered during the Holocaust. Not *just* the Jewish children in Amsterdam and elsewhere in occupied Europe, but *also* their parents and other adults who died in the service of a prejudice that none of us wishes ever to see again.

* * *

Thank you, Anne, for allowing us to "meet" you! In the course of our individual journeys with you and chatty friendship, I hope that none of us will disappoint and ask too much of you!

"MEETING" ANNE FRANK: AN ANTHOLOGY

MEETING THE AUTHORS

F IRST, LET US meet the worldwide writers for this anthology in order to learn more about their lives and interests before then turning our attention to a brief outline of Anne's life and my subjective overview of her enduring legacy; afterward, we will return our attention to how my contributors have chosen to "meet" and walk with Anne, her father Otto, her sister Margot, and her mother Edith.

Except for "getting to know" our cover artist, Helaine Sawilowsky, and our *foreword* writer, Joop van Wijk-Voskuijl, the order shown below corresponds to how each writer appears in the "Walking with Anne" section of our book. Except for some basic grammar and spelling changes and changing some of the biographical entries from third person to first person, I have left my contributors to introduce themselves on their own terms.

Helaine Sawilowsky, United States

I grew up in the Deep South in Meridian, Mississippi, where my father, Rabbi Milton Schlager, was the spiritual leader of Temple Beth Israel, a Reform shul or synagogue.

Growing up, I witnessed anti-Semitism firsthand when Temple Beth Israel was bombed on May 28, 1968. Parts of the school were destroyed, and the synagogue wall was damaged. This was during a time of bombings known as the Mississippi Burning era. I was then six years old and lived three miles away. I can remember the FBI in our yard with sharpshooters. We also had to have the FBI taking us to school. When I later visited the temple, I could see how the broken glass was still there, with some of the shards set into the temple's front windows to remember this earlier time of hatred.

At the time, my father was a member of an interfaith committee set up to address the "night bombings of houses of worship"—including, black churches; indeed, on the Friday night before the bombing of Temple Beth Israel, my father had been involved in coordinating a collection on behalf of the black churches.

In 2012, my husband and my two teenage children moved to Baltimore after having lived in practically every Southern state. The only state that we did not end up living in was Texas. I have since worked for some years now as an art teacher focusing on underserved communities.

Later, I would discover that I have a distant genetic relationship to the Frank family on my father's side through my great-great grandfather having a family connection to Alice Betty Stern, Otto Frank's mother. I had been told my whole life that I look like Anne and have her same color eyes. I am *not* an immediate cousin but close enough that you can see the connection on a family tree. My sister and I always thought that our parents knew but just did not want to share the information with us. My father disliked talking about the Holocaust, but I had always felt an affinity with Anne and the tragic story of her family.

When my children turned teenagers, I was able to pursue my art full-time. In honor of what could have been Anne Frank's ninetieth birthday, I completed an Anne Frank series of paintings that I then showed during an event at the Anne Frank Center for Mutual Respect in New York. This was the 2019 Spirit of Anne Frank Awards Gala held on June 17 at New York's Edison Ballroom in Manhattan's Times Square. Our guest speaker was Joel Grey, and I was excited as I had not been to Times Square before!

I knew that it was going to be hard because the only pictures of Anne that exist are in black-and-white. The challenge then was to bring her back to life, but in color. I felt that I needed to become like an actor to be able to understand her world and to be able to create different pieces based on that. This led me to having nightmares based on reading so much about the Holocaust.

I am currently painting a series of Holocaust images and want to be able to collaborate with museums on events about Anne and her life as well as the Shoah.

I am grateful for the opportunity to design the cover for this book and invite interested readers to visit my website.[23]

Joop van Wijk-Voskuijl, the Netherlands

I was born in Amsterdam in 1949.

My mother was Bep Voskuijl (Yad Vashem), or "Elli Vossen" as Anne chose to call her in her revised diary. My grandfather was Johan Voskuijl, the creator of the legendary revolving bookcase. I am a good dancer, and I love to play chess, just like my grandfather.

My degree is in mechanical engineering, human resources, and marketing management.

As producer of my own company, I have been involved in the realization of many corporate movies for several Dutch companies and institutes.

As marketing manager, I was connected for years to the Dutch national newspapers *NRC Handelsblad* and *Algemeen Dagblad*.

After my retirement, I became the coauthor and publisher of my mother's biography. The Dutch edition was republished in 2018 as *Bep Voskuijl, het zwijgen voorbij: een biografie van de jongste helpster van het achterhuis*.[24] The English/American edition was then published in 2018 as *Anne Frank, the Untold Story: The Hidden Truth About Elli Vossen, the Youngest Helper of the Secret Annex*.[25]

By selling these books (in reviews, the biography is often called an addition to the *Diary of Anne Frank*), I want to spread my mission of loyalty to every human being.

Melina Zaccaria, Canada

I grew up in the rural town of Lynden, Ontario. I now live in Toronto, where I am pursuing a law degree at Osgoode Hall Law School. I will graduate in 2022 and plan to live and practice law in Toronto.

I have been involved with school and community theater for much of my life, with some of my favorite roles including Helen Keller in *The Miracle Worker*, Wendla in *Spring Awakening*, and of course, Anne Frank in *The Diary of Anne Frank*. I am also a classically trained vocalist and spent much of my young life competing in the Kiwanis Music Festival. I am currently taking a break from the performing arts to focus on school, but I look forward to returning to voice and theater later in life.

I attended the University of King's College in Halifax, Nova Scotia, where I studied contemporary philosophy and French. I then worked for a year as an au pair in Paris. During that time, I had the opportunity to explore much of Europe, an experience that was greatly enriched by my prior academic endeavors in European philosophy, history, and languages.

I am grateful for the opportunity to take part in this project and am honored to speak about my experience with a character as vibrant, intelligent, and historically monumental as Anne Frank.

Federica Pannocchia, Italy

I live in Italy. I love to travel, and one day I hope to be able to visit India, a country where I have adopted a young girl. I am trying to give her a better life. I have always loved to read and write. One of the first books that I read was *Anne Frank: The Diary of a Young Girl*. It is now completely part of my life.

There is not a day in which I do not think about Anne or don't "talk" to her or her family. Not a day passes where I don't try to share her wonderful ideals. I think that I am extremely lucky to live in a time and in a country in which I am able to do what I love and in which I am free to be who I want to be. Of course, it is not easy, because prejudices are everywhere. Luckily, I have learnt to go on, to respect others, and be able to respect my ideas and ideals.

I would love to be an actress on a movie set, be able to dance, or be on the stage in theater. I like creating new projects, and I enjoy being creative. I have many hobbies, I love spending time with my family, and I can be happy both writing and reading. I also enjoy conducting school programs designed to educate the younger generation to embrace better attitudes and learn from the errors of our past.

I love to live.

Joy Gafa', Malta

I was born on April 21, 2005, in Saint Luke's Hospital in Pietà and raised in a wonderful town called Birżebbuġa. For eight years I attended Birżebbuġa's primary school, while for the past four years I have been attending Saint Benedict's College Secondary School.

Ever since I was a young girl, I have been interested in all sorts of things from the past. Today, I am extremely interested in the Second World War, the Holocaust, and the 1940s (especially the fashions). Over a year ago, I also started dancing the Lindy Hop, which is a type of dance from the 1930s and 1940s. I also love acting and performing as well as writing a lot of short stories, which most of the time find themselves in a forgotten file on my laptop.

Music is also extremely important to me. I do not sing or anything, but you will often find me playing music while I am carrying on with my work. As my great-grandfather Carmelo was a sergeant major in the Royal Engineers, collecting related items is something I love doing as well. Once a year, my great-grandpa's ex-colleagues and I organize an exhibition showing all our items. This is especially important to me.

In the future I see myself in a country where I can pursue my dream of taking my acting and writing to the next level. I also plan on graduating as a history or a drama teacher. Whichever path is the one for me, I am sure that history will continue to be a topic as close to my heart as it is now.

Tim Whittome, United States

I am originally from England and spent all my childhood and early adulthood there. Although I am now living in the United States, I have dual British and American citizenship and welcome the benefits of both!

I have a BA from the University of London in modern history, economic history, and politics, and a MA from Loughborough

University in library and information science. With respect to my first history degree, I feel validated by Anne Frank as I have since discovered that history was *her* favorite subject as well! Not just that, but she also hated math as much as I did at school!

In late 1997, I moved to Los Angeles to be with my future American and Jewish wife, Esther. We later moved to the beautiful Seattle area. I also live with the best and the worst of my recently diagnosed Asperger syndrome. I spend a substantial amount of time trying to help my adopted daughter, Cordelia, heal from her traumatic childhood and adolescence. This has meant that I have had to teach myself the basic principles of child development, special needs, and adoption. With the help of Xlibris Publishing, I put together my instructional *Denied! Failing Cordelia* trilogy documenting my efforts to navigate a safe and therapeutic path for my daughter through the maze of the Los Angeles legal system.

When I am not reading, writing, and photographing beautiful places in Seattle and across Washington State, readers should be able to find me at either one of the many Seattle Shakespeare Company and other theatrical performances held throughout the year, or at Seattle Sounders FC soccer games. I can be seen proudly and passionately wearing the colors of the Rave Green and cheering on the best and most successful soccer team in the MLS. The Sounders just won its second MLS Cup in front of 69,274 fans, the largest crowd to watch a sporting event in Seattle sporting history!

I am also a proud supporter of Arsenal FC in the English Premier League and watch as many games as I can on television and with other Arsenal fans.

I "met" Anne Frank when I was in my late twenties and have loved and followed her and her family ever since. This has since broadened to an interest in the lives of the helpers of those forced to hide in the Secret Annex and in all things Dutch. Because my grandfather helped to liberate and then secure the Netherlands toward the end of the Second World War, I have always been interested in how he helped the Dutch people. He developed lasting Dutch friendships.

Pine Delgado, United States

Rather than going by my birth name of Richard Siegfried Delgado in my daily, familiar life, I prefer to go by Pine, which I adopted as a nickname on a Saturday in June 2011 while I was riding on the way to a bookshop with my then life coach. I call myself Pine because my favorite tree is the pine and three of my favorite things are paper products, with paper, of course, being made from trees. These are *writing paper* (I love to write things such as limerick poetry and words to live by), *books* (I have two large private libraries in my home containing books on mathematics and books on Anne Frank—two of my favorite academic pastimes), and *stamps* (I have been an avid collector of stamps since 1980, when I was twelve).

I was born in San Diego, California, on September 30, 1967, outside wedlock to a drill sergeant in the US Marine Corps (who was originally from Chicago) and to a German immigrant who came to America after having lived in her native Berlin and then Great Britain and Canada.

While I had been given the assignment of reading Anne Frank's diary in my junior year of high school, it was during the first half of my senior year that I truly came to meet Anne thanks to my English teacher for that year. Janet Shanks was then in her first year of teaching at my school, Helix High School in La Mesa, California. This is a San Diego suburb. Janet was young, but I truly loved her, and I still do so more than three decades later. It was because of Mrs. Shanks's assignment of reading Anne's diary and the way that Janet presented her lessons on the Holocaust that I would go on to collect all manner of literature on the great wartime diarist years later.

When I first started collecting these books, my mother really did not approve of my acquisitions and even went so far as to denounce Anne Frank's diary as a hoax. My mom had even gone as far as to say that when my classmates and I were receiving lessons on Anne in school, we were all being brainwashed. So she was quite ignorant and narrow when it came to the subject of Anne and to the extent that there would be tension in the air between my mom and me whenever I would bring Anne's name up.

It was only after my mom had died that I was finally able to partake freely and openly in my indulgence of Anne Frank and her diary. I have since then purchased as many books as possible on my hero that I could afford to buy without any guilt or external interference from anyone. I am subject only to the constraints defined by my monthly budget, which is further based on my modest monthly government income.

By the way, I am a high-functioning autistic living independently in my own apartment unit in San Diego.

Sondra Learn, Canada

I was born and raised in Brantford, Ontario, Canada. I married in 1982 and moved with my husband to Burlington, Ontario. I then kept busy being a mom to my three sons. My middle son, Justin, is severely autistic and was diagnosed with multiple sclerosis a month before his twenty-first birthday. I became an advocate for my son, and with my husband, I helped to form the Halton Chapter of the Autism Society.

My two greatest passions are writing and theater. I have been involved with theater since my first high-school theater arts class taught by David Fox, who went on to star in movies and TV shows.

I have worn many hats with my involvement with community theater: stage manager, props, set design, set decor, workshop leader, producer, director, sound design, actor, acting and directing mentor, and playwright. I have won seven playwriting awards, and my plays have been produced in Canada and in the United States. I have also won awards for acting, directing, stage management, and set decor. I won Best Director and Best Production for my two favorite plays, *The Miracle Worker* and *The Diary of Anne Frank*.

When not active with theater, I am busy with my family, which consists of my husband, Chuck, and our three sons. I also continue to write new plays.

Yvonne Leslie, United States

I was born in Mesa, Arizona. I spent my school years growing up on farms in very rural areas of both Oregon and Arizona—I spent first through fourth grade in a one-room schoolhouse, complete with an outhouse!

During my time serving as a radio operator and then as a typist in the United States Army, I was stationed in South Carolina, Georgia, and South Korea.

I worked for many years in the collection department of the Internal Revenue Service.

I enjoy spending time with my family and working with children of all ages. Other interests include Holocaust studies, collecting books by and about Anne Frank, Judaica, ballet, music of the 1960s, herpetology, and reptile keeping.

Simon Rhodes, United Kingdom

I am English, having spent most of my life in England.

At the time of writing, I am living in Canada. I have two grown-up sons, of whom I am very proud.

When I not listening to music, I enjoy trying to play the ukulele, clarinet, and various other instruments—just not all at the same time!

Kirsi Lehtola, Finland

Although I have reached my middle-age years, I still feel rather young—except in the mornings!

I'm still trying to find out what I should do when I "grow up" but so far haven't found the answer. In the meantime, I work in the hospitality industry, which I enjoy tremendously. I love meeting new people, learning about new cultures, and expanding my language skills. I really enjoy it when I can provide an exceptional customer experience. I used to work in a completely different field that I didn't enjoy at all, *so* I took a risk and decided to try something else. Life hasn't been easy, but so far it has been rather good to me. I hope it still has some more good fortune waiting around the corner.

As my work has very tight schedules, in my free time I don't make many plans. I should exercise more, but every now and then, I manage to take myself for a walk. I enjoy being outdoors. I love knitting, and I'm a hopeless yarn hoarder. It is so satisfying to create something beautiful with one's own hands.

I love traveling more than anything, but unfortunately my limited funds don't allow for it too often. But when I have time and have gathered enough money, I am always ready for new adventures!

The Holocaust has long interested and touched me deeply. I read everything that I could find and watched every documentary on television. The need to know ever more became very important to me, and sometimes I couldn't even understand why it was so important.

Recently through ancestry research on www.geni.com, I found out that I am related to Raoul Wallenberg (https://en.wikipedia.org/wiki/Raoul_Wallenberg)! Raoul Wallenberg was responsible for saving thousands of Jews from the Nazis in Hungary. I was very excited to learn that he is a distant cousin of mine and am proud of what he did during the war to try to save as many Jews as he could.

I also found out that Nina, the wife of Claus von Stauffenberg, is another distant cousin of mine. Von Stauffenberg was involved in the famous plot to assassinate Hitler on July 20, 1944 (https://en.wikipedia.org/wiki/Claus_von_Stauffenberg). Anne Frank writes very excitedly about this attempt in her diary entry for July 21, 1944. I have to say that I am quite proud of this association as well.

Finally, I found out that I am a distant cousin of the actress Renee Zellweger.

Priscilla Smits, The Netherlands

I was born and still live in Holland.

I love my job as a receptionist as there are lots of things to do. I have been doing this for nine-plus years now, and I hope to stay there for a while.

My hobbies include reading. Other than Anne's diary, I like all kinds of subjects. These include music and reading the works of Dan Brown, Stephen King, and older English writers. I enjoy both writing and listening to music. I love rock and roll, rockabilly, Elvis Presley, and the other great rockers from the 1950s. Besides these big favorites, I also enjoy listening to the Beach Boys, the Doors, Janis Joplin, and Madonna.

Although I am an avid collector of memorabilia connected to Anne Frank, I also collect memorabilia on the British Royal Family—Princess Diana and her two children are among my favorites. I collect souvenirs relating to the Dutch Royal Family—both old and new members like Queen Maxima. I have been collecting Walt Disney memorabilia since I was about four years old. I started my various collections based on the early Walt Disney films, Marilyn Monroe, Elvis Presley, the Doors, the Beach Boys, and Madonna.

I also love watching movies. Depending on what mood I am in, I am a huge fan of horror movies. I mostly watch these at home. Besides Netflix, I have a large collection of DVDs, with all kinds of movies from *Harry Potter* to *Lord of the Rings* and everything in between.

I enjoy going to the theater and attending exhibitions. Many of these are on the Second World War, but other historical events and royal houses also interest me.

At home, I like spending time with my hobbies. In the summer I enjoy sitting on my balcony with a beautiful view of nature and lots of trees.

Fr. John Neiman, United States

I was born on July 4, 1953, in Santa Monica, California, the son of Col. Robert M. Neiman (New York) and Suzette Alexander (West Virginia). I was raised in Encino, California, and later attended

Hardin-Simmons University in Abilene, Texas, where I earned a BA and a MA in history (1975, 1979).

In 1980, I entered Saint John's Seminary in Camarillo, California, and was ordained as a Roman Catholic priest for the Archdiocese of Los Angeles on February 1, 1986. Among those in attendance at my ordination were Miep and Jan Gies, who traveled all the way from Amsterdam for the ceremony.

I was very involved in Holocaust remembrance activities in the Los Angeles area for many years. I helped organize Holocaust education seminars for teachers and gave several talks at local schools and synagogues. In June 1981, I attended the World Gathering of Jewish Holocaust Survivors in Jerusalem and then the American Gathering of Jewish Holocaust Survivors in Washington, DC, in April 1983.

I first met Otto and Fritzi Frank at their home in Birsfelden, Switzerland, in June 1976. Otto, Fritzi, and I became remarkably close friends. In fact, I credit my friendship with Otto and Miep with inspiring me to become a priest.

I served as an active priest in the Archdiocese of Los Angeles from 1986 until 2014, at which time I went on a medical leave of absence. After five surgeries, I retired on July 1, 2018, and, until recently, was living in Indian Wells, California, where I also cared for my ninety-seven-year-old mother until she died. I have since moved to Chester, West Virginia.

Ryan Cooper, United States

I was born in Los Angeles, California, in 1945.

From 1954, I lived in Monterey, where I was raised and educated. I studied art and cartooning, and in the late 1960s, I began doing freelance work for the California Test Bureau Publishing Company.

In 1972, I read *Anne Frank: The Diary of a Young Girl* for the first time. That inspired me to travel to Europe in 1973, where I first met Otto and Fritzi Frank, Miep and Jan Gies, and others who were part of Anne's tragic short life.

I returned to Monterey, where I took on a position as a staff artist with CTB McGraw-Hill Publishing Company, remaining there until 1980. It was during this period that I returned to Europe twice to see Otto, Fritzi, and Miep and Jan Gies.

In 1980, I took on a job as Art Director for Brook/Cole Publishing Company where I remained until 1982, after which I resumed doing freelance artwork.

In 1982, I moved to New England and continued my freelance work for various publishing houses in the Boston area and Chicago.

In 1983, I met my future wife Elaine, and we were married the following year. We settled in the village of Limerick, Maine, where we built our home. I continued freelancing, working exclusively for Riverside Publishing Company in Chicago.

In 1993, we sold our home in Limerick and purchased a house in Yarmouth Port, Massachusetts, on Cape Cod, where we currently live.

While still in California, my interests turned to collecting nautical artifacts. I carried my collection with me to New England, and for a while, I made a living selling artifacts until I could prove myself as a freelance artist. When my freelance career ended, I became an antiques dealer. This work now occupies me full time.

Over the years, I have carried Anne's legacy by speaking at schools, institutions, and synagogues.

In 2018, I donated all the letters and memorabilia that I received from Otto Frank, Miep, and others to the United States Holocaust Memorial Museum in Washington, DC.

In early 2021, my book about my friendship with Otto Frank, *We Never Said Goodbye: Memories of Otto Frank*, is published by Amphion Publishing and is currently available on Amazon.com.

Colleen Snyman, United Kingdom

I am a South African who is now living in the United Kingdom.

At a very young age, my fascination with books began in earnest. I would often be teased (not seriously) by my parents if they sent me to tidy my room only to find me *always* sitting on the floor reading after having started with the bookshelf tidying. Suffice it to say, not much tidying got done!

Not much has changed as I have grown. My room (flat, or *apartment* as they say in the United States) is not messy, but I still sit on the floor and read. I am a keen yogi and have developed my own meditation practice, which I do each day as a daily retreat.

After school, I studied public relations and then worked in the industry in an educational role for many years.

After moving to the United Kingdom, I took on something less rigid and more creative. I now build websites and create graphics for clients. I find the creative aspect hugely fulfilling.

My long-term partner, Petar, and I, are currently exploring his Jewish heritage. This is really exciting for me since I had "met" Anne Frank at an early age and then never had had any Jewish friends to answer all my many questions!

Amanda Tomkins, United Kingdom

I'm twenty-seven years old and originally from London. Now I live by the calming sea instead of the city.

Ever since I was small, I have loved history. With a father who loves the First World War and the Second World War, I had no chance in hating either. I even had a Second World War day at school where they would play the air raid sirens and bombing sounds in the classrooms. They would get us to close our eyes to make us imagine what it must have been like back then. This would come in handy when Anne Frank would talk about the noises while in hiding. It gave me a bigger picture as to what it must have been like for her in hiding.

I have grown up visiting places like the Imperial War Museum and even now, I go straight to the Holocaust section of the museum. I also read about Anne and what her life must have been like.

At school, I always felt as if I were the only one who was really interested in history. I would pick up any book that I could about any time in history—from the Stone Age to the Victorians. I thrived on knowledge and wanted to know as much about the earth, our world, and its history as possible.

By sharing my view here of the wonderful young girl who is Anne Frank, I hope that others will want to learn more about her, more about history and the Holocaust, and more about the people who have made an impact on our past as well as our future.

Anne Talvaz, France

I was born in Brussels in 1963 to a French father and English mother. I grew up there and later studied languages and literature in France. These days, I earn my living as a commercial and literary translator and am based in the Paris area with my husband and son.

My primary activity, though, is creative writing, which I do mostly in French. I have published three poetry collections, a travel book about China, and a novel about Lina Heydrich, the wife of Gestapo chief Reinhard Heydrich. Anne Frank has provided the inspiration for several of my poems, although she is mentioned by name only in the last, as yet unpublished, two.

Miranda Antoinette Troutt, United States

I was born and raised as a Seattleite. I began my performing experience as a classically trained singer, later earning a BFA in musical theatre at Cornish College of the Arts. I am currently making my career as a musical theatre performer and vocalist in the greater Seattle area.

The Seattle Children's Theatre summer student programs were where I first fell in love with theater, and it has been a delight to work professionally for them twice now in *The Lion, the Witch and the Wardrobe* and *The Diary of Anne Frank.*

Other acting credits include Village Theatre (*Into the Woods*, understudy), Taproot Theatre (Margo in *Bright Star*), the Seattle Gilbert and Sullivan Society (Phoebe in *Yeoman of the Guard*), and much more.

I can be heard singing with various groups within Naomi Morgan Entertainment, with the Dickens Carolers, with the Dutiful Dreamers (band), and with Cosmozoa (band). I have also been a guest artist with the Seattle Rock Orchestra.

Playing Anne was a unique and special experience because, although I have been able to do art that has incorporated my *Italian* heritage, this was my first opportunity to tell a story that put me in touch with my *Jewish* heritage.

I love cats, the outdoors, and social dancing.

Cara Wilson-Granat, United States

I am an author, inspirational speaker, vegan, nature, and animal advocate. Best, I am a mother, and I am Nana, which is my favorite role of all.

My books and talks embrace a universal theme of hope over adversity. I am the author of *Strength from Tragedy: Anne Frank's Father Shares His Wisdom with an American Teen*. My first book, *Love, Otto*, was excerpted in the 1997 *Reader's Digest* and then translated into many universal languages. It was also excerpted in two editions of *Chicken Soup for the Single Soul* and *Chicken Soup for the Woman's Soul*.

My most recent book is *Strength from Nature—Simple Lessons of Life Taught by the Most Unlikely Masters: The Nature Teachers*. I also cowrote with Mary Kate Scandone *Nick of Time—The Nick Scandone Story: A Champion Paralympian Turns a Death Sentence into Gold*.

My former career was as a copywriter (TV, radio, print) for award-winning campaigns in Los Angeles, Monterey, Sacramento, and San Diego. Presently, and in addition to freelance writing projects and speaking engagements, I Skype to classrooms worldwide, speaking about Anne and Otto Frank and their entire story.

A regular speaker for rotaries and schools, in 2018 and 2019 I held workshops at the Shine Girls Convention in Parker, Colorado, empowering young girls to "tap into their inner elephant" and learn about the matriarchal lessons of our planet's most massive and amazing species. I am also a board member on two 501(c)(3) nonprofit charities—ImpactAVillage.org (an organization that is committed to improving healthcare and education in villages around the world) and UpLiftUs. net (a movement of kindness dedicated to helping those in hunger and who are living a challenged existence). I have also been a TEDx Speaker ("What Matters—Lessons from Anne Frank's Father").

I am a UCLA graduate (BA with major in English and minor in dance and theater).

I live in Colorado with my husband, Peter, and our fat cat, Boo. Peter and I also perform in the timeless play *Love Letters* by A. R. Gurney. We spend as much time as possible loving the beauty and peace of nature together.

PART II

Getting to Know Anne

Having committed no crime at all, one day my family and I were shut off from the world and isolated from society.

—Nanette Blitz-Konig, *Holocaust Memoirs of a Bergen-Belsen Survivor* (2018)

A BRIEF LIFE

A S I SAID earlier, our anthology is not intended to add yet another biography of Anne to the Anneverse. Both Melissa Müller and Carol Ann Lee have published excellent and very comprehensive biographies of Anne and her family. Interested readers can find their works in our bibliography. At time of writing, I am not aware of any separate biographies of Margot or Edith, but as the above authors cover both in their biographies of Anne and Otto Frank, readers will know them well by the conclusion of their works.

However, I felt that it would still be helpful for our readers to have a brief outline of the salient aspects of Anne's life in this chapter as well as an overview of the power and meaning of her legacy in the next. I acknowledge the forerunner work of Melissa and Carol in putting together my own overview of salient moments in Anne's brief life.

Anne's Early Childhood and Life in Amsterdam

"[Anne] was likable, healthy, perhaps a little delicate, though I believe that showed up later on. She certainly was not an extraordinary child, not even ahead of her age. Or perhaps I should put it this way: in many things she was very mature, but on the other hand, in other things she was unusually childish. The combination of these two characteristics made her very attractive. There are many potentialities in such a mixture, after all."
—"Mr. van G." (Mr. van Gelder), Anne's first-grade teacher, in conversation with Ernst Schnabel, *The Footsteps of Anne Frank* (1958; 2014)

Annelies Marie Frank was born on June 12, 1929, in Frankfurt am Main, Germany. She was the younger of Otto and Edith Frank's two children. Margot had arrived over three years earlier on February 16, 1926. Their parents, Otto Frank and Edith Holländer, were married in Aachen, Germany, on May 12, 1925, the same day as Otto's thirty-sixth birthday; Edith who was born on January 16, 1900, was then twenty-five years old.[26]

Anne and Margot were both born during the time of the Weimar Republic in Germany, with Anne arriving more toward the end of its better years and not long before the Wall Street stock market collapse (October 29, 1929) brought about the Great Depression.[27]

Although the National Socialist German Workers Party of Germany (known also as the NSDAP, or more commonly as the Nazis) were already a growing presence in Germany and by 1932 were the largest single party in the Reichstag, it was not until January 30, 1933, that Adolf Hitler was appointed chancellor of Germany by President Paul von Hindenburg.[28] Anne Frank was still only three years old at the time. Thereafter, Hitler consolidated power and quickly eliminated opposition to the new Third Reich. The signing of the March 1933 Enabling Act effectively allowed him to make laws without the approval of the Reichstag.[29] It also marked the ignominious end of the Weimar Republic. After von Hindenburg died in 1934, Hitler then declared himself the *Führer* (supreme leader) and eliminated the separate posts of chancellor and president. The road to the renewal of war began in earnest from this point. Some have even seen the interwar years as merely a truce between the two world wars that have so scarred our attitude toward the last century.

Otto Frank does not appear to have wanted to alarm his daughters or wife unduly about the growing Nazi threat, and he would demonstrate a calmness in the face of adversity that I can only attribute to his past as an officer in the German Imperial Army of the First World War.

Nevertheless, in late 1933 and with the Nazis now in full control of Germany, Otto decided that the risk of staying in Germany was just too great. With the help of his brother-in-law who ran a subsidiary branch of *Opekta* in Switzerland, Otto decided to seize what was then a good opportunity to take a job in Amsterdam running a similar

"MEETING" ANNE FRANK: AN ANTHOLOGY

Dutch branch that was both dependent on its German parent company, *Pomosin-Werke*, and independently self-supporting.[30]

Opekta was both the name of Otto's firm and the marketing name given to the company's liquid and powder forms of pectin, an additive that was important in jam making. Otto focused his marketing attention on developing the retail needs of housewives, but when he first arrived in Amsterdam, most Dutch housewives had already made their jam for the year. The sale of pectin was more seasonal than I first realized when I read about Opekta.

Looking back, Otto's decision to immigrate to the Netherlands was obviously prudent and entirely understandable. Many other German Jews did the same given the extent to which the Nazis were consolidating their electoral rise in Germany. Otto moved to Amsterdam first and was then followed by Edith, who had been traveling back and forth for a while. Margot followed in time for the start of the school year in Holland on January 5, 1934. Anne stayed with her maternal grandmother in Aachen until she then moved over to Amsterdam in February 1934. In her diary entry for June 20, 1942, Anne notes how she was humorously "plunked on the table" as a "birthday present" for Margot's eighth birthday on February 16. Anne was still only four years old.

From when she arrived in Amsterdam in early 1934 until the circumstances of Margot's "calling up" for labor duty accelerated the decision to go into hiding on July 6, 1942, Anne lived with her family at Merwedeplein 37 (also known as the "Merry") in the *Rivierenbuurt* (River District or Quarter) of Amsterdam.[31] Many Jews who immigrated to the Netherlands ended up here and Merwedeplein has since become famous not just for the fact that the Frank family lived there but also for the presence of its architecturally plain but very visible twelve-story "skyscraper." This building separated the even- and odd-number buildings that branched off this central community focal point. A statue now exists in the main square to commemorate Anne's association with the complex.[32] Those who wish to visit Amsterdam to follow in Anne's childhood footsteps can rest assured that her former address still exists and is well-preserved.[33]

From what we know of Anne and Margot's lives before they went into hiding with their parents, both girls appear to have had happy and normal childhoods. They went to separate schools, with Anne going to the nearby free-spirited and informal 6e Montessorischool on Amsterdam's Niersstraat and Margot going to the more traditional Jekerschool on the even closer Jekerstraat.[34] Both schools would have been within easy walking or bicycle distance as they were both well under a mile from their home.

Educationally, Anne and Margot would reunite in September 1941 when both girls were forced to go with other Jewish boys and girls to the Jewish (Joods) Lyceum on Voormalige Stadstimmertuinen in Amsterdam.[35] By this time the Germans had been occupying the Netherlands for sixteen months, and in September 1941, Anne and Margot found themselves having to comply with new educational edicts demanding an educational segregation of Jewish and non-Jewish children.

Fortunately, we do have several iconic pictures of Anne at her Montessorischool. There is also a famous school picture of Anne from the Jewish Lyceum. In fact, we can consider ourselves fortunate that not only did Otto take so many happy pictures of Anne, but that the family photograph albums would later survive the chaotic arrest in the Secret Annex. Sadly, there are far fewer pictures of Margot and most that *do* exist, show us a serious young lady with the weight of responsibility on her shoulders.

Both girls learned Dutch quickly and with more fluency than either of their parents, with Margot developing habits every bit as studious and bright intellectually as her sister's predilections were spirited and rebellious. Anne was viewed as gregarious, curious, loud, and not a little indulged, with her "most adorable" father (as she described him in her diary entry for June 20, 1942) especially keen to indulge her various whims.

As I am somewhat of a literary persuasion, it might make sense to some readers if I could suggest that Anne Frank had a bubbly and witty personality not dissimilar to that of Miss Elizabeth Bennet in Jane Austen's *Pride and Prejudice*. Others might see a passing resemblance to the gossipy Emma Woodhouse in Miss Austen's *Emma*. At least Anne loved history and disliked math! She and I would have had a lot in common there!

*6e Montessorischool Anne Frank, Niersstraat
41–43, Amsterdam © Priscilla Smits*

*6e Montessorischool Anne Frank, Niersstraat
41–43, Amsterdam © Joy Gafa'*

*Jewish Lyceum (with crooked Star of David), Voormalige
Stadstimmertuinen, Amsterdam © Priscilla Smits*

Continuing with my Jane Austen ramblings, Margot, meanwhile, seems to have had much more in common with the serious-minded and faithful Anne Elliot in *Persuasion* or with the responsible Elinor Dashwood in *Sense and Sensibility*. I view Margot as being both far too intelligent to resemble Elizabeth Bennet's older sister, Jane, and much too empathetic to model herself after the bookish Mary Bennet; moreover, if I can unashamedly claim that Hermione is my favorite character in the Harry Potter series, it would be dishonest if I said that I did not have a huge soft spot for Margot and her constant studying.

Meanwhile, Edith seems to have struggled to understand and speak Dutch with any degree of fluency, while Otto presumably had to learn it for business reasons, if nothing else. That Edith found learning Dutch difficult and was seemingly reluctant to assimilate herself in the Dutch culture may seem odd in retrospect, given the alarming situation in her native Germany. Not so much, though, when you consider that Edith also expected to be able to return to Germany at some point.

Yet the fact that she *did* find it hard, provides us with a convenient reason to dispute the arguments of those who declared that the Dutch and the Germans were more than kin or that the two languages were overwhelmingly similar.[36] This viewpoint, of course, was perpetrated by both the Nazis and their Dutch sympathizers in the NSB or Dutch Nazi Party.[37] It seems that many Dutch despised their German neighbors and referred to them somewhat contemptuously as *Moffen*.

In retrospect, we can feel relieved and happy that, despite having more than her fair share of prolonged childhood illnesses that seemingly went on for months, Anne Frank does appear to have had a happy and cheerful, if completely indulged, childhood. Her Montessori schooling sounds idyllic, and both Anne and her sister made many friends.

On balance, I think we can say that the 1930s in the Netherlands were kind to Anne, Margot, and their parents. Yet much of these same years were still spent against a dark background of a growing fear that Otto, Edith, and other Jews of native and German origin could breathe, if not have their own personal reasons to touch. Otto and Edith did their best to shield their daughters from the anti-Semitism that was transpiring in Germany. Looking back, it is hard imagining how Jews desperate to leave Germany could have felt that *any* country in Europe would have been overwhelmingly safe given how widespread anti-Semitism was taking hold in response to Hitler's success in reviving the German economy. Of greater concern, though, was German rearmament and the seemingly inevitable march toward a renewal of war.

The Invasion of the Netherlands and German Occupation (1940–1945)

The Second World War was precipitated by the German invasion of Poland on September 1, 1939, and by the British and French declarations of war in response on September 3, 1939. Of all the major combatants in 1939, only Germany had spent years preparing itself militarily and psychologically for protracted conflict. Although they had certainly been taking some steps toward rearmament, the Allies were still largely unprepared at the start of hostilities for a quick and decisive war.

There is little doubt that the Second World War had a devastating and lasting psychological impact on the Dutch after their country's neutrality was violated, its borders crossed, and their cities and land seized by the Nazis following the invasion of May 10, 1940.[38]

Surrender followed swiftly five days later after the Luftwaffe extensively (and allegedly without permission) bombed Rotterdam and crushed any further Dutch desire to resist. It does not take much imagination to understand why the eventual liberation of the Netherlands (May 5, 1945) is still celebrated as an annual public holiday. Nor why football games between the Netherlands and Germany have such an added significance. Witness the 1974 World Cup final and the hopes some had for a repeat in the 2014 final.

The official reason given for the invasion was that the Netherlands needed "protecting" from possible Allied attacks. The Nazis also saw the Dutch as "kindred spirits," their land as easy to conquer, and the port of Rotterdam as a vital jewel in the Wehrmacht's desire to protect the Rhine and other strategic areas in Germany. The Netherlands was viewed as merely one segment of a strong Nazi-controlled Atlantic seawall that would quickly encompass both Belgium (May 28, 1940) and most of France (June 25, 1940). The entire military "wall" was designed to deter any future Allied invasion. It worked for the better part of four long years.

Another explanation given for the invasion was that the Dutch were violating their own neutrality by allowing the Royal Air Force to fly over Dutch territory en route to bombing strategic targets in Germany.

On balance, I find it extremely difficult imagining how the Netherlands could have thought that its neutrality at the beginning of the Second World War would *ever* have been respected by a Germany primed to spread its fascist culture and filled to the brim with the imagined glories of a lasting Nazi hegemony. Nor should we forget that the Nazis viewed both against a backdrop of historical and delusional grudges against neighboring states over land appropriated or lost in past conflicts.

When we consider the overall history of the Netherlands during the Second World War, we also need to be aware that the country ended up as among the last of the occupied Nazi territories to be returned to its prewar status as a free and independent state. Much of this was because Allied forces failed to secure a vital bridge across the River Rhine at Arnhem during Operation Market Garden in September 1944.[39]

Although much of the southern half of the Netherlands (including the cities of Eindhoven and Nijmegen) would remain liberated following the limited success of Operation Market Garden, Amsterdam and other areas would remain under German occupation until their eventual surrender on May 5, 1945.[40] On May 7, 1945, the British and the Canadians would assume full authority over the rehabilitation of the Netherlands at the conclusion of the Second World War.

It is important to understand that Operation Market Garden would not have had any bearing on the ultimate destinies of the occupants of the Secret Annex even had the operation succeeded. Sadly, they had already left Kamp Westerbork on the last transport train to leave the transit camp for Auschwitz-Birkenau on September 3, 1944. This was the same day that Brussels was liberated by the British Second Army, but it was also fourteen days *before* the start of Operation Market Garden on September 17.

That said, if the largest airborne invasion in history had succeeded in its key objective of holding the Rhine at Arnhem, then it is likely that eventual liberation might well have arrived sooner for Anne, Margot, and Mrs. van Pels given that the British would have probably reached Bergen-Belsen not that long after the three had arrived at the camp in late October 1944. That assumes, of course, that they would still have been sent there from Auschwitz. There are so many *ifs* involved in Anne's story, and I am afraid that the failure of Operation Market Garden is one of the many.

What the defeat at Arnhem *did* mean, however, is that the next eight months of Nazi occupation of the remaining parts of the Netherlands that were still under their control would be exceptionally hard. Gone was the hope of ending the war by Christmas of that year. It resulted in the Dutch being cruelly starved of what little remained of their food supply during the infamous Hunger Winter of 1944–45 as the occupying Germans stole what they could to give to their remaining Wehrmacht forces. The defeat at Arnhem also meant that American, British, and Canadian armies were forced to push into Germany from elsewhere. Bridges across the River Rhine in Germany would eventually be bridged by American and British forces in March 1945.

Let us now turn to what the occupation of the Netherlands meant for the country's significant Jewish population. Not forgetting, of course, that for two years of her life before going into hiding, Anne and Margot would have been just as vulnerable to the daily humiliations as the rest of the Jewish community.

Jewish Life in the Occupied Netherlands

The [yellow Star of David] made Jacqueline [van Maarsen] feel very vulnerable and gave her the feeling that every German soldier and Dutch Nazi in Amsterdam knew who she was. Whenever she passed a Nazi on the street now, she felt a huge threat coming from him, as though her life was really at risk. She knew she had to obey every law, because the star let the Nazis know that she was Jewish and, as such, someone whom they despised. It was a horrible feeling, and Jacqueline told Anne, "I'm scared to do anything, because everything is forbidden."

—Jacqueline van Maarsen and Carol Ann Lee, *A Friend Called Anne* (2007)

According to a Wikipedia entry on the "History of the Jews in the Netherlands," a staggering 70 percent of the prewar Jewish population died because of deportation and other decisions taken by the occupying Nazi forces to "free the Netherlands" of its Jews.[41] By any definition, this constitutes a genocide of horrific proportions.

It is also strangely bewildering that the percentage was so much higher in the Netherlands than it was in other areas of occupied Europe. A number of reasons have been suggested as to why this was, but as it is not the purpose of this anthology to explore these, I will merely suggest that interested readers take note of the extensive biographies of Anne and her family, the memoirs of her friends, and other works and websites regarding how the Dutch adapted to or resisted the German occupation.[42] Although I have read that the Dutch reportedly detested the Germans more than they felt overwhelming sympathy for the Jews, other evidence such as the February 25, 1941, strike contradicts this.[43]

It is important to know that the Nazis set up a *Joodse Raad* (Jewish Council) on February 13, 1941 to act as a chief liaison between the Jewish population and the occupying forces. The leadership of the Joodse Raad believed that by cooperating with the Germans, they could avoid or procrastinate the worst. The Joodse Raad was very involved in helping to find suitable premises for Jewish schools such as the Jewish Lyceum (which Anne and Margot both attended) in 1942.

For the Jewish population of the Netherlands, life after the subjugation of the country in May 1940 became incrementally challenging and restrictive as new laws and regulations issued by the occupying Nazis and their appointed *Reichskommissar*, Arthur Seyss-Inquart, stifled the life of the community.[44] The above February strike in support of the Jews inspired the occupying Nazis to even harsher countermeasures.

Yet for all the initial feeling that things might not turn out to be completely unendurable, the Jewish community *must* surely have been aware that the Nazis had crushed the Jewish population in Germany by a process of incremental relentlessness. This earlier incrementalism had allowed for any given measure to have time to take insidious root and grudging acceptance; even more alarmingly, to foster a false sense of hope that each step would be the last.

Thus, as one example, the 1935 Nuremberg Laws that had forbidden intermarriage between Jews and Christians and deprived Jews of their citizenship in prewar Germany were *not* imposed in the Netherlands the day after the Dutch surrender on May 15, 1940, but were delayed until March 1942.[45]

In further regard of this incremental point, we need to bear in mind that the transportation of Jews from the Netherlands to the infamous extermination camps in Poland such as Auschwitz and Sobibór did not take place until July 1942 as part of the country's enforced contribution to the Nazis' pursuit of their "final solution" to the Jewish "problem." Margot Frank would be among the first to be ordered to report for labor work in Germany and elsewhere when she received her infamous call-up notice on July 5, 1942.

By disguising their ultimate intentions for as long as possible, the Jewish population in the Netherlands was lulled by the occupying authorities into relying on a manufactured sense of ultimate safety that would only reveal itself as false when the time arrived for the Nazis to begin their deportations in July 1942. In other words, and *until* that point, the Nazis generated the impression that they would *obviously* be stopping well short of the deportation and extermination of the Jewish population. While both eventualities ought to have been viewed as inevitable when viewed through the power of hindsight, we should acknowledge that these final steps were opportunistically disguised until that act of concealment no longer served the occupying purpose. Did it really matter that all Jews over a certain age had to carry identity cards marked with a "J"? Not, until such a classification proved useful to the occupying authorities when it came time to put together the first transports to Kamp Westerbork and from thence to further concentration and extermination camps "back east."

As a final point here, the Jewish response to this stealthy and deceptive incrementalism may well have underpinned some of Otto Frank's willingness to comply too readily with the request that all Jews and Jewish businesses in Amsterdam and elsewhere register themselves with the authorities. Otto's refusal to turn in Margot's bicycle in June 1942, seems to have been a rare example of his unwillingness to cooperate. At least, it struck me as such. He didn't have to worry about Anne's as it had been stolen earlier in April. One of my fellow writers, Anne Talvaz, alerted me to a fascinating Amsterdam police report from April 14, 1942, noting how Anne reported the theft and valued her bicycle at 45 guilders.

Anne Frank: The Diary of a Young Girl

> *"When we were at the school with her, I asked, "Did you see anything special in Anne at the time?" She said she hadn't, but I think she was right when she remarked 'When a girl at that age is removed from friends, plants, animals—from everything, really—and you put her in a home with only adults, everything develops much faster. Who knows—if there had been no war, she might not have become a great writer until she was thirty.' Circumstances sped up everything, including her development as a writer."*
> —Theo Coster in *We All Wore Stars*, recounting a conversation about Anne between Hanneli Goslar and Mrs. Kuperus, their former teacher, and the principal of the 6e Montessorischool

> *Anne Frank: The Diary of a Young Girl* is a carousel of emotions.
> —Federica Pannocchia, *Siamo chi eravamo* (We Are Who We Were)[46]

Now let us turn our attention back to Anne. The brief overview of the history of the Netherlands during the Second World War and subsequent discussion of the many injustices meted out to its Jewish population constitute important background context to the arc of Anne's own story. It is hard to separate each element since so much of Anne's life after the occupation was determined by decisions made outside her control.

Based on the evidence of her diary entry for April 11, 1944, Anne clearly saw herself as Dutch and was probably the most virulently anti-German of everyone in the Secret Annex. Although some of these feelings would have probably been mollified under her father's influence had she survived, I do not see much point in ignoring Anne's strong Dutch feelings or looking for ways to discount her plans for future integration into Dutch society.[47] Others have tried to do this by advocating for changing her citizenship posthumously, a trend that is especially apparent in fictional portrayals of the lives of Anne and Margot as they *could* have been *if* they had survived the Holocaust.[48]

On June 12, 1942, Anne was given the famous red-and-white checkered diary (technically an autograph book) for her thirteenth birthday. This almost certainly came from *Blankevoort's* bookstore around the corner from where the Franks lived on Merwedeplein.[49] At this point, Anne would begin the writing that would eventually make her famous across the world. To date, her diary has been translated into some seventy languages, of which the Anne Frank Huis and Museum has around thirty versions for sale at last count.

Apart from the famous red-and-white checkered autograph/diary book, two other notebooks of original diary entries have survived for 1944. The surviving three books comprise Anne's "original" diary that we now refer to as the A version. In addition to the three original A diaries, separate sheets of a revised version of her diary, some thirty-four *Tales*, and an incomplete novel, *Cady's Life*, have survived. We also have Anne's accounting ledger book that she used to put together her *Book of Beautiful Sentences*.[50]

Anne Frank (5 or 6 years old), 1935 © Anne
Frank Huis and Museum Collection

Anne Frank (7 years old) passport photo, May 1937
© Anne Frank Huis and Museum Collection

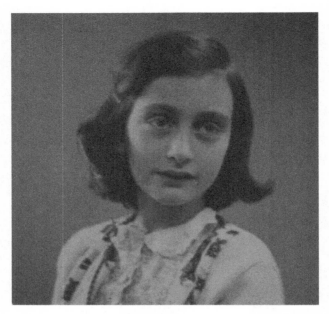

Anne Frank (9 years old) passport photo, May 1939
© Anne Frank Huis and Museum Collection

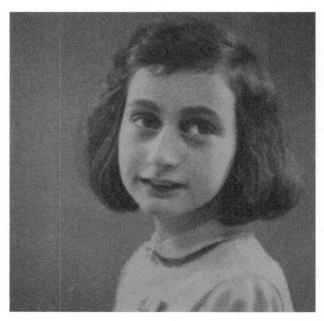

Anne Frank (10 years old) passport photo, May 1940
© Anne Frank Huis and Museum Collection

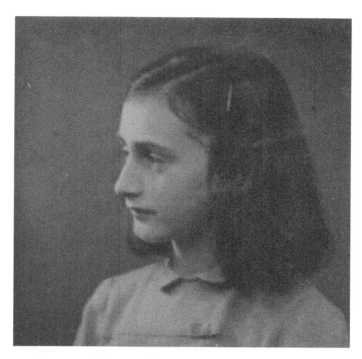

Anne Frank (11 years old) passport photo, May 1941
© Anne Frank Huis and Museum Collection

Edith Frank and Margot, 1929 © Anne Frank Huis and Museum Collection

Margot Frank (9 years old) passport photo, May 1935
© Anne Frank Huis and Museum Collection

Margot Frank (10 years old) passport photo, December
1936 © Anne Frank Huis and Museum Collection

Margot Frank school photograph (15 years old), Jewish Lyceum,
December 1941 © Anne Frank Huis and Museum Collection

Margot Frank (16 years old), passport photo, May 1942
© Anne Frank Huis and Museum Collection

Otto Frank passport photo (47 years old), May 1936
© Anne Frank Huis and Museum Collection

Edith Frank passport photo (35 years old), May 1935
© Anne Frank Huis and Museum Collection

Following an announcement on a Radio Oranje Dutch broadcast from London by Gerrit Bolkestein (the Dutch cabinet minister for education) that the Dutch government wanted to compile a war record of personal diaries and journals, Anne decided to revise her original diary entries for possible publication.[51] This revised version was completed on some 215 separate sheets of thin blue and pink paper through to March 29, 1944. It is now known as Anne's "revised" B diary. Anne would continue to write original entries in her third and final school notebook (as she was revising her earlier entries) through to her famous last entry on August 1, 1944.

The presence of "original" and "revised" versions of Anne's diary has become somewhat of a challenge for editors, publishers, and even readers over the years. The problem underpinning any decision to publish just the original A version is *not* that Anne decided to revise it, but that very little exists by way of original diary entries for 1943. The problem with *only* publishing her revised version is that it ends on March 29, 1944. Although such a decision would have captured more of what Anne intended to see published had she been able to, readers of just this version would miss out on some of the idealism for which Anne is now famous. Her original diary ends on August 1, 1944. Publishing just the B version would, therefore, eliminate the forty-eight original diary entry dates following the end of her revised version on March 29, 1944.

At first, readers would be offered a combined *third* version C by Otto Frank after the war. Otto, who also seems to have found editing his daughter's diary to be problematic, decided to use mostly Anne's revised B version up to March 29, 1944 before switching to the original A version for dates after that.

Het achterhuis: dagboekbrieven 12 Juni–1 Augustus 1944 was published in Dutch in 1947, before then being translated into English as *Anne Frank: The Diary of a Young Girl* in 1952. French and German translations appeared earlier in 1950. Our website resources include extensive links to the publishing history of Anne's diary. It is by turns fascinating for scholars and confusing for those of us who like matters to be obvious and uncomplicated.

It is worth pointing out that Otto did not eliminate many entire diary *dates* from the first edition of Anne's work, but rather some of the *content* as a way of appeasing the sensibilities of an age likely to be embarrassed by his daughter's vivid descriptions of her personal adolescent development. None of these early editing decisions appears to have satisfied everyone throughout the years and neither seemingly has been the decision to publish a more recent "definitive" version of Anne's diary.[52]

It was after Otto's death in 1980 that a decision was made with the concurrence of the Anne Frank Fonds in Basel, Switzerland, to provide the world with a fuller version of Anne's work; thus, we now have a *Definitive Edition* as edited by Otto Frank and Mirjam Pressler and translated by Susan Massotty. As part of the preparation for this new version D edition of Anne's diary, the Fonds agreed to the restoration of some 30 percent of the diary content that had originally been cut by Otto in 1947. Because this version has restored more of Anne's personal commentary on her growing development as a teenager, the age and gender appropriateness of the *Definitive Edition* are now much more to the fore as subjects for discussion, possible censorship, and inevitable complaint than either would have been in response to Otto's original edited C version. The original 1952 English version is still easily available, it must be said, for parents concerned about which version they should allow their children to read.

Whether Anne would have welcomed this later decision to publish intimate details of her personal growth as a teenage girl is also open to debate, given that she herself was somewhat embarrassed by what she had written earlier about such matters and by the sharp remarks she had made about her parents. We can see this in her added comment dated January 22, 1944, to her earlier diary entry for November 2, 1942.

Personally, I have only ever read the less confusing D version of the diary in its entirety as it has been the most widely available edition since I first "met" Anne in 1995; thus, I have not compared it textually to Anne's original A and revised B versions or to her father's edited C version beyond trying to determine the source dates for the three versions and the added 30 percent.[53] Anything more would probably confuse me with my autism or lead to my becoming overly enmeshed with trying to compare what Anne originally wrote with what she then revised. Readers who are interested in seeing extracts from her original and revised diary entries may appreciate that both Carol Ann Lee and Melissa Müller make full use of both the A and B versions when citing Anne's diary entries for their respective biographies. This way, we can get closer to the purer source material without having to bother with filtered editorial or publisher interference.

Nevertheless, for me to follow in their detailed footsteps would lead to a more scholarly book than readers of this anthology would welcome. Readers who *are* interested in reviewing the complete A and B versions may like to refer to the Netherlands Institute of War Documentation's *Revised Critical Edition* of Anne's diary where the two are compared side by side with Otto's combined C edition. The recently published *Collected Works* also has the complete A and B versions but chooses to present them alongside the D edition. Bibliographical details for both works are in our bibliography.

Lastly, and with apologies for such a lengthy diversion into the complexities of Anne's diary, we need to note how Anne develops her thoughts and ideals in her diary through the means of an age-old decision made by both real and literary children to invent imaginary friends. Anne famously chooses to confide in her imaginary and "patient" friend, Kitty.[54] At least, she does throughout in her revised version B diary. In her original red-and-white checkered diary (version A), Anne uses a variety of imaginary and real recipients.[55] Kitty is *one* of these recipients but only appears consistently in the second and third original surviving diaries.

*   *   *

Given the anxiety that must have existed for Jews who remained in Germany during the 1930s and then for the Jewish communities in the German-occupied countries during the war, it seems hard to understand how Anne was able to summon up as much calmness as she does in her early diary entries. These were the ones she wrote *before* she was forced into hiding. Even the innocuous fact that she could still cheerfully buy an ice cream seems so frighteningly unexpected given how the occupying

Nazis were imposing early Jewish curfews (between 8 p.m. and 6 a.m.) and restricting all Jewish shopping to just two hours each day (between 3 p.m. and 5 p.m.) from stores that bore the placard of "Jewish shop." This is yet another example of where the publishing history of Anne's diary is incredibly confusing because while Anne assigns this information along with other privations in her original (version A) diary to a "Thursday, July 1942" date, she decides to drop this useful overview from her revised diary. *Yet* it is restored to her father's edited version C diary with the date of June 20, 1942. The editors of the *Definitive Edition* decide to complicate this matter even further by maintaining the edited June date, but electing to drop the significant caveat (as mentioned by Anne in her original July 1942 diary entry) of Jews only being able to shop in stores bearing the "Jewish shop" placard. This is, again, one of those nightmarish scenarios that those of us with high functioning autism find it hard navigating!

The net result of all this prejudicial horribleness, is that Anne's ice cream *must* be bought from a Jewish ice-cream parlor such as *Oase* (Oasis in English versions of Anne's diary and located at Geleenstraat 1 near Merwedeplein) or from *Delphi,* which was also located close to Merwedeplein 37 at Daniël Willinkplein 1. In May 1946, and one year after the Allied victory in the Second World War, this square was appropriately renamed as Victorieplein. Anne describes her ice-cream predicament in a revised diary entry for June 20, 1942.

We see these same feelings at work with respect to how Anne talks about her thirteenth birthday party and a Rin Tin Tin movie that her father had to borrow and then show at home on a projector because Jews were no longer allowed to go to the cinema. Anne even sends out tickets to her friends! How is she able to describe all this with such apparent insouciance and normality! Much the same could be said regarding her walks with the young teenager who could have become her established boyfriend in more favorable circumstances: Helmuth "Hello" Silberberg.

This apparent blasé bravery extends to the point of including a glorious summary in her diary of the quirks, irritations, foibles, *and* ordinariness of her school friends at the Jewish Lyceum.[56] Anne is strikingly modern and fearless in her likes and dislikes—not strictly a "mean girl" so much as a loquacious and loud youngster who could be both generous and merciless. The final trajectory of her relationships with her school friends and classmates will never be known thanks to Anne being forced into hiding within weeks and never seeing most of them again. Well, she *does* manage to hear Hanneli Goslar and see Nanette Blitz, but as the girls only get to hear or see one another again within the restrictive confines of Bergen-Belsen, I feel that this barely counts.

Are we supposed to ignore this early chatter and commentary? Are we to believe that Anne was being self-delusional? Are we to think that the restricted life in the occupied Netherlands was more radically accepted by the Dutch—Jews and non-Jews alike—than we may want to believe it could have been? After all, and despite the fact that the Netherlands was placed under civilian and not military rule unlike other countries that were also occupied, the Nazis would have been *everywhere*. Members of the NSB (the Dutch Nazi Party) would also have been empowered by the occupation to snitch and betray. Suspicion of neighbors was rife and trust at a premium. Proclamations were being issued on a regular basis. The last of these to affect the Franks prior to the family going into hiding, would have been the registration and subsequent confiscation of bicycles owned by the Jewish population.

In addition, RAF bombers were regularly flying over the Netherlands en route to targets in the industrial heartland of Germany. Sometimes, the Allies would bomb strategic military installations in Amsterdam—the port of IJmuiden was one such target that Anne later talks about in her diary entry for March 29, 1944. These raids were not only terrifying to her in the confined circumstances of the Secret Annex—accompanied as they were by loud antiaircraft fire—but they would prompt her to leap into her father's bed for protection.[57]

Life could not have been *so* normal, could it? This prompts me to add that all of us writing for this anthology wish that Margot's diary could have survived as well, as it seems likely that her documented seriousness and thoughtfulness would have left us with a quite different perspective on Jewish life in Amsterdam as well as her own in hiding.[58]

This is not to discount, of course, the intoxicating value of Anne's rebellious spirit fighting to break through the ice of the restrictions slowly crushing the independence of the Jewish communities in the Netherlands.

Nor should we run away with the idea that Margot would have necessarily been a more reliable narrator than Anne. While Anne wanted to rebel against the growing dangers of Jewish life in occupied Amsterdam and unleash her feelings in perfectly healthy ways by writing in her diary, Margot pushed herself more toward accepting what she could not actively change. Both perspectives would have been needed to help them survive the restraints of life in the Secret Annex. Again, though, we do *not* have Margot's diary to compare with Anne's and I could be overstating Margot's willingness to accept the constraints under which she lived in hiding.

The Secret Annex, Prinsengracht 263, Amsterdam

Anne and Dr. Pfeffer's Room, The Secret Annex, Prinsengracht 263, Amsterdam © Anne Frank Huis and Museum Collection

> *It's hard to imagine a life in hiding, restricted to the smallest, quietest space. . . .*
>
> *I coped because I had to cope. Remember, the choice was stark: hide, or die. And I coped because when you are hiding you tell yourself that it is not for ever. The prospect*

of for ever really would be unbearable, so you hide until tomorrow, and then until next week, or even the next month. You wait one more day because you think freedom will surely follow the day after that. . . .

Our time in hiding was to be a mixture of two emotions— utter terror and mind-numbing boredom.
—Eva Schloss, *After Auschwitz* (2019)

I couldn't begin to imagine what they must be feeling to have walked away from everything they owned in the world— their home; a lifetime of gathered possessions; Anne's little cat, Moortje. Keepsakes from the past. And friends.
—Miep Gies, *Anne Frank Remembered (2009)*

By early summer 1942, it was clear that Otto and his family would need to go into hiding before much longer.

By this time, all Jews were being made to wear the infamous and obvious yellow stars that would come to symbolize the prejudice of the Holocaust for so many.[59] In June and early July, rules were drawn up for weekly transports of Jews to Kamp Westerbork. The Joodse Raad was held responsible for drawing up the lists of Jews deemed to be eligible for labor duty. These lists included those as young as sixteen which would later obviously upset Anne when she found out about Margot's call-up notice.

This would not have affected Margot, but after August 1942, most of those receiving call-up notices would have been expected to report to the *Hollandsche Schouwburg* in Amsterdam before then being taken to Amsterdam Centraal Station for further transportation to Kamp Westerbork.[60] The Nazis pressured the Joodse Raad to provide as many names as possible at any given time. From Kamp Westerbork, inmates were transported on a regular weekly basis (usually Tuesdays) to death and labor camps in Poland and Germany such as Auschwitz-Birkenau, Sobibór, and Bergen-Belsen.[61]

The sixteen-year-old Margot Frank was among the first to receive a call-up notice when it arrived unexpectedly on July 5, 1942.[62] This notice precipitated Otto's entire plan having to be rushed into activation a few weeks before everything was completely ready in his chosen place of hiding. The Franks (with the help of Miep Gies from Otto's office and her husband Jan) decided that they would have to go into hiding on July 6, 1942, the day following the call-up notice. "July 6" each year has since become one of the more sacred remembered dates for those of us who follow Anne's story.

Otto Frank's chosen place of hiding (which he had kept hidden from Anne until they were on their way there) was the rear annex (or *achterhuis*) of the Opekta's office building on Prinsengracht.[63] This "Secret Annex" now belongs to a select group of famous and meaningful addresses scattered across the world such as 1600 Pennsylvania Avenue (otherwise known as the White House), 10 Downing Street (the home of the British prime minister), Buckingham Palace (the most important of the British sovereign's homes), the Élysée Palace (home of the French president), and the Kremlin. Prinsengracht 263 may now be better known as the "Anne Frank Huis," but the address is the same.

On the wet morning that the Franks left for their place of hiding, they all endeavored to leave a convincing (and rushed) trail to the effect that they had fled to Switzerland where Otto's mother Alice lived. Although Anne's friend Hanneli Goslar believed in the ruse after she discovered Anne to be missing when she dropped by her friend's apartment, it is not immediately clear to me that this could ever have been *that* convincing a ruse. Bear in mind just how difficult and almost impossible it would have been to reach Switzerland at a time when the country was surrounded by German-occupied countries. They would have needed a *lot* of clandestine help.

It is only with the benefit of hindsight that the decision to hide in plain sight and in a place of business comes across as odd, slightly reckless, and not a little naive. Especially, it has to be said, when we consider that the warehouse workers (with the notable exception of Bep's father, Johan Voskuijl, who was the warehouse manager) were *not* brought into the decision-making process.[64] As Anne later makes clear in her diary entries for August 5, 1943, September 16, 1943, and April 21, 1944, everyone was very suspicious of Willem van Maaren, the warehouse manager who was hired to replace Johan Voskuijl after the latter was diagnosed with stomach cancer in summer 1943, and had to retire.

Notwithstanding, the hiding was still exceptionally well planned. By all available accounts and not just their own, Miep and her husband Jan Gies, Bep and her father Johan Voskuijl, Johannes Kleiman, and Victor Kugler were clearly extremely trustworthy helpers who could be depended upon to be as discreet as they were helpful at a time when the Germans were providing every financial incentive to be otherwise.

Although Anne *does* describe arguments between those in hiding and the helpers in her diary, most of these concerned the helpers' need to vent at the careless safety errors made on occasion by the occupants of the Secret Annex. We must acknowledge the considerable strain on the helpers who could not have anticipated having to be responsible for the hiders for over two years. We only have Anne's word for it, but it does *not* appear that she was responsible for any of the carelessness, as she periodically blames others for leaving wallets and other objects behind in the main front office and other areas during their evening and weekend wanderings around the rest of the building. This comparative freedom could only take place when the office was completely free of the warehouse workers. As the offices were open on Saturday mornings, their freedom at weekends chiefly comprised Saturday afternoons and evenings and then all day on Sundays.

Inevitably, some degree of carelessness was always likely to creep in across the twenty-five frustrating months that the eight were in hiding. Oddly, given the strange circumstances that gave rise to it, in her diary entry for April 15, 1944, Anne documents the occasion of Victor Kugler's anger at arriving at work and finding the front door locked. Peter van Pels had the responsibility of making sure that the main front door was unlocked before everyone arrived but forgot on this occasion. I am not quite sure why Mr. Kugler would not have had his own key.

I also find it surprising that no one appears to have been asked to stay behind at Opekta in the evenings to perform any overtime. Then again, as Anne does not write in her diary every day, I could be overthinking this one. As part of a later interview, Otto Frank said that his daughter chiefly only wrote when she was stressed or when something interesting had happened.[65]

Finally, we need to be aware of the fact that those in hiding in the Secret Annex lasted in *one* place for twenty-five months at a time when other Jews in hiding were often forced to move around. Those in hiding were known as *onderduikers*.[66] With the benefit of hindsight, being able to stay in one place was both unusual and remarkable. It is testimony both to the resilience of the occupants of the Secret Annex and to the strong and determined characters of those helping them. The risk of precipitate action on the part of the occupants and betrayal by any of those helping them were *not* issues that those who follow Anne's story have to be concerned with today. The latter concern was certainly an issue for others in hiding.

The fact that those in hiding were eventually betrayed on August 4, 1944, by persons still unknown for certain to this day does not change the fact that Otto's plan *almost* worked out. With the Allies having already launched their invasion of Europe the previous June 6, there was every reason for optimism that liberation would arrive *before* the fearful worst had a chance to happen.

For her part, Anne was initially excited by moving into the Secret Annex and declared in her diary entry for July 11, 1942, that it was like "being on holiday in some strange pension."

Later in her diary entry for May 3, 1944, Anne looked back at her initial arrival in the Secret Annex as a moment that was akin to an "interesting adventure, full of danger and romance."

* * *

Anne and her family moved into the Secret Annex on July 6, 1942. Margot got to ride there early with Miep Gies on her unregistered bicycle. Anne, Otto, and Edith came along within hours but had to walk the distance of approximately three miles (as calculated by Google Earth) in the warm rain. Anne dressed herself in multiple layers as carrying suitcases would have looked suspicious. In her diary entry for July 10, 1942, she notes how she helped her father organize the chaotic rooms while her mother and sister were shell-shocked. This must have been difficult to achieve while the workers were in the warehouse.

Hermann and Auguste van Pels (the van Daan family of Anne's diary) and their son Peter and his cat Mouschi moved in a few days after the Franks on July 13.[67] With the exception of the cat, the van Pels family's arrival was always part of the plan. Hermann van Pels had been working for Otto since 1938 as part of *Pectacon*, the spice side of the business.

Anne and Margot initially shared one room and their parents another on the same lower (second) floor, while Mr. and Mrs. van Pels shared space upstairs on the next floor that also doubled as a community space for everyone during the day. Peter had his own small living space off this main communal area. Peter's room also had a ladder leading to the famous attic from where Anne could look out at the changing leaves on the horse chestnut tree. Her complex and brief relationship with Peter would later flourish in the dubious privacy of the attic. The attic also had a loft.

The only major change in everyone's living arrangements happened when Miep Gies's dentist Dr. Fritz Pfeffer moved into the Secret Annex on November 16, 1942, and joined Anne by replacing Margot. Margot moved into her parents' room, leaving Anne and Dr. Pfeffer to develop a frosty and confrontational arrangement for most of their remaining months in hiding. Anne liked him initially, but that feeling lasted all of twelve days before she was writing negatively in her diary about her new roommate being an "old-fashioned disciplinarian."

Many feel that Anne's adolescence could have been her chief advocate in changing this admittedly odd new arrangement. The van Pels family *could* have agreed to swap sleeping spaces with the Franks; Peter and Dr. Pfeffer *could* then have shared Anne and Margot's old room; Margot or Anne *could* have had Peter's small space beneath the attic for herself. Anne does not suggest in her diary that there was any discussion regarding Dr. Pfeffer's future sleeping arrangements prior to his arrival and nothing on the day itself either. Any final solution would have needed to consider the fact that Anne would have needed quick access to her parents' room or sleeping area as she was often frightened and overwhelmed by German antiaircraft guns aiming their noisy fire at RAF bombers flying over Amsterdam.

In the end, the greater need was for everyone to survive, and in trusting Otto's judgment on the matter, I believe that he would not have countenanced Anne feeling or being harmed.

Nevertheless, Anne's clashes with her "Mr. Dussel" would become the stuff of legend as far as readers of her diary are concerned. Surprisingly, given what we know of Anne's romantic and generous nature, she seems to have ridiculed her Mr. Dussel's relationship with his then Christian girlfriend, Charlotte Kaletta.[68]

As with my growing feelings of empathy toward Edith and Margot, I have developed a lot of sympathy for Dr. Fritz Pfeffer, and I do feel that his shared sleeping arrangements must have been as intolerable for him as they were for Anne. He needed space and time to learn Spanish, while Anne needed a private area where she could write and consider her life as a teenager. Neither understood the other's respective adult and teenage needs.

Although life was never easy in the Secret Annex—with unavoidable restrictions on talking, coughing, and taking lavatory breaks during the working day for the offices and warehouse downstairs—it seems that it became routinely bearable. Early on in her diary entry for November 17, 1942, Anne described the Annex as "ultrapractical." She writes of the pressures of eight people living together in camped circumstances and having to be "reasonable" about everything (December 22, 1942), and then of the boredom inherent to knowing the "punch lines" of everyone's jokes (January 28, 1944).

Margot and Anne (and Peter van Pels to a much lesser degree that Anne felt bordered on laziness) were expected to maintain some semblance of "home school" learning and reading while they were cooped up. This gave the day some structural expectation and focus. Outside supervising his younger daughter's home schooling, Otto seems to have assumed the general role of peacemaker between everyone and Anne, a role for which he was temperamentally and paternally well-suited. His love and tolerance for his daughter shines through as much during the twenty-five months spent in the Secret Annex as it is known to have done during the preceding years.

Notwithstanding the delightful bursts of wit and humor about her fellow inmates that we all love and cherish, Anne clearly conveys throughout her diary the evolving fabric of a life composed largely of depressing solitude, enforced restriction, petty arguments about food, and how best to buy cigarettes for Mr. van Pels. On July 23, 1943, she writes that if they were liberated, she would be "so overjoyed [she] wouldn't know where to begin." Then on November 8, 1943, Anne conveys her obvious frustration by noting how she and her companions resembled "a patch of blue sky surrounded by menacing black clouds."

Later in her diary entry for May 26, 1944, Anne would speak of wanting "even an air raid" to take the place of the otherwise "crushing" anxiety of waiting for an unknown end of being among the "victors or the vanquished."

These are clearly not the musings of someone who was always happy and resigned to life in hiding but rather the angry bursts of someone who was fighting burdensome privations and restrictions each day. Anne clearly cherished what remained of her former childhood freedoms after the invasion and occupation of the Netherlands. It was natural, therefore, that she would have looked forward to a future time without any of the humiliations that had done their best to constrict but not entirely ruin her existence before she went into hiding.

Not long before she was arrested on August 4, 1944, Anne writes in her diary entry for July 15, 1944, of the sheer impossibility of building her life "on a foundation of chaos, suffering and death." She then speaks of the desperate need to "hold on to [her] ideals" with the hope of being able to realize them one day.

Before moving on, I do not believe that my autism would have allowed me to have coped easily with life in hiding—at least, it would have taken me a long time to calm down enough to rationalize the experience. The studying and the reading would have been easy for me, but everything else about living in such confined and unpredictable circumstances would have been hard. I also believe that I would have been as noisy and as frustrated as Anne was and probably just as difficult. That said, any diary that I wrote would have helped me just as it did Anne. Much as I now love and admire Margot, I could not have felt as resigned to the situation as Anne so defines her older sister. On balance, it is to Anne's credit that she was able to function at all, let alone as well as she did at first and then with as much perseverance as she displayed as time dragged on without resolution.

Arrest, August 4, 1944

I believe no psychologist could have helped me understand my years in a concentration camp better than I did on my own. After all, how can you comprehend what is incomprehensible? Someone who never lived the horrors of a concentration camp can never imagine what it was like.
—Nanette Blitz-Konig, *Holocaust Memoirs of a Bergen-Belsen Survivor* (2018)

The Frank girls were so emaciated. They looked terrible. They had little squabbles, caused by their illness, because it was clear that they had typhus [...] They were terribly cold. They had the least desirable places in the barracks, below, near the door, which was constantly opened and closed. You heard them constantly screaming, "Close the door, close the door," and the voices became weaker every day.
—Rachel van Amerongen-Frankfoorder in an interview with Willy Lindwer for his documentary and book, *The Last Seven Months of Anne Frank* (1991)

Then on August 4, 1944, the worst of intrusions, the inevitable, and the jarringly unexpected happened. Life in the Secret Annex would come to an emotionally violent end, with only a modicum of surprising respect accorded to the fact that Otto had once been in the German Imperial Army in the First World War.[69] Anne and her family, the van Pels family, and Fritz Pfeffer had been in hiding for twenty-five months by this time—which, as I said earlier, was remarkable on one level but, in the end, not enough.

As Anne had been writing her last diary entry on August 1, the Allies had been advancing slowly across northern France toward the eventual liberation of Paris on August 25. For at least two months, there had been a healthy degree of reasonable optimism that the war would soon be over, and liberation assured—both for the greater Netherlands and for everyone in the Secret Annex. Nor should we forget the relief that the helpers would have felt given their need for constant discretion, self-policing, and endless vigilance.

As both the dramatic arrest on August 4, 1944, and its immediate aftermath have been extensively covered by both Melissa Müller and Carol Ann Lee in their respective biographies, there is no need to duplicate too much of their thoroughness in this narrative.[70]

On August 8, Anne and the others from the Secret Annex were taken to Amsterdam Centraal Station. A locked train then took them to Kamp Westerbork. Otto Frank says that Anne loved looking out at the changing scenery through the windows of the train. Fortunately, this was a regular train and not a cattle car.

On arrival at the camp, they were placed in barrack 67 which was also known as the "S" barrack for political prisoners and those who had tried to elude the requests to report for labor camps through becoming *onderduikers*.

Compared to Nazi-run camps elsewhere, living and medical conditions were not totally intolerable at Kamp Westerbork and Anne appreciated the fresh air and continued closeness to her family. Ronnie Goldstein-van Cleef in discussion with Willy Lindwer even went so far as to refer to the camp as the equivalent of a "vacation colony."[71] Anne was given the pointless task with Margot and her mother of breaking up old batteries.

The camp commander, Albert Gemmeker, was known for appreciating orderly transports down to the point of apparently wanting to help the elderly and children onto the weekly cattle cars.[72] Unfortunately, he had no issue with then ending his concern beyond encouraging those who remained in his camp to relax for the next six days. Those whom he had helped on the trains would be left to experience little food and water and only poor sanitary arrangements. Several would die before even reaching their final destinations. Gemmeker later dubiously claimed not to know what happened in any of the camps beyond his own.

On September 3, 1944, Anne and everyone else from the Secret Annex were deported with over one thousand others on the last of the cattle-car transport trains to leave Kamp Westerbork for the three-day trip to Auschwitz-Birkenau in Poland.[73]

After arriving on the main railway line's infamous spur track directly into the glaring heart of the Birkenau (Auschwitz II) women's camp on the night of September 6, 1944, the struggle for survival took on added urgency.[74] While all eight survived the initial selection for work as opposed to immediate gassing, Anne and Margot saw their father for the last time as they went with their mother and Mrs. van Pels to barrack 29. Otto, Hermann van Pels, and Peter were marched off to the main men's camp (Auschwitz I).

* * *

Hermann van Pels was the first from the Secret Annex to die as he was one of the last inmates at Auschwitz selected to be gassed after one month of labor. According to the Jewish Virtual Library, Heinrich Himmler, as head of the Nazi SS, ordered the gassings to cease at Auschwitz in November 1944, but too late for Mr. van Pels.

Fritz Pfeffer managed to survive Auschwitz before dying of enterocolitis on December 20, 1944, at Neuengamme concentration camp in Germany.[75] He was transported there via Sachsenhausen, which was yet another concentration camp in Germany for political prisoners.

Edith Frank died from starvation at the infirmary in Birkenau on January 6, 1945, just three weeks before the camp's liberation by the Russian Red Army. Edith had an end that was particularly heartbreaking, as she still believed that Anne and Margot were with her until the end as she continued to look for and hoard food for them long after both girls had been transported to Bergen-Belsen. The trauma of Edith's last weeks and death were later reported by Rootje (Rosa) de Winter to Otto Frank when their journey home after the liberation of Auschwitz was interrupted in Katowice. There will be more on Rosa's role later in this story.

Joop van Wijk-Voskuijl stands beside the poignant memorial at Kamp Westerbork (Drenthe Province, The Netherlands) to the 102,000 who never returned from being transported to camps "back east" such as Auschwitz-Birkenau, Bergen-Belsen, Sobibór, and Theresienstadt. When viewed from above on Google Earth, the memorial appears shaped in a map of the Netherlands © Joop van Wijk-Voskuijl

Closer view of the memorial to the 102,000, Kamp Westerbork,
Drenthe Province, The Netherlands © Joop van Wijk-Voskuijl

Remains of a former barracks at Kamp Westerbork, Drenthe Province, The Netherlands © Fr. John Neiman

Replica Cattle Car, Kamp Westerbork, Drenthe Province, The Netherlands © Joop van Wijk-Voskuijl

Peter van Pels survived the horrors of Auschwitz but died after a forced march to Mauthausen, a harsh labor camp with a mobile gas chamber in Austria. It is believed that Peter died from starvation on or around May 10, 1945, a few days after the Second World War finally came to an end in chaotic fashion across Europe and five days after the Germans were finally forced to surrender in the Netherlands.

Meanwhile, Anne, Margot, and Mrs. van Pels were shipped off to Bergen-Belsen in Germany sometime toward the end of October 1944. Much of this hasty activity (along with the cessation of gassings and the subsequent blowing up of evidence) toward the end of 1944 was a consequence of the advancing Russian Red Army making slow but steady progress across Poland.[76]

Auguste van Pels was again moved at some point from Bergen-Belsen to the Theresienstadt (Terezín) ghetto, which seems to have been marketed by the Nazis as being akin to a holiday camp compared to their other placements. We are not sure of the exact date on which Mrs. van Pels died, where, or how.[77]

Somewhat miraculously in Anne's case, given her always fragile health, both she and Margot not only survived the transportation to Bergen-Belsen, but they were also able to keep going for another three or four months. Although Bergen-Belsen was not technically one of the infamous Nazi death camps, both girls later succumbed in February or March 1945 to a virulent typhus epidemic that spread throughout the camp.[78]

Margot Frank is said to have died after falling out of the "bed" that she shared with Anne. It is highly likely that she did not even remember her nineteenth birthday on February 16, 1945, if indeed she even made it that far. New research conducted by Erika Prins on behalf of the Anne Frank Huis suggests that she did not. See note 78 above for further information on this research.

Anne Frank died a few days after her sister. She was still only fifteen years old and died covered in the fleas that she hated so much and with only the warmth of a flea-ridden blanket to keep away the cold.

Both girls died around two months before the British Army liberated the camp on April 15.

A striking memorial plaque has since been placed for both Anne and Margot alongside that of many others at the camp's former location. Their memorial resembles a shrine complete with the flowers left by well-wishers as it sits in what is now an open field. Margot's name appears first which is interesting and welcome.

It is believed to be significant that both Anne and Margot died not knowing that their father had survived the liberation of Auschwitz on January 27, 1945. Hanneli Goslar, who amazingly came across her friend at Bergen-Belsen after learning that Anne was there from Mrs. van Pels, felt that if Anne had known that her father had survived, she might well have found a further will to live.[79]

We will never know the answer to this. Nor will we ever know what effect it would have had on Margot if she had known. I can imagine Margot and Anne feeling a keen sense of responsibility for each other once they both left Birkenau, and I feel a poor sense of relief that both girls were together at the end. Likewise, that Anne was able to receive some hugs from Nanette Blitz, who had also ended up at the camp. Although they had never been close, Anne and Nanette had been classmates at the Jewish Lyceum and Nanette did manage to secure an invitation to Anne's thirteenth birthday party at which everyone viewed the aforementioned Rin Tin Tin movie. Just as importantly, their shared hugs are a brief reminder of the humanity that could exist in the darkest of places. Readers can learn more about Nanette's story as a "classmate of Anne Frank" in *Holocaust Memoirs of a Bergen-Belsen Survivor*.

Anne's scattered diary and her other notebooks, a broken comb, her pictures of film stars and members of the British and Dutch royal families on the wall of her bedroom in the Secret Annex, dashes and dates outlining her height (alongside those for Margot) on the wall of the Secret Annex, and the memories of Otto, other family members, and her surviving friends constitute the chief of what helps us to connect with her today. Let's also not forget the all-important family photograph albums. Sadly, far less remains of Margot, but I remain ever hopeful that one day her diary *will* be discovered either hidden in the Secret Annex itself or in the drawer of some random piece of furniture that would have found its way to Germany after the Annex was cleared in August 1944.

Anne's dreams of becoming a writer or a journalist and of becoming a proper Dutch citizen after the war died with her. Margot's dream of becoming a nurse in Palestine (later Israel) after the war died with her.

We should not forget, though, that Anne and Margot were among some fifty thousand "statistics" who died at Bergen-Belsen from starvation, typhus, or other causes in the last months of the war. I imagine that Anne was probably more resilient than her sister through to the end and that she inclined more toward the angry than toward the depressed with their situation. That said, it is not often understood the extent to which Anne had rarely been among the healthiest of children and that she succumbed to frequent and prolonged illnesses throughout her childhood. Within the Secret Annex, her ailments must have often been the cause of alarm, as can be inferred from some of Anne's comments in her last diary entry (August 1, 1944). Notwithstanding, she must have exuded a certain healthy presence of mind to have passed the ruthless selection process at Auschwitz-Birkenau and almost to liberation at Bergen-Belsen.

* * *

The Nazis destroyed as much evidence as they could of the infamous crematoria and gas chambers at Auschwitz-Birkenau. They left behind only some buildings, up to seven thousand "survivors" languishing in the infirmaries and elsewhere, and an infamous sign. Auschwitz was finally liberated by the Russians on January 27, 1945. What remained now stands preserved and open to the public as a memorial to the Holocaust and a stark reminder of the worst of humanity. Pictures of Birkenau today and the chillingly precise spur line into the camp look especially ghoulish and stark when set against a backdrop of winter snow—as if the whole former nightmare has become frozen in time. I wonder when the birds came back…?

"MEETING" ANNE FRANK: AN ANTHOLOGY

The Second World War ended in chaotic fashion over several weeks in May 1945, with most of the Netherlands being among the last areas to be conceded by the Germans.

Meanwhile, the war with Japan continued in the Far East until the Japanese finally decided to surrender after atomic bombs were controversially dropped on Hiroshima on August 6, 1945, and on Nagasaki three days later. The formal surrender needed to wait until September, with some Japanese soldiers taking several decades to acknowledge the end of the war. Our website resources section contains important links to the surrender of Axis forces throughout Europe and Asia.

Otto Frank

Of the eight people who had been forced to go into hiding on or after July 6, 1942, in the rear annex of Prinsengracht 263 in Amsterdam, only Anne's father Otto survived the Holocaust. He was among those still alive in the infirmary after the liberation of Auschwitz.[80] Otto's survival has obviously meant that we are now able to read Anne's words and try to live up to her hopes for humanity.

As I examine my thinking surrounding this well-known fact, I find myself feeling as strongly for what we have missed in Margot dying without leaving us with, at least, a diary as I welcome the fact that Anne, at least, left us with one. While I think that Otto would have still published his younger daughter's diary if Margot had survived without her sister, there is little doubt that she would have been able to provide a lot of clarifying and valuable edits of her own. Anne's diary would have become more of a collaboration between her father and sister; however, this belongs to the many *what-ifs* of publishing history. I also think that Otto would have published Margot's diary if it had been found with or even *without* the survival of Anne's. While Anne almost certainly would have published something after the war if she had survived, it is less clear to me that Margot would have published her own diary. As far as we know, she did not really have the aim of becoming a writer in the same way that Anne did.

After the Second World War, Otto chose not to dwell on what happened to him and his family in a destructive way. In fact, he returned to work for Opekta in the very same Prinsengracht 263 building that he had once been arrested in, which may seem amazing to us who have grown up in an era of PTSD, antidepressants, and other therapeutic interventions. Talk about exposure therapy!

Otto's generosity toward answering so many letters from children, teenagers, and adults around the world has since become legendary. We can be left in little doubt that he was always trying to focus the attention and thoughts of others on the hope of his lost younger daughter and that he rejoiced in the lasting spirit of Anne's words as others interpreted them.

Many who grew into adulthood in the decades following the conclusion of the Second World War in 1945, and especially those like Cara Wilson-Granat who were traumatized by the emotional and political divisions of the Vietnam War and the assassinations of President Kennedy, his brother Bobby, and Martin Luther King, ended up thrusting a lot of their hopes and idealism on Otto's shoulders. To an extent, indeed, that it is not always easy to tell whether it is *Otto* responding to us or his *understanding* of what his younger daughter would have wanted from him. On the other hand, and given what we know of his famously measured disposition, I do not think that anybody can seriously claim that Otto was never himself after the war or that he had no idealism of his own separate from his interpretation of Anne's.

Otto Frank would go on to live until he was ninety-one years old, dying on August 19, 1980. He was survived by his second wife, Elfriede (Fritzi). Although he had probably known Fritzi and her daughter Eva reasonably well from their earlier time on the Merwedeplein, they became much closer during their journey back to Amsterdam after the liberation of Auschwitz-Birkenau. They became closer still while putting together what was left of their lives in Amsterdam after the war. Fritzi and her daughter were able to move back to their apartment on Merwedeplein while Otto was able to move in with Miep Gies and her husband after discovering that his old Merwedeplein 37 apartment had long been taken over. Elfriede Geiringer had lost both her husband and her son during the Holocaust and was thus able to eventually marry Otto on November 10, 1953. Eva Geiringer would subsequently become known to many of us as Eva Schloss, the "posthumous stepsister of Anne Frank."

Otto and Fritzi were very happy to share Anne's story with all those interested in learning more about her. They spent most of their lives together in Basel, Switzerland.

Otto opened the former Secret Annex as the Anne Frank Huis to visitors on May 6, 1960, and then later established the Anne Frank Fonds (Foundation) in Basel in January 1963. Both organizations have since published a wealth of printed and online information on Anne's story, including the role of the helpers, biographical information on other members of her family, and details on the complex publishing history of her diary. Our website resources section contains valuable links to each of these informational subsets.

He bequeathed Anne's diary and other papers to the Dutch government as part of his will, but any commercial use of the diary in books about Anne must go through the Anne Frank Fonds, which retains the copyright to her work.

THE LEGACY OF ANNE FRANK

T HE OPINIONS IN this chapter are very much my own. While I am confident that my fellow writers will share most of them, some of my thoughts with respect to Anne's legacy will reflect a more decidedly personal view of the world.

* * *

If the life of Jesus Christ for Christians across the world derives much of its unique power and meaning from his miraculous *transcendence of death* and subsequent appearance to his disciples, Anne Frank's life derives almost all of its transcendent power and meaning from the fact that she *died* in the state-sponsored grip of one of the cruelest of all ideological and genocidal dreams—namely, that the world would be infinitely better off without there being any Jews left to envy or despise. *Did* Anne have to die at Bergen-Belsen and—as far as we know—*not* rise again and *did* Jesus have to die on a cross and then rise again in accordance with Christian faith for their current martyred reputations to exist today?

On one level, it might seem presumptuous to link these two historical figures and fellow Jews, but on another, we need to bear in mind that Anne's diary has become one of the most well-read and translated books in the world after the Bible.

Anne is now widely regarded as a teenager who was not only extraordinary in in terms of her writing abilities, but also preternaturally wise beyond her years in highly challenging circumstances. As we saw earlier (as recounted in *We All Wore Stars* by Theo Coster), Anne and Hanneli's former teacher at the 6e Montessorischool, Mrs. Kuperus, believed that the compressed circumstances of the Secret Annex may have been responsible for accelerating the growth of Anne's wisdom. The proximity of so many adults in hiding must have led her to see the best in the adult wisdom around her but also to become contemptuous of the worst of an adult world that she held responsible for the misery around her. There is plenty of evidence of both in her diary, with generous commentary regarding instincts and comments that she liked mixed with icy contempt for those that she disliked, and which offended her. Very adolescent! It appears that her father may well have shared many of his daughter's feelings, which may explain why he included so many of Anne's icier observations in the published version of her diary.[81]

Thus, Otto and even Mr. van Pels to a degree (when he wasn't smoking) emerge well from the pages of Anne's diary, while Edith, Margot, Mrs. van Pels, and the hapless Dr. Pfeffer do not; however, we still need to recognize that some of Anne's criticisms can be attributable to the workings of her fertile and imaginative literary mind and to her adolescent mindset. In other words, we can put *some* of them down to simple misunderstandings and not always to the recipient's just desserts.

Nowadays, Edith, Margot, Mrs. van Pels, and Fritz Pfeffer are each rightly appreciated for the depth and unnecessary nature of their enforced suffering and for their basic humanity in challenging circumstances. I am convinced that Edith parented her younger daughter much more instinctively than Anne gives her credit. If Edith was not as flexible as Otto in terms of addressing Anne's famous temper, it is worth remembering that *both* parents only wanted her to be happy at school, that *both* championed the principles of the Montessori curriculum, and that *both* dismissed any concerns about negative school reports. For many children today, this type of schooling and parental response would sound ideal!

Although Anne may not have fully appreciated either her sister or her mother while they were in hiding, it is worth mentioning that their relationship changed for the better once they were confined to the horrors of Auschwitz-Birkenau. Bloeme Evers-Emden would later tell Willy Lindwer that she saw little evidence of the discord that Anne relates so often in her diary and that it had obviously been "swept away" by "existential need." She also says that Edith and her daughters were "always together" at Auschwitz. I love this imagery and believe it to be closer to the reality of their relationship. This is *not* to deny that there were problems between Anne and her mother, but to suggest that their underlying love for one another likely kept things from totally spiraling out of control. As a final point here, I would like to draw the attention of our readers to a famous photograph of the Frank family from 1941 in which Edith is clearly holding Anne's hand. Anne would have been eleven or twelve at the time; for me, it not only tells us a lot about Edith as a mother, but also about Anne as a daughter not rejecting her mother's protective care. I love this one! As I am unable to download it for inclusion in our book, here is a link to it from the Anne Frank Huis and Museum website collection of photographs in the public domain: https://www.flickr.com/photos/collection_annefrankhouse/31902941952/in/album-72157678631610275/

Notwithstanding the relatively cheerful and witty vignettes of her school friends in her early diary entries, we still need to recognize that Anne's general outlook would become predominantly determined by her understanding of some adults whom she loved (chiefly her father), those whom she loved but viewed as flawed (mainly her mother), those whom she probably never wanted to see again at the conclusion to the war (chiefly Mrs. van Pels and Fritz Pfeffer), and those whom she truly respected (chiefly Bep Voskuijl and her father, Miep Gies and her husband, Victor Kugler, and Johannes Kleiman).

If Anne is now considered to have been wise, thoughtful, and idealistic beyond her years, paradoxically, she is also viewed as someone who was typically adolescent in her tempestuous moods, tempers, rudeness, and selfishness—at least, as those around her saw her. Many of my fellow contributors to this anthology view her in the same way and love her for the resonance of her rebelliousness as much as they do for her wisdom and idealism. It is right that we celebrate this side of Anne as much as we do the more serious and idealistic side of her character as revealed through her more introspective diary entries. The "two Annes"—as she herself would describe her predicament in her diary entry for April 28, 1944—resonate equally with the global teenage and adult fan base that she now has.

For example, when I was reading *We All Wore Stars* by Theo Coster, I did not get the impression that Anne Frank was completely liked by everyone who knew her, and it is entirely possible that she *may* have overestimated her overarching popularity among other girls and her attractiveness to boys. As I noted earlier, some have suggested that Anne might have well been one of the "mean girls" of Merwedeplein.[82] I leave it to our readers to decide whether the attributed conduct was "mean" or "normal" for a girl of Anne's age and vibrant temperament. We have to assume that flirtatious girls of eleven or twelve must have seemed as intimidating to shy boys and less extroverted girls in Anne's time as they can be now.

Regardless of how she later confided her seriousness and self-awareness to Kitty in her diary, Anne recognized that in public she was always struggling with the authenticity of the "two Annes" and how best to reveal or conceal each of them. The livelier of the two versions was the one that everyone usually saw and just as usually disliked. Unfortunately, it was *also* the version that they were most ready to trust. This must have caused Anne several problems when in hiding because no teenager likes to be seen as "inauthentic" in terms of their feelings. If even Otto claimed not to know his own daughter properly until after he read her diary and became acquainted with the deeper and more serious Anne that we all cherish today, it is hard imagining how anyone else in the Secret Annex would have trusted her growing self-awareness and thoughtfulness.

In conclusion at this point, Anne Frank must have been both a difficult and an amazing child and teenager to have been around. Otto certainly understood both in terms of the livelier side revealed by his daughter in public, but he must have been shocked by the thoughtful and serious side that Anne showed to Kitty and which he only discovered later when reading her diary.

It is in a spirit of honesty and frankness that Anne records both her more volatile feelings *and* the exasperation of others at seeing them on display. In doing so, she is being faithful to herself and to the perception of her faults by those around her. We must applaud her self-critical honesty even if sometimes she uses her faults to expose the failings of others. Only Otto is adjudged to have understood the public version of his daughter. By report, he was clearly keen to forgive Anne everything. As I explain later, with my own daughter, this forgiveness is easy to pursue as a parent once one understands the circumstances that give rise to its need.

* * *

Over the years, Anne Frank's life and death have taken on both real and mythological proportions that show little sign of abating on either count. Nor will they while the Holocaust remains as such a powerful symbol of genocidal oppression and while we continue to celebrate or honor the important anniversaries of events such as D-Day, the liberation of the concentration camps, other important battles such as the Battle of Britain and Pearl Harbor, and the overall ending of the Second World War. Nor will they while we continue to believe that Anne displayed the enduring signs of an idealistic sense of purpose and raw young literary talent that were cut tragically short.

Nor *should* we be looking at the end of any of these celebrations or at any concluding ceremony for Anne's symbolism and her resonance with so many people. The Second World War is widely considered to have been the most necessary war in history, effectively silencing the morality and purpose of any previous or subsequent war. Paradoxically, Anne's life and death exist within one of the darkest corners of that moral and purposeful interface. Yet that very darkness defined the brightness of the light that guided the "greatest generation" to an unqualified victory.

The war was never fought, of course, to rescue Anne, her family, and any of her friends held in various concentration camps throughout occupied Europe. Yet it *was* surely fought to rescue humanity from the prejudice, expansionism, and hatred threatening to engulf much of the world.

It is also true, though, that in rescuing what remained of Anne after the war—her diary and other written and photographic artefacts— Miep, Bep, and Otto allowed her to "go on living after [her] death" as she told us she wanted in her diary entry for April 5, 1944. By securing an ultimate victory for humanity and democracy over Nazism and fascism, the Allies allowed Anne and others who had left behind written testimony of their lives during the Holocaust to speak to the future of the horrors of the past. This observation applies as much to Jews who lost their lives during the Holocaust or who survived it as it does to those who documented the dangers of life under occupation but who had no risk of deportation because they were not Jewish. An Allied defeat would have meant suppression of such pillars of witness and a continuation of the horrors endured.

*   *   *

Throughout her short life Anne was often sick with normal childhood illnesses that somehow became prolonged. She was also gregarious, highly inquisitive, and mostly happy. She disliked math and she loved history. She had a mostly normal life while the Netherlands remained free. Yet Anne's premature death from unaided starvation and typhus in 1945 meant that she could not *physically* transcend a time in history when ascendant and rampant fascism in Europe defined both itself and what others should believe as well. Nazism had nothing to offer outside Germany and was an illusion to those inside the country. It was built around a culture of hate, demonization of the other, Aryan supremacism, and ideological purity.

The Holocaust was the tragic result of this warped way of thinking and Anne Frank's early death and truncated promise must be viewed as inseparable issues from the historical turmoil and revenge around her if both are to be understood and accepted for their iconic meaning today.

The German invasion of the Netherlands on May 10, 1940, put an end to any lingering illusions of security for the Jewish community, affecting those who had been born in the country and those who had emigrated there from a hostile Germany in the 1930s. Anne clearly tried to live a normal life as far as she could (which seemingly included going to the beach at Zandvoort with Margot the same summer that the country was invaded) and for as long as she could before having to endure the privations of an enforced life of abnormality in hiding. After the arrest of those in the Secret Annex on August 4, 1944, Anne lived a life of brutality, pointless work, and conformity to rules based on fanatical prejudice.

However, Anne *was* able to transcend the reality of being a statistic in a horrible genocide. She did so by leaving us with not just her beloved and inspirational father but also with hundreds of pages of illuminating diary entries that sadly "died" some seven months *before* their author.

The question here is the extent to which the reality of the older and wiser *teenager* dying with so many others in such horrific and traumatic circumstances after her last diary entry on August 1, 1944, invalidates the idealism shown by the younger and more hopeful *writer* in the younger diary. This question is rarely asked, although a few of us have asked it in this anthology, and so too has Eva Schloss, Anne's posthumous stepsister.

Arguably, some would say that we do not need to ask this question because Anne's idealism and deeper purpose (as defined by the "second Anne" unknown to others, including her own father) are primarily what we now cling to. Everything else *outside* this consideration of Anne as a serious writer risks invalidating her idealism if considered. Many would find it difficult trying to travel this road.

These qualities—her essential humanity and complexity, and the hauntingly beautiful photographs that remain of her—are what resonate with us today, and we have to be grateful that Anne had a father who was interested not just in publishing his daughter's diary, but also in the *promise* and the *creative* side of photography. Otto Frank's Leica camera has taken on an iconic status in the years since the publication of Anne's diary in 1947 and in line with the fascination that has grown around her brief life. Otto later gave the Leica to his stepdaughter Eva Schloss after the war to help her develop her career. Ryan Cooper also got to use it for one of the photographs that he asked me to include in this book.

In addition, we also have a compelling record of photographs taken by others in school settings and elsewhere that both Otto and Edith must have loved and which they decided to preserve in their photograph albums. Even Anne's passport photographs have assumed iconic status, and she would end up including many of them (as well as others taken elsewhere) in her famous red-and-white checkered diary. Sadly, there are no known photographs of Anne or anyone else in the Secret Annex.[83]

The decision by parents to create a record of the lives of their children through photographs and other ephemera goes a long way toward showing any child that he or she is worth the effort taken to parent them. As a father myself now, I have taken lots of pictures of my own daughter to memorialize stages and events in her life.

Yet are we being fair by continuing to fix Anne Frank in our minds to just her feelings and idealistic hopes as a teenager? This is certainly *not* about questioning whether Anne is still worth the attention paid to her life and ideals as everyone writing for this anthology loves this youngster, cherishes her life, is angry about her early and pointless death, and extracts inspiration from what she did, wrote, and hoped for herself and others.

Notwithstanding, and perhaps controversially, I believe that we *must* still ask whether, as Anne famously declared to Kitty on July 15, 1944, she would have continued to believe that people were "truly good at heart"? This point has been raised by Eva Schloss, among others.[84] Given the extent to which we also have to face the fact that some of the most traumatic events of her life—her arrest, her transportation to Kamp Westerbork, her deportation to first Auschwitz-Birkenau and then Bergen-Belsen—had yet to happen when her diary concludes on August 1, we *have* to wonder if this comment would have stood the test of revealed time.

If Anne had survived and continued to write after the war, *would* she have maintained the sunny idealism and optimism shown throughout her diary but which she was already interlacing with thoughtful seriousness, worldly cynicism, and inner wisdom the longer she was exposed to adult ways of thinking and behaving in the Secret Annex? We need only look at her controversial comments in her diary entry for February 8, 1944, about her parents' marriage and about Edith as a less than perfect mother to prompt us to ask the extent to which Anne could suspend her critical faculties long enough to believe that people *are* "truly good at heart," and with that observation serving as *more* than just a passing serious or idealistic whim. These critical comments only appeared in 1998 and have been added since as four long paragraphs to her February 8, 1944, diary entry. Otto Frank had withheld them as too upsetting, but the Anne Frank Fonds has since given permission for them to be included as part of a recent updated *Definitive Edition* of Anne's diary.

Much the same could be said of the upsetting letter that she wrote to her father and which she includes "more or less" as she wrote it in her diary entry for May 5, 1944.

With so many circumstantial pressures to adapt to, it is not surprising to me that Anne felt so many contradictory impulses and why she then came to so many reasonable but paradoxical views of her world. Some of her views were unquestionably fixed but I see others as mere whims with little in the way of a permanent sticking point. The only problem is determining which is which. I also cannot tell whether the observation that people are "truly good at heart" belongs to the serious Anne that was then under strong development or to the naively optimistic and idealistic Anne who would have probably shed such feelings if she had could have made it home after enduring life in Kamp Westerbork, Auschwitz-Birkenau, and Bergen-Belsen.

Anne was certainly obstinate and rude to her elders in a way that many teenagers would recognize to this day. We also recognize that she was forced to vent in cramped circumstances that she could not easily escape without getting killed and risking the lives of everyone else.

Today, most teenagers do *not* have to resolve their feelings in circumstances similar to Anne's, but, instead, can freely and safely vent to friends and in locations both known and unknown to their parents. One of my coauthors, Joy Gafa', often talks to another of my coauthors, Yvonne Leslie, and to me over Messenger about some of her hopes and fears. Anne did not have this luxury, and Twitter, Facebook, Messenger, email, and text messaging obviously did not exist as ways for her to connect with her friends outside the Secret Annex. Nor would it have been safe to write letters, although she did try in some of her earlier diary entries. She famously describes dreaming of her friend Hanneli Goslar on several occasions.[85] She could *only* vent in front of her parents, sister, four others, and up to six helpers, and she could *only* resolve her conflicts and feelings through writing in her diary to "patient" Kitty. She also *only* had the famous attic of the Secret Annex to escape to and the rest of the office building in the evenings and at weekends. Everyone was judgmental to varying degrees and to an extent that would annoy most teenagers, but Anne's "Pim" clearly also understood her. So too did Bep Voskuijl, who, as one of the helpers, developed a healthy and compatible relationship with Anne.[86]

All of us who have written in this book ache for Anne to have survived, but which Anne are we looking for when we have both the *person* and what one of my contributors, Pine Delgado, has referred to as the "great wartime *diarist*" to think about? What would an Anne who survived have been like? Should we be frightened that there are at least two Annes to consider just like we have several versions of her diary? She was a Gemini after all. To what extent can we combine these *two* Annes into a coherent *single* Anne who can speak to us both through the wisdom, humor, and growing self-awareness of her diary entries *and* through the likely cynicism and trauma of her subsequent experiences. This issue is different to that of the "two Annes" that Anne struggled to manage *within* herself.

This question both intrigues and frightens us because I am not sure that many of us even *want* to consider the idea of a permanent fun-loving Anne Frank who exists outside the received literary wisdom of her diary. Still less, of a potentially bitter Anne Frank who might have suffered from complex PTSD had she survived Bergen-Belsen and returned to Amsterdam with or without any other surviving members of her family. We prefer to think of the teenage Anne becoming a wiser and even more informed adult with her earlier sunny optimism and ideals fully intact.

The novelist David Gillham, however, wants to offer his opinion on all this and does so in the form of his recent novel, *Annelies*. Mr. Gillham has bravely written a fictional account of a "resurrected" Anne living an angry, tormented, and unforgiving life in Amsterdam for several years after the end of the war. His *imaginary* Anne who survives is clearly deeply traumatized and depressingly unlikable in terms of her anger toward her father, a vivid portrayal that is at odds with how most of us prefer to think of the *actual* Anne who died, who left us with a beautiful diary, and who considered her father to be the most "adorable" of fathers. It is far easier thinking of her generous, warm-hearted, funny, and hopeful disposition. The former *imaginary* Anne of Mr. Gilham's world is unknown, of course, while the latter actual Anne is the lively young girl whom we all feel we know from her diary and from the testimony of her father and other friends.

I do tend to see it as authentic that Mr. Gillham's Anne would have shed many of her illusions about how "truly good" mankind really was when set against the horror of the atrocities ultimately perpetrated against her and millions of others. At least, she would have done so at first. I also agree that if Anne *had* survived, she would have returned to Amsterdam with unspeakable trauma, survival guilt, and a sense of profound shame when thinking about how dismissive she had been earlier of her mother and sister.[87] Both Edith and Margot would have punctuated Anne's dreams in ways that could only now be addressed through therapy. In a way, Mr. Gillham addresses this point by creatively adding Margot's ghostly presence in *Annelies* and by effectively setting her up as Anne's conscience.

The imaginary Anne's trauma, postwar pettiness, and anger (irrational or not) would be instantly recognizable today; and even if it could *not* have been addressed successfully, there is no doubt that the real Otto would have marched her to the nearest therapist if his younger daughter had survived and showed such symptoms. He would have surely done the same for Margot as well if she had survived with or without her younger sister. It is significant, I think, that Otto would always remember the panic in his older daughter's eyes when they were separated at the platform at Birkenau. This haunting image was brought up in a recent bookazine publication centered around Margot's life. Please see our bibliography for further information on the "Anne Frank: 75 Years Later" series.

Annelies is certainly compelling, but, as an example of the *what-if* genre, it will be not entirely satisfying for some because of how the historical Anne died in such horrific circumstances and who never did get to reunite in Amsterdam with the father whom she loved and adored.

In this anthology, we have avoided imagining what Anne would have been like if she had survived the horrors of the Holocaust and been able to rejoin her father in Amsterdam. In the end, it is just too powerful a line of thought to be addressed rationally and without otherwise drowning in an emotional swamp.

* * *

When I read Anne's diary today and think about her life, I keep coming back in my mind to the fact that her story involves many "almost" achievements. Had any one of these been successful, it could have saved Anne's life, the lives of her sister and mother, and the lives of the other four who died from the Secret Annex.

Despite the fact that there was always a certain inevitability about their presumed betrayal and then their arrest and deportation, Anne and her fellow hiders (Otto included) *almost* survived their time in hiding.

They were *almost* justified in feeling super optimistic respecting the likelihood of their eventual liberation after the D-Day landings of June 6, 1944. Yet such hope was more a veneer designed to mask the greater likelihood of their betrayal and arrest as the occupying Germans became ever more desperate to cling to whatever occupied territory that remained to them in the now waning days of the Second World War.

They *almost* survived the comparatively reasonable conditions at the transit camp of Kamp Westerbork but were placed, instead, on the last of the transport cattle cars sent to Auschwitz on September 3, 1944. The Allies were a mere 168 miles away liberating Brussels at the time. Much would happen, though, before Kamp Westerbork was eventually liberated on April 12, 1945. The occupants of the Secret Annex could surely have survived at that camp, *but* for that final transport to Auschwitz.

Mr. van Pels *almost* outlived the order given by Himmler to stop the gassings held at Auschwitz in November 1944.

Edith Frank, who died on January 6, 1945, *almost* made it through to the liberation of Auschwitz on January 27, 1945, by the Russian Red Army.

Anne and Margot *almost* survived to the moment of Bergen-Belsen's liberation on April 15, 1945, by the British Army.

Peter van Pels and his mother *almost* survived the end of the war in their respective Mauthausen and Theresienstadt concentration camps.

Of those who eventually died from the Secret Annex, only Fritz Pfeffer died long before Neuengamme's eventual (and late) liberation on May 4, 1945.

It is worth bearing in mind that many other *onderduikers* from the Netherlands would have had their own *almost* moments built into their own desperate efforts to avoid the end that they could not ultimately escape.

Concluding Remarks

We know as much as we do about Anne today because her father survived and famously devoted the rest of his long life to preserving and cherishing his beloved daughter's memory and ideals. Not a little time was also spent challenging the arguments of those who believed that Anne's diary was fake. I said earlier that we would not be exploring this topic outside the links provided in our website resources section.

Anne's diary spoke to Otto when Miep handed it to him in July 1945 after it was confirmed that his daughters had not survived. Even then, it took him a while to listen to the message, and he found Anne *almost* unrecognizable when he did. Publishing his younger daughter's work was clearly as therapeutic for Otto to do as it has been illuminating for us to read.

Anne's legacy now flourishes across the world. It is fortunately rare to find her life or work dishonored or commercialized in sordid ways, although examples of commercial tastelessness do appear occasionally. Where once Anne was just an excitable daughter who seemed destined for a bright and colorful future had the Nazis not invaded the Netherlands and redirected her life, now we have an Anne who unites us through her essential humanity and the power of her writing. The number of possibilities as to how best to connect with her seem endless and equally true! Many of these are explored throughout this anthology and this is how fame interacts with and transforms those who follow in its wake.

That Anne Frank tried to control many of her feelings through her writing is amazing, quite frankly. As I say in my own story later in this anthology, I tried to instill this *reconciliatory* power into my own daughter when she went through a traumatizing experience in Los Angeles. I chose to follow my own advice when I wrote my *Denied! Failing Cordelia* trilogy. Just as Anne has inspired me to write and try to transcend my own traumatic experiences, so too have some of my cowriters in this anthology addressed Anne as their own "Kitty."

That Anne *was* able to write a diary was not as rare as it is sometimes assumed to be, and we do need to acknowledge the powerful accounts of other Jews who were able to write of their experiences in the occupied territories during the Second World War prior to their capture and deportation. For example, Etty Hillesum's letters from Kamp Westerbork have been published along with her diary of life in the occupied Netherlands. She subsequently died in Auschwitz-Birkenau. Her last letter was thrown out of the train that she was deported on and found by someone who posted it.

Others who survived the Holocaust have written retrospectively of their suffering. Elie Wiesel famously published several books relating to his experiences in Auschwitz and Buchenwald. I have *Helga's Diary: A Young Girl's Account of Life in a Concentration Camp* newly beside me as I write this. I had never heard of Helga Weiss and her account of life in the Theresienstadt ghetto and then in Auschwitz-Birkenau until recently; not surprisingly, her diary has been compared to that of Anne's, but then many are! Renia Spiegel's diary was found recently and published by her sister. Renia has been dubbed "the Polish Anne Frank." Publishing details for each of the above works can be found in our rich bibliography.

*   *   *

Anne Frank's messages of critical self-inquiry and hope for a better world continue to resonate to this day because extremism continues to be a problem across Europe, the United States, and other parts of the world. I often wonder what Anne would think of the present world and the place of her ideals within it. Were her thoughts on everything and everyone around her just impulsive and changeable whims and musings or, instead, well-considered and lasting ways of seeing that were tragically cut short?

Would Anne's ideals as expressed while she was in hiding and the subsequent jarring reality of her arrest and afterward have clashed and led to her idealism emerging as the ultimate victor? Or would her ideals have *merged* with the traumatic reality, leading to each becoming diluted and transformed by the benign and hostile influence of the other? Would they, perhaps, have *diverged* into different compartments of her life and found themselves unable or unwilling to speak to each other again but with *both* capable of living and breathing? I am not sure what these two Annes would have looked like! For what it is worth, I think that Eva Schloss has probably merged her ideals and her experiences and used both creatively; however, there were fights between the two with Eva displaying some notable ambivalence about her stepfather Otto's preoccupation with Anne and her mother's tolerance of it coming to the fore on occasion—at least, that is what I pick up from reading *After Auschwitz*.

In deciding to pose these important questions, I have no intention of disrespecting either Anne or the power of ideals that I have no doubt were sincerely held by her during her time in hiding and which millions of her more ardent followers cling to today. We need to respect this while also being aware that her early death placed both her life and her ideals in a lasting cage.

While she was exploring her growing identity as a serious adolescent with a sense of purpose in the confined space of the Secret Annex, with typical honesty, Anne also recognized that she wanted to go back to school, have fun, and not know what to do with herself should she ever be freed from the Secret Annex.[88] We must see these as Anne being typically honest and expressing valid teenage feelings.

Although it might be tempting to think that Anne would have sympathized wholeheartedly with a recognizable buffet of current and worthy environmental, political, and social causes, it is also possible to argue that she would have been wary of anything that smacked of any extremism that would have precluded fun and escapism. I consider it far more likely that Margot would have wholeheartedly joined such causes.

Anne Frank *could* have turned ninety years old the year that I first started to think about this book in 2019. Two years on and we are somewhere in the middle or toward the more hopeful end of a horrible pandemic that (as of February 2021) has stolen over 400,000 lives in the United States and over 100,000 in my former homeland (the United Kingdom). Some seventy-five years ago this month when I first wrote this chapter, the *real* Anne died at the age of fifteen, caught up in a virulent typhus pandemic that was raging unabated throughout Bergen-Belsen.

* * *

Before we move on, let us consider some concluding and ever-revolving thoughts here:

First, I often wonder if Anne had survived whether she would have just ripped up her original and even the revised versions of her diary, destroyed or discarded her now famous red-and-white checkered book, and then started anew with trying to interpret the bitter experiences of her last seven months. Would she be adding her voice to those trying to transcend their unspeakable trauma and loss with published and speaking offerings of an even deeper and darker nature? Would Anne have developed a voice more in the mold of Elie Wiesel with his seminal works about the horrors of Auschwitz and Buchenwald, or become a public speaker like Eva Schloss? Going down the path of Elie Wiesel seems entirely possible given Anne's obvious talents as a writer and her beautiful ability to render the mundane as psychologically interesting.

Second, because Anne is so frozen in the time that she lived in and the age that she was when she wrote and then revised her diaries, her feelings about the world around her and her attitude toward what it meant for her future are frozen alongside the difficult circumstances under which she wrote. Her tragic death before the end of the Second

World War had the paradoxical and unsatisfying effect of liberating Anne from having to be accountable for such feelings and emotions had fate allowed her to grow older in safety and comfort. In other words, they are left as they were first expressed. This dovetails with my earlier discussion about Anne's future commitment to people being "truly good at heart."

Third, and speaking personally, it will always be the beauty of Anne's relationship with her father that will ever inspire me. While there are other father-daughter and family relationships that also inspire me with hope such as the Holderness family from North Carolina and Mat and Savanna Shaw from Utah, I will always have a special affection for Otto and Anne.[89]

Fourth, we should forever be thankful to Miep Gies and Bep Voskuijl for rescuing what they could of Anne's writings and to Otto Frank for having had the emotional strength to publish his daughter's diary. We can also cherish the fact that he loved *both* his daughters enough to create such a comprehensive and iconic photographic record of Anne and Margot as they were growing up. Taking and developing photographs were obviously much harder tasks in the 1930s and early 1940s than both are now, and it took more commitment to realize the ambitions of both.

Fifth, while she was still alive, Anne Frank as a young girl was *more* than the sum of what has survived of her and *more* than the widely cherished wisdom and ideals of her original or revised diary. Yet since her death, Anne has become paradoxically both *less* and *more* than the words and ideals that have surrounded her. By virtue of her untimely death, her obvious talent, and the loving decisions made by her father and others to keep her memory and ideals alive, Anne has acquired a stunning megaphone that has allowed her to become the voice of *all* the children who died during the Holocaust and with their talents so cruelly cut short. Only a few are unable to accept the responsibility that posterity has given to Anne, and none of those few is writing for this anthology.

In saying that Anne was "less" than the myth that now surrounds her, I am wondering how much of the real Anne would still want to stand behind that megaphone if she had survived. In saying that she is "more" than the myth that now surrounds her, I am honoring the fact that Anne was a warm and generous child and an extremely self-aware, normal, and lively teenager who was loved deeply by *both* her parents and in ways some of us can only dream of today. This beautiful normality haunts me today and will likely haunt many of our readers as well.

Anne was thus forced by tragic circumstances to become preternaturally extraordinary while still only a teenager and then preternaturally mythological once we reflect on the legacy of her inspiring words and consider how posterity has handled them. Would she now be linking hands with Greta Thunberg and Malala and endorsing political and populist movements such as the Extinction Rebellion? Many writing for this anthology and elsewhere are of the firm belief that she would be very active today. If Otto were alive today, he would probably believe this of his daughter as well. Yet I think that Anne would have preferred to live a happy and carefree life filled with all sorts of experiences *outside* the political and activist realm. Beyond wanting to become a journalist or a writer after the war, I do not pick up any sense from reading her diary that Anne had any future activism in mind —at least, not as the term is meant today. That said, if she had become famous with any book published on the Secret Annex, I am sure she would have been delighted with seeing Prinsengracht 263 turned into a memorial and a museum and I am confident that she would have given meaningful talks to younger audiences wanting to learn more about her experiences. Anne loved children.

Lastly, for those of us *writing* in this anthology and for those of you *reading* it, I am asking that you view Anne Frank as both a victim of the Holocaust that ultimately engulfed her *and* as the extraordinary writer of a diary that allowed her to transcend her own death. This transcendence was due in no small measure to the loving decisions taken by her father to publish his daughter's work and allow his younger daughter to live on in the hearts of millions. By being able to look into the world of a teenager trapped by fate only to be able to live freely in the uncertain world of the 1930s and to die by being engulfed in the horrors of the 1940s, we are privileged to be able to hear the busy thoughts of one who was strikingly modern, self-aware, and compassionate in her ideals, and refreshingly bright, generous, and warmly engaging in her emotions. This is a rich legacy indeed!

The suffering and needless death of the 1,500,000 children and 6,000,000 overall who died during the Holocaust do not speak to us through *just* Anne's truncated dreams and words, of course. Yet Anne has become our most famous "access point" (a library science term) into understanding the horror. Fame has allowed her to transcend the fate of most of the 1,500,000 children who died and who have disappeared anonymously into history, unremarked by all except those in their families who survived them. Reminding ourselves of this sober fact should lead us to a perspective that is sometimes forgotten and shouldn't be. My Jewish wife often reminds me of this fact when she wants to complain about the burden that Anne Frank is forced to carry as a perceived spokesperson for all the children lost in the Holocaust.

Statistics such as these defy any rational explanation and lie beyond any words that could possibly convey the comprehensiveness of the horror. Indeed, any general attempt to describe the Holocaust in words demeans it by adding rational boundaries to an irrational horror. Our understanding should have *no* comfortable boundaries. There are *no* insurance codes that medical insurance companies could possibly use to define all the trauma that survivors felt in the years and decades following the end of the Second World War. Do triggers today still include the sound of slow trains clacking over railroad ties with horns blaring, the sight of armed police, the voices of command over loudspeakers, the sight of fires and smoke from chimneys, the use of words such as "the East," the screech of a loud car at night, sudden footsteps, and knocks at doors?

None of the above has stopped many from writing about it. That so many have done so, suggests to me that at the *individual* level much therapeutic energy is still needed to process the horror.

Yet because we *have* empowered Anne's words to speak for the lost generation of the Holocaust, and because Otto Frank made it abundantly clear after the war and for decades afterward that his beloved daughter deserved to be heard, we are where we are today with this anthology. It is why my fellow writers and I have chosen to add multiple echoes to this talented Jewish girl's thoughts and hopes for a more tolerant future.

The last two chapters have been the hardest to write and edit for this anthology, and not least, because of not knowing what to exclude and still make Anne's living journey and posthumous legacy meaningful and vibrant for our readers. As I noted at the outset, I am indebted to both Melissa Müller and Carol Ann Lee for providing us with a substantial history of Anne Frank and her family and it would be hard for any writer to find anything worthy of adding to their seminal works. That hasn't been our purpose at all here. I have found that full biographies of famous people are actually infrequent, and if they are *really* good, they can silence any thought of wanting to supersede them for decades. In these last chapters, I have only wanted to share the salient points of Anne's history as I see them and some of my opinions respecting how I relate to her life and the legacy of her writing.

The following contributors to this anthology will now take this journey forward and describe more of how they "met" and were inspired by Anne in their own lives. Although I do return with my own piece and various editorial comments on those written by others, I can assure readers that my own contribution will not be anything like as long as the last two "introductory" chapters!

PART III

Playing Anne

An Interview with Melina Zaccaria

TORONTO, CANADA, JANUARY 2020

M ELINA ZACCARIA PLAYED Anne Frank in *The Diary of Anne Frank*, as directed by Sondra Learn in February 2014 for the Theatre Burlington, Burlington, Ontario.[90]

I sent Melina the following interview questions via a Microsoft Word attachment to an email in December 2019. Melina, who was studying for her law exams at the time, graciously agreed to answer my questions once her exams were over. I thank Melina for her time spent recalling her experiences performing as Anne in *The Diary of Anne Frank*. Later in this anthology, we will also be hearing from her director, Sondra, respecting her side of producing and directing the play.

Melina asked that I not change any of her answers beyond the odd typo and edit for further emphasis or clarity. My questions and her answers are as follows:

1. *How did you become involved in Sondra's play, and how excited were you to play the part of Anne? Was it a dream role for you and one that you had always wanted to play?*

When I was in my first year of high school, I had the good fortune of working with Sondra on *The Miracle Worker*. It was a wonderful experience, and I really respected Sondra's vision and directing style. When I auditioned for *The Diary of Anne Frank* three years later, I was familiar with Anne's story but had not read the book or play. I wouldn't say that I had always wanted to play the part because I didn't know very much about the production at the time, but as soon as I saw the script, I felt attached to Anne. From then on, it became a dream role.

2. *Before playing her, how familiar were you already with the story of Anne's life, her time in the Secret Annex, and what happened after the arrest on August 4, 1944? How did you prepare for the role? I know from your interview with Gary Smith from*

the Hamilton Spectator that you said you visited a "number of Holocaust memorials and Anne Frank memorials." Did this include Merwedeplein 37, the Secret Annex, Westerbork, Auschwitz-Birkenau, and her grave site in Bergen-Belsen?

Prior to Sondra's production, I was familiar with Anne's story but not particularly knowledgeable about her life. I had visited a small selection of Holocaust memorials, specifically in Germany and the Netherlands. Since then, I have visited others such as Merwedeplein 37 and the Secret Annex in Amsterdam, as well as the Auschwitz-Birkenau memorial in Poland. I am particularly grateful to have visited these sites after having played Anne.

However, while preparing for the role, I found it important to focus on Anne's personality rather than the circumstances of her death. Without ever forgetting the tragedy of the Holocaust and Anne's eventual murder at the hands of the Nazis, Anne was a human being with a great many thoughts and interests. While she was aware of what was happening to the Jews of Europe and she thought about it a great deal, it was not her sole focus. She did not know herself as a victim of the Holocaust, and so while it is impossible to read about, write about, or think about Anne Frank *without* [also] thinking about the Holocaust, one must in some ways separate her from that tragedy in order to do her character justice.

3. *How did Sondra want to direct you in her version of The Diary of Anne Frank, and did you talk about difficult issues such as Anne's relationship with her mother and her jealousy toward Margot? How do you think our impressions of Anne would change if we had the legacy of Margot's diary or could interview her mother today?*

Sondra's directing style involved a lot of conversation about how you imagine your character feeling in different contexts. We frequently discussed Anne's relationship with the women in her family, and especially with her mother. Carla Zabek, who played Mrs. Frank, is a wonderful actress and person, and the two of us worked with Sondra to tackle the difficult tension between the two women. If we were able to interview Mrs. Frank today, I believe we would find that the tension between Anne and her mother was of the normal kind that occurs between mothers and daughters and that it would not, in fact, alter our perception of Anne.

4. *How did you as Anne and Michael Hannigan as Otto decide to approach the much-loved father-daughter relationship? Was this something that you both discussed at length with Sondra? Do you think that Anne and her father would have continued to understand one another if both had survived the war?*

Another phenomenal actor and person! Michael was amazing to work with and made my job easy. I was fortunate enough to audition with him and immediately felt that we worked naturally together. We did discuss the relationship with Sondra frequently, and we spent a lot of time on the intimate moments between Anne and Otto. I really feel that, with the help of Sondra and the rest of the cast, we were able to render a true representation of the understanding and dedicated relationship between Anne and her father.

5. *With my "Meeting" Anne Frank anthology, I invited my contributors to describe how they first "met" Anne and how they were then inspired to go on a journey with her. For some, this meant literally making pilgrimages to many of the places associated with her life and tragic end. It sounds as if you did in fact do this, but I am curious as to whether you approached this journey as a kindred spirit or more as a means of preparing for the role? You said to Gary Smith that you did not think you could "get all the emotions across without feeling all those things that Anne had inside her." You also said that it would mean "chipping away at what is Melina and finding what is Anne." Can you elaborate on the success or failure of this interesting observation?*

Anne is a character who is simultaneously relatable and inaccessible. I found it important to discern between the situations where I understood what Anne was thinking and those where I was wholly unable to comprehend. "Chipping away at what is Melina" was, for example, a lot easier where Anne described the impossible conditions of the Annex (a situation that is unfathomable in the context of my life) and a lot harder where she described her first crush (a situation with which I am familiar). I remember one week where the character seemed especially prominent in my real life when I began to have nightmares akin to what I imagined Anne to be dreaming about in the nightmare scene from the play.

By the end of rehearsals, I think I succeeded in finding a balance. This required pulling from my own experiences where I felt that I related to Anne and doing the necessary research and practice to represent her in places where I could not relate. If I were to restate my comment to Gary, I would likely describe the task more as a remolding than a chipping away.

6. *You told Gary Smith that you admire Anne's belief that "in spite of everything, people are truly good at heart." Some of us who have been writing for this book as well as David Gillham in Annelies, his recent fictional account of how Anne would have acted had she survived, feel that Anne would have modified this opinion that she wrote before her arrest, before her transportation to Westerbork in the Netherlands, and before her subsequent transportation to Auschwitz-Birkenau and Bergen-Belsen. How do you think Anne would have felt about much of the chaos in the world today? With respect to her opinions, do you view Anne as a historical forerunner of, say, an activist such as Greta Thunberg or as someone who—while she would have certainly thought as richly as Greta—would have also allowed herself to be easily distracted by the richness of life? Anne in her diary speaks several times to the existence of "two Annes" with one Anne who was silly and frivolous and one who was deeper and more sensitive. Would you agree that*

this speaks to Anne's ability to understand and define a positive identity for herself, but also to her willingness to have fun?

It is difficult to conjecture about what kind of person Anne would have been and how her perceptions of the world might have changed had she survived the Holocaust. With that said, given Anne's observant character, I imagine that she would have been struck by the social and political climate of this decade.

7. *I liked your comment to Mr. Smith that you needed to remember that Anne does not know her end when she is writing her diary. As a result, she expresses a lot of hope in her entries as well as despair over what would have probably seemed completely trivial if she had survived and become the writer or journalist that she dreamt of becoming. Do you think Anne would have published the same diary as her father chose to do on his daughter's behalf and as a way of keeping Anne alive in his mind?*

I'm not so sure about that. My impression while playing Anne was that she understood her diary to be very personal and she might not have wanted to publish it. Of course, and in light of the tragedy that befell her family, her diary is an important historical document, and I do believe that Otto Frank did the world a great service in publishing it as he chose to do. If she had survived, I believe she would have been a writer but that she might have been hesitant to publish her diary as it was.

8. *Lastly, after working with Sondra on this play, did your school friends say what they liked about it and whether they would now go away and read Anne's writings to learn more about the Holocaust and its effects on a teenager similar to you and to them in age?*

I have to admit that the play occurred right around exam and university application time, so I'm not sure any of us were reading as much as we would have liked. With that said, I think that my friends were struck by how relatable Anne's character is for young women in a totally different place and epoch.

PART IV

Walking with Anne

It's amazing how a girl's story from years ago
Can make a heart decades later break with sorrow.
How one diary can give a whole perspective
Of a reality which was, oh, so destructive.

So many innocent people died
While Hitler in the "perfect nation" found pride.
So many children for their mother screamed,
Tears from their fearful eyes streamed.

You would think that after seventy years people would
learn
But yet we see a repeated pattern:
Children being ripped from their parent's arms
While pointed to their head are firearms.

Why are people still suffering because of their race?
Or because of their birthplace?
When will people ever learn
That only if we remove hate, will peace return?

—Joy Gafa', "A History Repeated" (2020)

I too could have grown up here
in these flat serene streets
without mystery but isn't it just
because they are broader than where we live

At the center, the photos showed a wasteland
the trees are sixty-five years old today
and cast heavy shadows. Under them
you can settle down to read

some book or other in the stagnant heat.
Later get up, because in the end
you end up feeling like a voyeur.
An ordinary citizen on an average street,

you pass in front of the school, the tearoom
and get back into circulation. On the cafe terraces
people are happy to chat, laugh.
I know why I came here. I don't need to explain.

—Anne Talvaz, "The River District" (The
Rivierenbuurt, Amsterdam); translated for the
Scottish Poetry Library by Brian McCabe (2002);
translation revisions by Anne Talvaz (2020)

FEDERICA PANNOCCHIA, LIVORNO, ITALY

M Y NAME IS Federica Pannocchia, and I am the founder of the Italian charity *Un ponte per Anne Frank* (A Bridge for Anne Frank)[91] I am now thirty-two years old, and I opened my organization in 2015.

When I was a teenager, I had a wonderful opportunity to read *Anne Frank: The Diary of a Young Girl* and be able to learn more about Anne Frank's story and life. I was very touched by her sense of hope, ideals, and love of life.

Since I was seven years old, I have always loved to write. I started writing short stories, novels, and then books. One of my books was published in 2016. It is called *Quando dal cielo cadevano le stelle* (When the Stars Fell from the Sky), and it tells the story of Lia, a young Italian girl who lived during the Second World War. Due to the fact that she is Jewish, she has been captured with her family during the Raid of the Ghetto of Rome.[92] The fact that Anne Frank also loved to write so much really made me feel even closer to her. I felt her to be like a sister and like a girl I really wanted to know and talk with.

I did not accept that human beings during the Holocaust could have done what they did to other human beings. Why discriminate against people? Why force human beings to live in fear? Why capture Jews, handicapped people, political opponents, homosexuals . . . Why?

I was thirteen years old back then and did not realize how I could behave to fight against it. I was young. Then I focused on my studies, opened a dance school, lived in London, and traveled to the United States. But I could not forget it—I could not forget Anne Frank's diary and did not want to.

Her words and her ideals were within me all the time. I knew that we could all learn from the errors of the past. I knew that discrimination and indifference were still part of our society.

I decided to write a book about the Holocaust—*Quando dal cielo cadevano le stelle*. In doing so I had the wonderful and fulfilling opportunity to read more testimonies, read books, learn more about our history, and see the reactions of many Holocaust survivors. I was filled with their love and hope. I felt inside me that this was a fight I could not leave anymore.

As part of my research, I connected with Cara Wilson-Granat. She is a wonderful American author who is still one of my closest friends.

Cara immediately opened her arms to me and let me know that she corresponded with Otto Frank (the father of Anne Frank) for twenty years until the moment when she came to Europe to meet him and his family. I was so touched by her story, hope, strength, and love. Cara published her correspondence with our beloved Otto Frank, and she daily inspires people to learn more about Anne Frank and her family, to fight for their beliefs, and to see the good in others. Cara became my inspiration. She is such a good-hearted woman, and I love her deeply. It is thanks to her that I also had the opportunity to reach Buddy Elias (Anne Frank's cousin) and to connect with him.

Buddy and I exchanged several emails, and he was always so kind and loving. I keep him with me each day. He was such a good, inspiring, caring man. I wrote to him about my dream of opening an organization in Italy to honor Anne Frank since I needed to continue her legacy, I needed to talk about her, I wanted to share her story, and I wanted to encourage others to embrace better attitudes to being able finally to fight against any form of discrimination and indifference.

Un ponte per Anne Frank (A Bridge for Anne Frank)

Buddy always encouraged me to keep doing it. In 2015, I finally officially registered my organization, *Un ponte per Anne Frank* (or A Bridge for Anne Frank). It made me very emotional to register it; I was scared and curious, and I wondered how would people see it? And then a new life opened in front of me. A lot of people reached out and connected with me and to my organization. I understood then that I had made the right decision. People needed an organization like this and still do, as much as I need it. I want to continue to share Anne Frank's life and ideals, and to help those who are still suffering today.

My organization nowadays counts so many supporters and educational programs. I can develop and spread these words of thanks to the work of my volunteers. I collaborate with teachers, municipalities, Holocaust survivors, educators, librarians, families, and organizations. I daily try to encourage people to learn from our past and to reflect on our society today. Is there anything that each of us can do to build a better world?

One of my favorite quotes of Anne Frank is, *"How wonderful it is that no one has to wait, but can start right now to gradually change the world!"*[3] And I do believe that this quote has become my motto.

We also focus on children in need and on actual issues like migrants and refugees. We focus on all those people who are still discriminated against today.

> *We can choose what to do with our life, how to react*
> *We can choose to love and not to hate*
> *We can choose to live and to help*
> *We can choose to start to improve our world*

*   *   *

The story of Anne Frank literally changed my life. She opened a new world to me—a world that was maybe *already* inside my heart, but that needed to be enriched and encouraged by the words and courage of this wonderful and special young girl who lived during the Second World War.

I will always be grateful to Anne Frank and to her dad, who decided to publish her diary and her thoughts. I will always be grateful to those who helped me during this journey and to those who daily help others, no matter what.

Because despite all the atrocities that surround us, we still must hope and have a light in our heart.

> *To help,*
> *To believe,*
> *As Anne Frank always did!*

JOY GAFA', BIRŻEBBUĠA, MALTA

I AM JOY GAFA' from Malta, and I "met" Anne Frank for the first time when I was seven years old during my social studies lesson. It was our last lesson of the day. We were discussing her story, and something struck me about her. After that lesson, I kind of forgot about Anne until my seventh-grade English teacher, Ms. Spiteri, mentioned the diary during her lesson. That evening I went to the library, but unfortunately someone else had borrowed it.

The next weekend I went to Valletta (Malta's capital city) with my Aunt Violet and my Uncle Leonard. My aunt went into a bookstore to see if they had a particular book, and while I was looking around, I saw *The Diary of a Young Girl*. She bought it for me, and I started reading it immediately on the bus. When I finished, I put it on the shelf and left it there for a few months. I think that I did not really understand it on my first reading. After some time, I picked it up and read it again. It took me longer to read this time, and it left an enormous impact on me mentally and emotionally.

I watched documentaries about Anne and watched the movies over and over again. I saw Anne Frank as a friend I never had the chance to meet, and I realized that I had a lot in common with her. I related to her with regards to her thoughts, doubts, and insecurities. During this period, I joined group chats and pages on both Facebook and Instagram where I met other people my own age (fourteen) and those who were younger and older who were also struck by Anne's story. I built some of the best friendships that I will ever have in my lifetime. Some of them are even writing in this book!

Just like others here, I would like to know more about the other residents of the Annex—especially Auguste van Pels, Hermann van Pels, Peter van Pels, and Fritz Pfeffer. Of these, I think I would be more curious to know about Peter's life. In the diary we see that he was a very mysterious and private young man who never shared enough information for us to know what he was like.[94]

In November of 2018, after months of waiting in anticipation, I went to Amsterdam with my parents to visit all the sites related to the girl who had now changed my life. Reality hit me only when the plane landed. If I felt close to Anne Frank the moment that we landed at Amsterdam's Schiphol Airport, you can only imagine what it felt like to be in front of the Anne Frank Huis facade. It was half past seven in the evening. I was on my way to a vintage clothing shop. As it was dark, I did not realize that I was at Anne's hiding place until I saw the sign on the door.

The following day was the day when I visited her former home. It was a surreal and unexplainable feeling. It felt as if all the people inside that building weren't there and that it was just me and Anne. Walking through the narrow corridors and steep staircases, I sensed how each step was getting me closer to the bookcase. I could not help but feel strong guilt that an innocent girl my own age once walked past this same bookcase only to come out two years later, guarded by Nazis. Her freedom and dignity being taken away and the fear that she must have felt at that moment are heartbreaking to think about.

Inside the museum we found some of their belongings on display, including Anne's marbles and Margot's call-up papers. There was a whole room dedicated to Anne's diary and her other works, including her other journals and the first draft of *Tales from the Secret Annex*. I think that that was the room where I felt the most emotion and where I felt closest to Anne Frank.

I also visited the apartment where the Franks used to live on the Merwedeplein square. Unfortunately, we could not go inside, but it was nice to see where Anne spent her best years and where she was at her most happy and carefree. On the way I came across the 6e Montessorischool that Anne used to attend, and which is now called the 6e Montessorischool Anne Frank.[95] At the Anne Frank monuments in Amsterdam I often saw fresh flowers and notes, which were sweet reminders that her story and significance are not close to being forgotten. We also went on an Anne Frank walking tour, which took us to all the sites connected to the Holocaust, including the Holocaust memorial monument where we all paid our respect to the victims by placing a stone on the letters forming the phrase "NOOIT MEER AUSCHWITZ" (Never Again, Auschwitz).[96]

On Malta, I often meet people who ask me who Anne Frank is when they hear me talk about her or see me reading an Anne Frank book. I have also met people who are oblivious of what the Holocaust was, and I find this very alarming. We often hear on the news about acts of anti-Semitism and other types of discrimination. This is not only happening to the Jews but has grown to a larger scale.

Anne always saw the beauty in the misery that was surrounding her, and that could be something that you and I should remember—that there is always something positive even in dark times. The world is now facing some dark times, so let us take the opportunity to speak up for peace, diversity, and equality. This is something that Anne Frank would do if she were still alive.

If we take a closer and deeper look into *The Diary of a Young Girl* and at Anne's other writings, we will see various pieces of advice that are still valid for today's world. Remarkable from a fifteen-year-old!

In a time of abhorrence and suffering, this iconic girl managed to stay as positive as possible, to love, to be inspired, and to stay in touch with her interests as she grew and matured. All this has made her an idol to many teenagers and adults even decades later.

Still, by teaching Anne's story in schools and then ending it there, the students will not know about the wider harm done during the Second World War and the Holocaust. Students should know about how and why the Holocaust happened, about the propaganda, and Hitler's election. If we do not educate, history will repeat itself, and we are very close to repeating it. The world is still divided by race, religion, and culture. With all the problems that the world and society are facing, we need to overlook these borders and combat the problems cooperatively.

Joy Gafa' outside the Anne Frank Huis in Amsterdam © Joy Gafa'

Joy Gafa' with the statue of Anne commissioned by the Boekhandel Jimmink (formerly Boekhandel Blankevoort's where Anne spotted her red-and-white checkered diary) and then unveiled in 2005 in the Merwedeplein, Amsterdam © Joy Gafa'

Joy Gafa' with a Stolpersteine (memorial plaque to victims of the Holocaust) in honor of the Frank family outside their former apartment at Merwedeplein 37, in the Rivierenbuurt Quarter, Amsterdam © Joy Gafa'

A closer view of the Frank family Stolpersteine outside their former apartment at Merwedeplein 37, Amsterdam © Joy Gafa'

Outside Merwedeplein 37, Amsterdam © Joy Gafa'

Joy Gafa' outside the door of Anne's house,
Merwedeplein 37, Amsterdam © Joy Gafa'

I would also like to comment about the people claiming that that Holocaust is *not* a fact or that Anne's diary is fake. We have witnesses—many of whom who were not Holocaust survivors—to corroborate that the Holocaust existed. We also have videos and pictures. I do not think that anybody would make up such stories of cruelty. Focusing on Anne's diary, most of us have come across people trying to prove that the diary was "really written by Otto Frank" after the war. I personally saw the diary with my own eyes, and it is clearly visible that the diary was written in ink and not with a ballpoint pen. Even if it were, ballpoint pens were used in Europe during the early 1940s.[97]

So instead of spreading the negativity and doubt, we need to spread the inspirational legacy that Anne Frank left behind her and help her to live on for more decades and centuries.

TIM WHITTOME, SEATTLE, WASHINGTON STATE

WHEN IT CAME to my turn to reflect on what I asked of my fellow writers, I concluded that I have probably "met" Anne Frank five times in my life—six, if you also include the writing and editing of this book. As I write this, I do feel as if Anne has been looking over my shoulder and—*hopefully*—smiling or laughing with her father. I am sure I will be meeting her again many times in the future. At least, I *hope* so, depending, of course, on whether she likes this work!

I believe that much of my interest in Anne Frank stems from the fact that I have always loved the Netherlands. That Anne came to do so as well after she immigrated to the country in February 1934, fills me with confidence that we share something fundamental in loving all things Dutch.

One of the things that I have long known about my maternal grandfather as a former soldier in the British Royal Artillery during the Second World War was that he was involved in either trying to liberate the Netherlands from Nazi occupation or helping in its reconstruction afterward. Like many returning veterans, my grandfather was always vague about what he did during the war, but I don't think he took any part in Operation Market Garden in September 1944. Sadly, he is no longer here for me to talk to him about postwar life in the Netherlands, where he went, what he did, and whether he would feel proud with my opening dedication to him in this anthology.

It is far more likely that my grandfather was involved in helping to stabilize the Netherlands after the war. As far as I know, he was stationed in the Arnhem area. Because I like to fantasize that he *could* have been part of the earlier efforts made during Operation Market Garden, I recently bought a commemorative coin from the Royal Dutch Mint honoring the air and land campaign's seventy-fifth anniversary. This sits nicely alongside my other commemorative coin honoring "100 years of Dutch aviation." I have also just received a third commemorative coin celebrating the seventy-five years that have elapsed since the liberation of the Netherlands in May 1945. These are all significant moments in Dutch history, and I feel attuned to each one of them.

I *do* know that my grandfather did make some Dutch friends who remembered him fondly for many years; I can testify to this when I got to meet several of them at their homes in Oosterbeek near Arnhem. It was 1990, and I was visiting Holland with my parents. Sadly, we did not visit Amsterdam, and I lost a chance of being able to see the Anne Frank Huis and Museum. As I had yet to read Anne's diary, this was not the emotional disappointment that it would have been today. I had also missed another chance of visiting Prinsengracht 263 three years earlier when I went to Amsterdam with a friend and had to spend a significant amount of time acting as his "bodyguard" in some of the sleazier parts of the city. He *only* wanted to visit these and not anywhere cultural, which I still regret to this day!

My growing love for the country did, however, grow into an affection for Dutch culture and emblems of national identity. While this naturally included a fondness for tulips and for the golden age of Dutch art in the 1600s, it also included an interest in the fortunes of KLM Royal Dutch Airlines and worrying about how busy Amsterdam Schiphol Airport might be compared to other airports in Europe and worldwide. This fills me with a huge sense of pride that may not make much sense to someone who does not experience life as an Aspie! Having vivid and intense interests are integral to what it means to be an high-functioning autistic.

KLM continues to fascinate me to this day. Schiphol, meanwhile, is consistently ranked among the busiest airports in the world, which is remarkable for a country the size of the Netherlands. It is the third busiest airport in Europe by aircraft movements and one of the ten busiest airports worldwide for international travelers. It has a fascinating runway layout, with one of the six runways (the Polderbaan) positioned some 3.1 miles and a fifteen-minute taxi ride by plane from the rest of the airport, according to Schiphol's Wikipedia entry. It is also in a different Zip Code to the rest of the airport!

Nor should I forget to mention my love for the national football team. I followed the Netherlands (or just Holland as it is also known in the World Cup) as it progressed toward the finals of the 1974, 1978, and 2010 World Cups. To the chagrin of some among my American friends here in the United States, I also followed the Dutch Women's National Team through to the recent 2019 Women's World Cup final. I may even have some Dutch ancestry, but this is unconfirmed at this point.

*   *   *

As I said, my interest in the life of Anne Frank can be seen as a natural extension to this love for "all things Dutch." It also explains why I take umbrage at any efforts to make her a posthumous American citizen.

Although I certainly knew about Anne from an early point in my life, I cannot recall exactly when I first heard of her. All I can remember is that I probably connected with her story as part of a wider general empathy for stories that were rooted in the challenges of living through the Second World War. I think, also, that Anne's suffering was integral to my overarching goal of wanting to find interesting ways of talking to my dad who lived in Kent and close enough to the Luftwaffe bombing of London during the Blitz to remember red skies over the city. It has only been in the last twenty-five years that I have come to view Anne more as an understanding spirit during various interesting and challenging times in my own life.

I had just turned thirty when I really "met" Anne for the *first* time. My girlfriend, Debbie, was at Cambridge University, and I amused myself by reading interesting books while she was attending lectures on classical pots and Greek and Roman authors.

I think that I must have discovered Anne's diary while I was perusing the shelves for something else. Hitherto, I had been focusing much of my attention and energies on obsessively working my way through the entire works of Shakespeare and reading books on the *Titanic* disaster, while also listening to Bob Dylan and collecting recordings of his concerts. It *may* have been Debbie herself who first suggested that I should think about reading Anne's diary as a way of distracting myself with something different. She felt that Anne's story was more than likely to resonate with me once I had made the decision to learn more about her life, her death, and her positive relationship with her father. Things may not have unfolded *quite* in this way and my memory is fuzzier than I would like it to be after twenty-five years.

Following Debbie's advice, it wasn't hard finding a copy of *Anne Frank: The Diary of a Young Girl*. I remember jumping straight into buying what was then regarded as the *Definitive Edition* of Anne's diary as translated by Susan Massotty. At the time, I knew nothing of the different versions of Anne's diary or how they came into existence. I was not prompted to think about what an earlier and less complete version might have looked like. As far as I was concerned, I was "sold" on the idea of a "definitive" copy! Why buy a smaller or lesser edition!

As part of what quickly became a rapid growth in my interest in Anne and her life, I also jumped at the chance to buy a remainder copy of the famous *Critical Edition*. This acquainted me with the fact that there was probably more to the publishing history of Anne's diary than what I had just read in the *Definitive Edition*. I was now able to see that there were different versions of Anne's work and how Otto's original C edition from 1947 then matched up against them. I wasn't sure, though, that I was *that* emotionally invested at the time in what those differences were, but I bought the remainder copy just in case I might want to become even more involved in Anne's story. I didn't need to read the *Critical Edition* to be convinced of the authenticity of Anne's diaries, but it was nice to see the forensic efforts made to prove it.

As I was not studying at Cambridge University but there in my capacity as Debbie's visiting boyfriend and emotional support, the *Critical Edition* seemed more important as a means of impressing her that I could discuss certain topics as critically as she was able to discuss a pot from ancient Greece. She was, unfortunately, about as interested in Anne Frank's life as I was in the finer artistic details of black-on-red or red-on-black classical designs for her beloved pots.

After discovering how emotionally supportive and interesting Anne's diary was, I decided to enroll in a Dutch language evening class so that I could one day challenge myself to read *Het achterhuis* in its original language. Sadly, the class ended up being canceled due to insufficient numbers. I come back to this idea periodically.

As I became progressively fascinated by Anne's life and times, Debbie bought me *Anne Frank: Beyond the Diary* as a Christmas present. Details for this important book by Ruud van der Rol and Rian Verhoeven are in our bibliography. Debbie knew that I was affected by Anne's end in Bergen-Belsen, and she thought that *Beyond the Diary* would go some way toward enlarging my understanding of Anne's life outside the confines of her diary. I needed to familiarize myself with the effects of the Nazi occupation on the wider Jewish population of the Netherlands.

Regrettably, my relationship with Debbie did not survive, and we went our separate ways—or rather, she did in early 1997. Although Anne Frank came with me, I should point out that my interest in her story was *not* part of our breakup; however, Anne did slip away for a brief (and, hopefully, restful) sleep before I would have the chance to "meet" her again. I do not believe that I had been too much trouble for my new friend, and I trust she was pleased with my efforts to become better acquainted.

* * *

I "met" Anne Frank for a *second* time when I was dating my future American wife Esther in London in September 1997. Esther was initially "concerned" that I might not like her because she was Jewish, and she had relatives who had survived the Holocaust. My affection for Anne convinced her to think otherwise, and she was reassured on all points! Nevertheless, Esther could not understand quite why so many non-Jewish folks were fascinated with the life of Anne Frank when so many other children of anonymous promise died during the Holocaust.

Although reasonable as far as her question went, I did *not* think that rejecting the prevailing view of Anne as a tragic poster child for the suffering of 1,500,000 Jewish children during the Second World War was entirely valid or helpful.

Fortunately, I was able to persuade Esther that following in the footsteps of Anne's life and tragic journey was always going to be a powerful way of transcending the overall statistical and anonymous trauma of the Holocaust and of understanding the horror at an acutely personal level. I told her how Anne "speaks" on behalf of the millions of children and adults who died during the Holocaust and how she has become their posthumous advocate. Not intentionally, of course, but by happenstance.

Furthermore, I suggested how reading her diary could act as an appropriate access point (that term from library science again) for especially young children and teenagers attuned to Anne's core messages of resilience and hope for a better world to understand why the horrors that engulfed her should never be forgotten.

As I explained to Esther at the time (and still do on occasion), the statistics, pictures, films, and other anonymous evidence of the Holocaust only take us so far along the road to understanding the trauma. Reading more personal works such as Anne's diary and the recollections of others caught in Nazi concentration camps takes us much further along the road toward where we need to go—to thinking about how best to structure a world where such prejudicial horrors are unlikely to be repeated. Anne vividly tells us what was happening around her and the fear involved in trying to keep safe. She also shows us the promise of what *could* have been in an alternate universe where Hitler was unknown and where Jews could be accepted as children, teenagers, and adults with the same feelings, anxieties, and dreams as non-Jewish children, teenagers, and adults.

The reader should be imagining at this point that I have had lots of discussions like this with my wife over the years. In 1997, though, Esther chiefly needed to be satisfied that I was *not* anti-Semitic. She had been concerned because she had heard that British people were supposed to be anti-Semitic. I pointed out that I did not know anyone who was like that and would have rejected their company if I did. My wife's concern for anti-Semitism in the modern British Labour Party is one of the main reasons why she feels she could not have supported any of their candidates in the last 2019 British election.

Once all this was sorted out to Esther's satisfaction, Anne disappeared again for another long rest and would not wake up again for ten more years. That said, I also knew that my new kindred spirit would be sighing with eager relief that I had no intention of discarding or forgetting her during these years, and as I moved forward into married life.

> Sal [de Liema who was in the same barracks as Otto in Auschwitz-Birkenau] remembered one other thing he was able to do to help Otto. One day Otto asked Sal to call him Papa, even though he knew that Sal's real father was hidden in the Netherlands. At first Sal refused, finding it a peculiar request, but then Otto broke down and confessed he found it impossible to live without his children. He cried, "I'm the type of man who needs this, I need somebody to be a Papa for." Sal understood that and was filled with sympathy for Otto, who from then on became "Papa Frank." Otto's morale picked up again; he drew great strength from hearing himself addressed once more as "Papa."
>
> —Carol Ann Lee,
> *The Hidden Life of Otto Frank* (2000)

It was 2007 when I would "meet" Anne again for a *third* time. By then I had been living in the United States for ten years. It would be under quite different circumstances, as our "meetings" would take place at first in the hopeful light of sunny days and then in the darkness of stormy nights with few stars and no moon to appear through any brief breaks in the clouds. It must have been bewildering for Anne to be summoned forth in such a manner, but there were reasons for my urgency that I knew she would understand once I had explained the challenging circumstances:

"So, Anne, my wife and I have decided to adopt an older child. We—or rather I have, but with my wife's consent after a brief battle—decided this; however, our chosen child is a traumatized twelve-year-old girl, Cordelia, from the Washington State Department of Children and Family Services (DCFS) network of "waiting" children. These are children, Anne, who have been in foster care but who are now legally free and adoptable by new 'forever families.' These children need parents who can love them unconditionally because they have experienced a lot of past attachment trauma."

Put like this, I knew Anne would understand and that she would find this effort fascinating and absorbing. She loved children and she would have known instinctively about the challenges facing teenagers and also those facing their parents. Otto would have felt the same. He understood the need for a father to love his children unconditionally. I know this more now, but Edith would have agreed with this observation just as I already knew that Otto did. Also unknown to me at the time, but Margot would have understood all this as well and I am confident that she would have supported my lofty hopes. In short, and after all her earlier trauma had been comprehended and addressed in therapy, Cordelia *needed* a Margot for a sister, she *needed* an Otto for a father, and she *deserved* a mother like Edith.

Nevertheless, parenting a teenager diagnosed with reactive attachment disorder (RAD) was always going to be a challenge. Cordelia would find being receptive to the idea of being my "forever daughter" very hard. For children with RAD, the instinct to *survive* trumps any instinct to *belong*.

Although a natural choice for helping Cordelia to adjust would have been to have her read about Anne Shirley's journey toward acceptance by Marilla and Matthew Cuthbert in *Anne of Green Gables*, I remembered how Otto Frank had connected so well with his younger daughter. Although Anne Frank clearly did not show any signs of poor attachment, it was her father's patience, reasonableness, and empathy that I most wanted to emulate when considering how best to parent my new daughter. As a result, it quickly became clear to me that Cordelia could derive two immediate benefits from learning about Anne's relationship with her father:

First, that the father-daughter relationship can be unique and rewarding across a range of normal and challenging circumstances. Otto was *always* accessible to Anne, took her on holiday with him, and was highly respected by her friends. He was a calming and distracting presence during the Nazi occupation of the Netherlands. Cordelia's survivalist and control issues would dominate her life and ultimately be harmful to her if she couldn't learn to trust that her new father would always be there for her.

Second, that reiterating how Otto tried to keep his younger daughter calm during air raids was a means of having my daughter understand why she should be able to relate to Anne's life on a traumatic level. Cordelia had not been persecuted for her race or religion as Anne had, and neither had she been subjected to bombing, but she *had* been forcibly removed from her birth mother without her consent and she *had* been moved through many foster homes with mixed success before she was rendered legally free for adoption by a forever family.

I also appreciated how Otto was Anne's advocate during their time in hiding. She was her father's main focus and, while this attracted a certain resentment from Edith and perhaps from Margot as well, it was successful in keeping Anne calm. At Kamp Westerbork, Otto tried to have Anne assigned to easier duties. These positive father-daughter connections were worthy of emulation as far as I was concerned as a new parent.

When we adopted Cordelia in 2008, she was then at the same age as Anne was when she was given her famous diary on her thirteenth birthday. While I *intentionally* gave my daughter on her thirteenth birthday what I hoped would become an enduring and loving family-focused future, Anne's father gave her the diary that would *unintentionally* become his younger daughter's future, centered on an involuntary fame that was destined to become her lasting legacy.

Clearly, Anne's trauma would surpass anything that Cordelia had already experienced. Yet in explaining my daughter's attachment trauma in ways that I have just done, I am more interested in conveying the demonstrable *existence* of trauma bonds than I am in *ranking* what both girls had or would endure at different times in their lives. From my perspective as a new father, I looked to Otto to show me the type of responsive and empathetic parenting most likely to be able to address typical adolescent challenges and—in Cordelia's case—the lingering effects of past trauma.

Although I obviously encouraged Cordelia to read *The Diary of a Young Girl*, it was in fact the play *The Diary of Anne Frank* by Frances Goodrich and Albert Hackett that resonated with her more than anything else. We saw this play performed at the Intiman Theater in Seattle in 2008; it starred Lucy DeVito as Anne and was directed by Sari Ketter.[98] That it must have had an impact on my daughter's way of thinking can be confirmed by the fact that she wanted to see it again. Just as importantly, she has always remembered having seen it. Given everything that has happened to Cordelia in the years since, this should be regarded as an achievement.

Looking back at this difficult time throughout most of 2007 and 2008, I can see that I did not allow Anne much rest as I was always asking her to "meet" me somewhere or other to tell me more about her father. She must have thought that I was not very strong or independent, but I knew that Anne would listen to me over several coffees in Starbucks. Parenting adopted children with attachment trauma is not an easy undertaking under the best of circumstances, and given Anne's curious and engaged nature, what better person to try and explain all this to!

* * *

The *fourth* time that I "met" Anne happened in April 2009, when I read an article in the *New York Times* that mentioned the fact that the horse chestnut tree that Anne could see outside the windows of the Secret Annex was dying.[99] All was not lost, though, because it was also announced that there would be a competition among interested and qualified organizations in the United States to secure one of several saplings that had been saved from the tree.

When I went to a Seattle "Green and Clean" event that same month, I caught up with our then mayor Greg Nickels and asked him if he could try and get a sapling "won" for Seattle. He had not heard about the competition, but he put me in touch with Tim Gallagher, the then head of the City of Seattle Parks Department. Tim promptly put me in touch with the city's chief arborist, Mark Mead. Mayor Nickels had been very keen to learn of the project, and I was thrilled that both the Parks Department and Mr. Mead were also enthusiastic. At some point, someone must have obviously contacted the Holocaust Center for Humanity in Seattle.[100]

By the end of that same year, but with circumstances very changed in my own life, I discovered that that we had indeed won one of these cherished saplings and that Seattle would shortly have some kinship connection with Anne and her immediate world outside the Secret Annex. Although the horse chestnut tree is not mentioned all that much in her diary, when she *does* talk about it, it is clear just how symbolic it was for her, representing both changes occurring in her own life, freedom outside, and nature's ever-changing but consistent sense of its own fundamental beauty.[101] Maybe Anne longed to join the tree in its mocking and beautiful indifference toward the suffering going on in the real world.

Sadly, there would end up being endless delays before Seattle's sapling would eventually get planted at the Seattle Center on May 1, 2016. It now sits in the Peace Garden, protected by the pleasant shadow of the Space Needle. This all happened some *six-and-a-half* years after we first learned that we would get our important connection to Anne's world, and *three* years after the sapling had arrived in the city as a much smaller version of itself. After incessant pestering on my part to know what it looked like, I did have an early opportunity to see it in a greenhouse pot when it was not much more than a few feet high. It was not that much bigger by 2016, but our arborist had to make sure that it was resilient and thriving before he was prepared to risk planting it in the Northwest's demanding climate.

"Anne Frank tree," Seattle Center © Tim Whittome

"Anne Frank tree" memorial stones, Seattle Center © Tim Whittome

Closer view of the "Anne Frank tree" memorial
stones, Seattle Center © Tim Whittome

Horse chestnut leaves, "Anne Frank tree" © Tim Whittome

"Anne Frank tree" with the Seattle Space Needle,
Seattle Center © Tim Whittome

The author and the "Anne Frank tree," Seattle Center. This photo was taken a few days after the Seattle Sounders emphatically won the MLS Cup in 2019 © Tim Whittome

By May 2016, however, I was so frustrated with the prolonged quarantine process that the saplings had been necessarily forced into by the United States Department of Agriculture and then by the further delays in Seattle that I did not want to go to the dedication ceremony. I am sure that the Holocaust Center for Humanity shared my frustration with the endless delays, but in the end, I just felt too disappointed and overwhelmed to attend a ceremony that I had once hoped would be very elaborate and attended by people who had, perhaps, once known Anne.

I have seen our Seattle sapling many times since it was planted, and I can report that it does look extremely vibrant, well-maintained, and healthy. As you can see from my selection of photographs, it is now much more of a recognizable tree. Though it is close to the Space Needle, it is not well highlighted and there are no signs pointing visitors to its location. Modest memorial rocks surround the tree at its base, and I have included photographs of these as well. If I had once hoped for something more visible and elaborate, on further reflection, I think that the modesty of the display is probably right, and it is certainly respectful. At some point, I am sure that they will have to move the tree to a new and more open location. Maybe then, there will be a more visible display with, perhaps, a statue of Anne.

There is also something appropriate in the tree sitting in the shadow of the tall Space Needle standing in for the tall Westertoren in Amsterdam! While in hiding at Prinsengracht 263, Anne relied on the vibrant and loud bells of the nearby Westertoren to remind her of the passage of time and the passing world outside.[102]

Ultimately, I was as proud as I was disappointed in my—albeit slight—role in helping to bring a horse chestnut sapling from Amsterdam to Seattle. I have a sense, though, that Anne would still be delighted both in my small role and in the subsequent resilience of the tree that symbolized so much for her.

The words wounded Edith and made her cry. "I can't make you love me," she said to her daughter. Anne knew she was not being kind, but she could not apologize. She was too angry with her mother—and with the world.
  —Kem Knapp Sawyer, *Anne Frank: A Photographic Story of a Life* (2004)

His choice was only to write or to remain silent. He chose to write, his heart demanded it. For the rest, the reader must be his judge.
  —Jacob Presser, *The Destruction of the Dutch Jews* (referenced in *Anne Frank and After* by Dick van Galen Last and Rolf Wolfswinkel, 1996)

The *fifth* time that I "met" Anne, it was in the darkness of a personal and family tragedy. While it did not end as ignominiously as Anne's obviously had done in the squalor of Bergen-Belsen in 1945, it nevertheless stirred in me complex thoughts and dark affinities. For long stretches, I could barely let go of Anne's hand as we wandered across a bleak landscape. These would not be occasions for chats over coffee but for desperate discussions of ideas fermented in the mind's war room.

I chose to write extensively of this nightmare in my earlier published works, and interested readers can follow my parenting and adoption journey in my *Denied! Failing Cordelia* trilogy. Here I only need to talk about my "meeting" Anne Frank in the dark and twisting alleyways of this trauma and how I was forced to be afraid of those who chose *not* to understand anything other than the fruits of their own prejudices. Anne's fear of the Gestapo coming angrily to the door of the Secret Annex and then of arresting her and her family for the Nazi-codified "crime" of being Jewish resonated strongly with me. Parenting mistakes made within the overarching context of trying to address my daughter's special needs with the therapeutic parenting needed to help her would lead me into a protracted court battle with the Los Angeles Department of Children and Family Services (DCFS). I had to transition my life from Seattle to Los Angeles for the duration. How Cordelia ended up in Los Angeles in the first place is a nightmare in itself that my earlier published trilogy fully explains.

In the small room of a Los Angeles Motel 6 where I waited with Esther for court hearings, I always felt as if I were in hiding from aggressive and uncompromising social workers steeped in the judgmental and social prejudices of a society primed to believe the worst of parents. Where once such authoritarian prejudices had centered on anti-Semitism or in the construction of laws justifying slavery and the oppression of black people, it was *too* easy telling myself that parents, especially fathers, were the present inheritors of the same scorn, hatred, and misunderstanding. Families could be broken apart and children separated from loving parents as the consequences of a broken system steeped in prejudice and protected by laws designed to shield social workers from any accountability for error.

Although clearly many readers will see this as hyperbolic, I met many overly strident social workers who were not as far removed as I would have liked or expected from the attitude of the Nazis who occupied the Netherlands and who then terrified the Jewish population with their Nuremberg Laws, rolling restrictions, sudden roundups, and cruel deportations to extermination camps. Yes, it was a Kafkaesque world that Anne lived in, and it was just not enough of a stretch to believe that I too lived in a similar world that readers open to the experiences of my other works would understand. I have already alluded to the fact that many of us who have Asperger's live in a world of connections that may not be readily apparent to those who are not on the autism spectrum.

For those who do *not* know much about the detailed reach of cases involving child welfare, it is important to know that there are social workers, therapists, lawyers, and judges, who mistrust you as a parent and who are empowered to decide *when* you can visit your child, *with whom*, and *where*. Dehumanizing and arbitrary *restrictions* on parent-child contact dominate the proceedings, and just as Anne experienced severe separation anxiety from her father in Auschwitz-Birkenau and from both her parents in Bergen-Belsen, so too did I experience similar feelings of intense loss and separation in Los Angeles after my daughter was taken into care. Not knowing *when* or even *if* I could see my daughter again and not knowing *if* I would still be allowed to be her "forever dad" when all the misunderstandings involved in parenting her had been cleared to everyone's satisfaction overwhelmed me with fear and uncertainty.

Trauma is trauma irrespective of the severity, nature, or prolonged intensity of the source. It is either something you experience, or you don't. The triggers are still there today when I come across homes that look dysfunctional, when I encounter police on the streets, when I hear that my state is about to allow cherished businesses to fail because of COVID-19, when I receive the hasty judgment of others over disagreements, and when I learn of loving parents judged for presumed parenting mistakes that are far from obvious or intentional. Life feels a lot more threatening to me now than it did ten years ago when I trusted more people and accepted their decisions. Now I am irritable, argumentative, and defensive, and I do not trust social workers as I once did.

I always had Anne's diary with me in the Motel 6 that Esther and I were staying in, and I found myself quickly collecting other books on the Holocaust and the experiences of Jewish children and others who were presented with the choices of hiding or facing open and daily persecution during the Second World War. Those in hiding were seeking to escape a world of strangers with hostile and arbitrary agendas in much the same way that I was trying to hide from hostile professional and legal forces seeking to encircle and define my life. My imagination was unrestrained and at its darkest throughout the duration of the case. Although I like to think that Anne and I are united in our shared ability to express ourselves, I would have to admit that the feisty and rebellious Anne had a far greater range of humorous insight.

I had to try to rationalize my anxieties for my daughter's future and for my own as a father. In one of our late-night chats, I "listened" as Anne told me about her experiences and feelings during the war and how she searched for life's meaning through the power of the written word. Anne told me to write and find ways of trying to make sense of what my daughter and I were going through. I decided to keep a very full Microsoft Excel diary and wrote emails constantly to friends and others during the prolonged nightmare. While Anne was sadly denied the opportunity to publish her thoughts and writing on her own terms, I eventually empowered myself with my self-published instructional trilogy and with the goal of reaching my target audience of other parents, social workers, therapists, lawyers, and judges on my own terms. With the exception of other parents, each professional grouping had misunderstood me and invalidated my parenting efforts.

Anne's diary was also one of the first items that I tried to send to my daughter through our social worker. Even a book had to pass through the various legal *checkpoints* designed to control and manage parent-child contact. In actuality, such checkpoints existed to impede reconciliation and reunification. I told Cordelia that it would help her to write about her preadoptive and adoptive experiences as Anne Frank had done as a way of distilling some of her past and present trauma into something recognizable and understandable. Anne was afraid, but she also saw enormous value in her imaginary Kitty's "patience" and in the willingness of the written word to listen and stay silent. Anne could confess, share, and be heard by Kitty in ways that I hoped would resonate with Cordelia and which I believed I was also doing with my own diary and then with my subsequent trilogy.

My journey through this three-year nightmare has flowed into the writing of my contribution to this anthology in more ways than I had once imagined. At times in my parenting journey, I would feel as rejected by my troubled daughter as Edith felt when Anne would only look to her father for understanding and comfort. It didn't make any more sense for Edith than it did for me. The hurtful letter that Anne—as a more rebellious older adolescent—later wrote to her father and which she shares in her diary entry for May 5, 1944, captured the essence of the rejection that I felt as a parent. Anne, at least, was open to understanding the pain. The social workers and the court were not in my situation.

As we saw with Sal de Liema's recollection of Otto's time at Auschwitz, Otto *needed* to be a father, and to be honest, this should not surprise any of us who have followed his journey and relationship with both his daughters and their friends. I, too, *needed* to be Cordelia's father whether she was willing to accept it or not, and this instinct drives many parents of children with special needs to believe in themselves and to advocate for their children's best interests.

As Otto had done with his decision to publish Anne's diary and disseminate her ideals to the best of his considerable parenting resources, I hoped that my *Denied! Failing Cordelia* trilogy would become my way of honoring my daughter's early childhood and teenage struggles. If Otto managed to keep Anne alive by publishing his daughter's diary, I, in my turn and through my own self-publishing work, had to show the strength and importance of the father-daughter bond that the authorities in Los Angeles had otherwise tried so hard to destroy. Anne Frank and Cordelia would *not* be united by any shared end, but rather by their shared connection in my mind to the efforts of others seeking to subvert their adolescence and destroy the family bonds that were supposed to be keeping them safe. There was nothing safe about guarded Kamp Westerbork, Auschwitz-Birkenau, or Bergen-Belsen for Anne, and there was nothing safe about Cordelia's locked residential treatment facilities.

Otto's efforts to edit Anne's diary and then defend the authenticity of her writing represented both a labor of love and a necessity. We can read about his postwar efforts in *The Hidden Life of Otto Frank* by Carol Ann Lee and in the testimony of Father John, Ryan, and Cara later in this anthology. Otto *had* to talk about Anne, and he *had* to write to all those who had grown to love what his daughter stood for. I would come to feel the same way as I tried to process my own experiences and those of my daughter.

As a final point here, it is worth mentioning that my therapist at the time thought that bringing Anne's diary into the legal proceedings and then explaining to the social workers how I wanted my daughter to respond to it constituted an unintended and provocative "threat" to those seeking to determine her best interests. Because of the historical power and symbolism of the diary, my actions would have been viewed as dragging a document into the proceedings every bit as significant and religious as the Bible; notwithstanding, my heightened response to everything that had happened, or which could happen if left in the hands of others unfamiliar with my daughter's history, was actually not that unusual.[103] I have seen children wrenched from their parents outside the Los Angeles courtroom, and I have seen the confusion and horror enveloping parents unable to navigate the expectations of an unresponsive legal system.

It is entirely normal for a father to want to honor his bond with his daughter. As one example, I keep seeing fathers singing lovely modern and classical songs with their daughters on the internet—Mat and Savanna Shaw, for example, embody the true spirit of Otto and Anne in the way that they have singing "conversations" in the course of their wonderful father-daughter duets. They have taken the internet by storm during the current pandemic and I invite readers to join them in their musical and parenting journey. I also see entire families bonding in beautiful ways—the Holderness family, for example. It was normal for Otto when he decided to publish *Het achterhuis*, and it was normal for me when I published the first book in my *Denied! Failing Cordelia* trilogy in 2014.

It is not presumptuous to claim that Otto and I had found similar ways of telling the world that those who did, or tried to, destroy our relationships with our beloved children had lost their power. In doing so, we were transcending our earlier powerlessness to stop them.

No one understands why the Holocaust had to happen eighty years ago, but it did anyway. I will never understand why the authorities in Los Angeles decided to take my daughter away for three years, but they did anyway.

As Otto found after learning of his daughters' deaths at Bergen-Belsen, the quest for finding ongoing meaning is akin to hoping that a candle will continue to burn in life's darkness when the air is otherwise stale. We urgently breathe into the flame, and by doing so, we illuminate everything ever so brightly for a second, a minute, an hour, and maybe a week, a month, or a year if we are lucky. Unlike with Anne, whose flame is now eternal and protected by fame, I am repeatedly forced to breathe into the flame to keep the toxic darkness at bay and to ensure the instructive meaning of my daughter's trauma remains relevant for parents and others who work with families.

Postscript June 2020

Under normal circumstances we sometimes take these little things for granted, and how good they make us feel. In turn, when these things are taken away, the shock is frightening—you lose your sense of reality.
                         —Nanette Blitz-Konig, *Holocaust Memoirs of a Bergen-Belsen Survivor* (2018)

When I first wrote this postscript earlier in 2020, COVID-19 was still restricted to bats and was largely unheard of outside the medical and scientific community. Many of us in the Seattle area where I live were looking forward to spring and hopefully to another beautiful display of tulips in the Skagit Valley. I was personally looking forward to visiting my mother (who was then bedridden with Alzheimer's) in June, and then of walking in Anne's footsteps around Amsterdam.

I had every intention of *finally* being able to visit Amsterdam after so many prior attempts to really appreciate the city had fallen short of their goal.

On my agenda were the Anne Frank Huis and Museum, Merwedeplein 37, the 6e Montessorischool Anne Frank, Margot's former Jekerschool, the Jewish Lyceum where both girls went, and the famous Blankevoort's bookstore (now the *Boekhandel Jimmink*) where Anne probably first spotted her red-and-white checkered diary.

I also felt that I *needed* to see the location of the former German SD headquarters (a converted school) on what used to be called Euterpestraat, but which is now the Gerrit van der Veenstraat and the site of the Gerrit van der Veen College. Anne and everyone else from the Secret Annex were interrogated there on the day that they were arrested. I knew that I *needed* to visit the *Huis van Bewaring* (House of Correction I) on Weteringschans where Anne and the others from the Annex were imprisoned for three days before being transported to Westerbork. I also *needed* to visit other places associated with the suffering of the Jews in the Netherlands such as the Hollandsche Schouwburg where many were held before being moved to Amsterdam Centraal Station for transportation to Westerbork. Anne and the others did not go through here, but Anne's friend Susanne Ledermann did, according to Carol Ann Lee in *Roses from the Earth*. In hoping to visit each of these places so linked to Anne's life in her happier moments and then her suffering, I was not being voyeuristic but expressing a need to acknowledge the importance of where she lived and her trauma. As Lear shouts in *King Lear*, "Reason not the need!"

I would not only be "meeting" Anne for a *sixth* time and Margot for what I believed would be my first real chat, but I would also be walking in their footsteps around the places most associated with their brief lives. I would have wanted them to be my guides. In my heart, I knew both girls would have welcomed me joining them and we could have linked arms.

Seeing where both girls lived, where they went to school, and where they were both forced to hide for twenty-five months would have meant a lot to me and especially after writing and editing this anthology. I felt sure that the journey would bring much-needed emotional form and focus to places I had hitherto only been able to visit on Google Earth. My daughter says that I am always only ever taking Google Earth vacations and never actually going anywhere. However splendid the world may look on some zoomed-in *Satellite* or *Street View*, everything and everywhere still takes on a cold Martian appearance. I knew that I would need to unfold Anne's personal and special world in ways impossible to achieve on *Street View*.

Then, of course, the coronavirus assaulted our world and destroyed all my hopes and dreams for the near future. Not long after I wrote the above and had gone so far as to book my flights, hotels, a tour of the Houses of Parliament, a Shakespeare performance at the Globe, and Eurostar to Amsterdam—everything, in fact, except for tickets to the Anne Frank Huis and Museum which cannot be bought more than two months in advance—governments across the world were reduced to imposing international restrictions on the airlines and on tourism in general. I reacted with unrestrained horror to the United Kingdom's restrictions on seeing parents and other elderly relatives in care homes and to the closing of museums in London; still further, to what turned out to be a prolonged "temporary" closure of the Anne Frank Huis and Museum and other places of interest in Amsterdam. My hopes of "seeing my mother who has Alzheimer's and Anne Frank" as I expressed it on Facebook scattered with the last winds of March and with every evidence of April's imagined cruelty in the pessimistic words of T. S. Eliot. I was forced to cancel everything.

*   *   *

As of August 2020, I was still hoping to get to London in September to see my mother before she died, and to Amsterdam to "meet" Anne and Margot.

*   *   *

By September 2020, my mother had died, and the airlines were still unable to resolve their bankruptcies and provide us with any route stability. The United Kingdom had also not relaxed its two-week quarantine restrictions for travelers arriving from the United States.

*   *   *

As of now (October 2020), I am hoping to get to see my dad in London and Anne and Margot in Amsterdam early next spring—assuming that reliable COVID-19 treatment options, safe vaccine approval, and consistent air bridges between approved countries will permit me to go. None of these is guaranteed to be in place at time of writing.

PINE DELGADO, SAN DIEGO, CALIFORNIA

W HEN I WAS a student in junior high school almost forty years ago, I had noticed that many of my fellow schoolmates were walking around campus with uniform copies of *The Diary of a Young Girl* by Anne Frank. I had not one idea as to who Anne Frank was or what her position in life was. At first, I thought that she was a farm girl from the Midwestern United States. Perhaps someone from the 1930s, around the time of the Great Depression. When I was in the eighth grade, however, I would come face to face with Anne for the first time.

In late 1980, a made-for-television movie was released that was based on the play, *The Diary of Anne Frank*. This movie starred Maximillian Schell and Melissa Gilbert as Otto and Anne Frank. And as an in-class assignment, my eighth-grade English class took turns reading from the script of the TV movie, *The Diary of Anne Frank*. I read the part of Mr. Dussel the dentist (portrayed in this movie by Clive Revill). I also remember that one of my classmates, a *girl*, read the part of Peter van Daan (played in the 1980 movie by Scott Jacoby), who was the son of Mr. and Mrs. van Daan.

But as we read our assigned lines from the movie, I had a better sense of who Anne Frank was and the difference that she and her diary had made in human history—a difference that she *continues* to make.

Yet despite this exercise in elocution, I was still a bit naive and a little ignorant about Anne, her diary, and her message. Even after I hit high school and was given the assignment of reading her diary for the first time during my junior year, I'm sorry to say that the assignment and my junior year English teacher who gave it to us left very little impression on me.

It was not until the next year when I was a senior during the fall of my 1984–1985 school year at Helix High School that things all changed for the better. My English teacher that year was young and new to full-time teaching. But she was *exceedingly good* and tops in her field—or, at the very least, *very, very, good*. So when I received lessons on Anne Frank's diary and the Holocaust from our new teacher, my interest was awakened. Even though I did not finish reading Anne's diary (just as I had not finished it the year before), I became much more interested in her life and diary. Her interactive classroom discussions along with the assignments given to us in her class (along with photocopied handouts derived from a reproducible teaching aid called "The World of Anne Frank" by Betty Merti) really got my attention! And because my teacher was (and is), of the Jewish persuasion, her lessons were personally, and perhaps even historically, influenced by the practice of her faith.

This "young and new" English teacher was Janet Shanks. I have always felt some thirty-five years later that Janet has taught me more about the great wartime diarist Anne Frank than *any human* has in my entire life. I have thanked her incessantly for this since we became friends on Facebook. In fact, I regard Janet Shanks not just as my *favorite teacher* of any I have *ever* had but also as the older *sister* I never had as a kid growing up and as one of my many "best" friends—one of many.

It is because of Janet's great influence on who I am today that I have been keeping and maintaining a private library of books, CDs, and DVDs continuously, with great enthusiasm, and with dedicated relish on the subject of Anne Frank since 2015. The library material consists of multiple copies of Anne's diary, including some foreign language translations as well as compilations of her short stories. I have adult and children's biographies of Anne, members of her family, and the people who hid them. My collection also includes picture books, scholarly essay books, and compact disc sound recordings of her diary and her other writings as well as music that has been composed in Anne's memory and honor. There are likewise DVD dramatizations and documentaries of the great diarist's life. So for these reasons, I will be forever grateful to Janet Shanks for the remarkable impact that she has made and for the wonderful influence that she has had on my life. *No* amount of my human thanks would be able to do her *any* bit of justice! In fact, she is like Anne in very many ways, which is why I see Anne *in* Mrs. Shanks!

I know I have just said that I could never thank Janet Shanks enough for the huge part she has played in my life, but let me just say again, *"Thanks, Shanks!"*

*   *   *

I thought that I would give readers some "coming from the heart" background information about my love and admiration for the great wartime diarist Anne Frank and what it has taken for me to get to the stage that I am with it. Readers will have been able to appreciate some of these feelings from what I have just said respecting my indulgence and passion for all things and people connected to Anne. But here is what I have *not* yet told you interspersed with what I have said already.

As I said earlier, my interest and love for Anne Frank dates to late 1984 and during what was then my senior year at Helix High School.

Fast forward a few years to the moment when I had been out of high school for a number of years. My interest in Anne Frank is rekindled after a few years of lying dormant. But my mother was not having any of it. In fact, she once angrily growled, "Why do you want to study a teenage girl?" And if this were not enough, when we were living in Spring Valley in California, and after I had gone to Grossmont Center (a shopping mall in nearby La Mesa) to buy some books about Anne Frank, my mom told me to go back immediately by bus and trolley and return the books to the bookstore and get my money back.

My mom had no tolerance for my indulgences and passion for my hero Anne Frank. And she had little of it for any discussion about her unless it was demeaning in nature. In fact, my mom went so far as to say that my classmates and I at Helix had all been "brainwashed" as we were being taught about Anne Frank. She even held onto the hysterical belief that her diary was a hoax, believing instead that it had been written by her father (Otto) or even by a third person![104] I'm *super sorry*, everyone! I must apologize for my mother, as I would *never* have held or harbored such thoughts on my own.

One would think that my mother, who had been brought up in Nazi Germany during the Second World War, would know better. Then again, my mom was an adult with a long list of skeletons from the very start. I also need to tell you that in the ensuing later years, whatever reading material on Anne Frank I purchased and that I did not feel forced to get rid of, I felt I had to buy in secret and away from the glare of my hypercritical mother.

Now that she has gone, I feel liberated and endowed with much academic freedom to indulge my interest in Anne and quote her as much as I want! I just wanted to let readers know what has been on my mind for quite a while as I reiterate and reaffirm my great passion for Anne Frank. And while we are dealing in indulgences, I beg *yours* as this posted status does seem a bit long-winded; however, I must remind you that I am being sincere and honest in ways that I could not have been when my mom was still alive.

https://www.facebook.com/groups/annefrankbookclub/

I started the Anne Frank Book Collectors' Club on the Facebook social media site on April 16, 2019, as a way for collectors of mass media materials regarding the great wartime diarist Anne Frank to unite and freely discuss in a common forum the books, CDs, and DVDs that they read, hear, see, and collect. Contributors are free to express what they feel when they make use of these materials after reading, listening to, or watching them.

Though I've been doing some form of intermittent collecting of reading and viewing material about Anne Frank for many years with varied levels of personal interest in her, it wasn't, as I said earlier, until after my mother passed away in late 2014 that I felt free to openly indulge in my passion for Anne as much as I wanted to. Now my personal funds—borne forth from a monthly government income in the manner of Social Security benefits—permit me to indulge myself.

Pine Delgado's Anne Frank
library © Pine Delgado

Pine Delgado's Anne Frank
library © Pine Delgado

Pine Delgado and his Anne
Frank library © Pine Delgado

Now, some five years later, I have a personal Anne Frank library beyond my boldest of dreams. I even own books, CDs, DVDs, and other media material on Anne that the branches of my hometown library system do not possess in their stocks! So let me happily say, as an Anne Frank collector, that I am a *child* of Anne Frank! We who have succeeded Anne in her physical demise—as her fans and followers—*are* her offspring and heirs.

As such, it is our continuing duty to disperse and perpetuate her message and ideas as contained in Anne Frank's *perpetual* voice—her diary! *That* is why I created the Anne Frank Book Collectors' Club.

Anne Frank is a passion and an interest of mine—and I am not giving either up! Thank you much for your support and for reading!

SONDRA LEARN, BURLINGTON, CANADA

I DO NOT ACTUALLY recall *not* knowing about Anne Frank. It seems strange to say that, but for as long as I can remember I have known about Anne. I knew that she went into hiding when she was fourteen years old and that she died before she turned sixteen. Even now, I mourn her death.

I wonder how different the world would be had she survived. I imagine that her diary would still have been published, but I also imagine that she would have progressed to other wonderful things. Maybe she would have married and raised a family. But we will never know what the world lost with not only the death of Anne Frank and most of her immediate family but also the deaths of the millions of other Jewish people who died.

*　　*　　*

Anne and I did not have a lot in common when we first "met." But I felt in her a kindred spirit. *She* dreamed big dreams, and *I* dreamed big dreams. *She* wanted to be a writer, and *I* wanted to be a writer.

Anne did not get along with her mother. *I* did not really have a good relationship with my mother when I was a teen either. *Anne* adored her father, and he was a strong a presence in her life. Sadly, *I* never knew my father. My mother divorced him when I was so young that I have no memories of him, although I did meet him once when I was eleven. There were times when I envied Anne and the close relationship she had with her father.

As Anne did, I loved movies and movies stars. I also enjoyed Disney movies, Elvis Presley, and Bobby Curtola.

As a child and young teen, I read Anne's diary more times than I can count. I watched the movie *The Diary of Anne Frank* whenever it happened to come on television.[105] I read as many books about her as I could. I have watched other VHS, DVD, and Blu-ray versions of the original movie many times, as well as other movies and documentaries about Anne Frank.[106]

As a child I was quiet, shy, and withdrawn. I would get books out of the library every week. By Wednesday I would have them all read, so I would read them all again. I lived for Saturdays, when I could take the bus to the library and then get a whole new set of books. I loved books about animals (horses, dogs, and cats, in particular). I loved mystery books and thrillers. I loved Nancy Drew, and I loved the classics.

Having a vivid imagination, I would propel myself into the world of the characters and people I found in the books and plays that I read.[107]

I spent countless hours reading, dreaming, and imagining alone in my room or, in the summer, under the lilac trees in my backyard.

I also spent many hours in my room living as I read Anne had lived when she went into hiding—quiet during the day and active in the evenings. I would tiptoe in my room, as if fearful that I would be caught. I would look out my window and watch the clouds drift by as I breathed the fresh air that came through my open window. The large mulberry tree in my neighbor's front yard became Anne's chestnut tree.[108] I watched the birds fly around and sing their songs. They were free to fly as high as they wanted. At night, I watched the stars and made wishes on the first star. I wonder if Anne ever did that—ever wished on the first star? What would that wish have been?

And although I knew she would never read them, I wrote letters to Anne. I never mailed the letters, of course. Unfortunately, they are long lost. But I can reimagine what those letters might have said:

Dear Anne,

My name is Sondra, and I am twelve years old. I live in Canada. I have a pet cat named Boots and a dog named Paddy.

I think you are the most inspirational person I know. The words you wrote and the courage you had to write your innermost feelings are so inspiring. I know, I already said that, but I can't think of a better word.

Maybe someday I will write another letter to you.

Sondra

My school years were both a sanctuary and a menace. They were a refuge because when I was at school, I was free of the emotional and verbal abuse of my alcoholic stepfather. They were a menace, though, because I endured endless bullying, teasing, and name-calling. This continued throughout my school years. But my saving grace in high school started on the first day of tenth grade, and in my theater arts class.

That is when I found the play, *The Diary of Anne Frank*.[109] I have read it so many times that I have lost count. And I dreamed of someday playing Anne Frank in the play. As I outgrew the age at which I could play Anne, I adjusted my dream to play one of the other characters. When this did not come to fruition, my dream changed to directing the play. That dream finally came true in 2014.

But I backtrack. I will tell more of that journey later.

I soon learned that I could live vicariously through the characters in plays. What a wonder that was! I could be anybody *but* me, and I could feel safe and happy and loved for a time.

I wrote another letter to Anne:

Dear Anne,

Hi, it's me, Sondra. I wrote a letter to you when I was twelve. Now I am sixteen. You died just a few months before you turned sixteen. When I was younger, I "played" at being in the Annex and living the way you lived. I know now that never in my wildest dreams could I begin to imagine the horror that you lived through when you were in hiding and then when you were in the concentration camp. I cannot fathom why the Germans did this to you and countless other people. Just because you were Jewish? What is so wrong about believing in God and having a different philosophy than other people? I will never understand. And what I am going through with the bullying and teasing pales in comparison to what horrific torture you endured.

Since I started high school, I have discovered theater. What a wonderful thing this is!

I will forever love you and admire you. You give me strength.

I hope someday to honor your memory.

Sondra

I imagine how Anne might have acted in plays or written plays. I know she wanted to be famous someday—a famous writer. Maybe I could make *her* dream *my* dream, make the footsteps she never would make.

*   *   *

Now, years later, I look back on my life and realize that every day that I lived and carried on despite the childhood and school years I endured, I was honoring Anne. I was following my dream and Anne's dream of being a writer. I have written plays and won playwriting awards for them. I was making footsteps of my own.

I promised to tell you how the story of directing *The Diary of Anne Frank* changed my life, the lives of the cast and crew, and the lives of the audience members who came to see the play.[110]

The play dates were set. I had had my auditions and had my cast. In the role of Anne Frank, I cast Melina Zaccaria. She had played Helen Keller for me when I directed *The Miracle Worker* in 2011.

Working on this play was a wonderful journey that was full of discovery, hope, and a tinge of sadness. The sadness being that this was the story of real people who lived, laughed, cried, smiled, loved, and tragically died.

For one of our first rehearsals we attended a synagogue and got a tour of the beautiful building and an explanation of the many symbols of the Jewish faith. This tour was led by Enid Aaron, a member of the synagogue, who was also our properties mistress.

Another particularly good thing that was an amazing insight into directing the play was that a traveling Anne Frank exhibit was on display in that same synagogue. I and many of the cast members went to the exhibit. Melina (who played Anne) and I both spent hours at the exhibit. It was very disturbing to see real and tangible items as well as photos of the horror of the Holocaust. Until then, I had only seen photos in books or documentaries on television.

Not that the deaths of millions of Jewish people were not tragic, but the one fact that especially hurt my heart was learning that not only Jews were victims. Children and people with disabilities were also taken away and murdered. Many experimented on in horrific ways. You see, I have a son who is severely autistic and nonverbal. It is frightening to think that my Justin would have been taken away from us if we had lived in that place and time. I cannot imagine what horrors might have been done to him.

Now on to the eight weeks of rehearsals. Our tech Sunday rehearsal day was very special. For those of you who do not know, the Sunday before a play opens in the community theaters that I am involved with is referred to as *tech Sunday*. It is a long day, usually starting in the early afternoon and ending late in the evening. This is when all the lighting and sound cues are incorporated into the play.

There is always a dinner break. As cast and crew, we collectively decided to have a Hanukkah meal. Our properties mistress, Enid, helped with planning the menu, providing many of the foods, and explaining to us their significance. We even had her say the Hanukkah blessing before we ate the delicious food!

Our dress rehearsal was especially poignant. We had a group of Dutch home-schooled students, many of whom had grandparents or other relatives who lived or died in the concentration camps. In lieu of paying for tickets, we asked that they bring donations for the local food bank. I was able to give over one hundred pounds of food to the food bank.

Next came three weekends of performances. There were many full houses and audience members leaving in silence. Many left the theater in tears.

I watched every performance filled with gratitude to the cast and crew who took on the challenge of telling Anne Frank's story. Closing night, and after the curtain fell, I could hear sobbing from backstage. The cast and crew were mourning the end of the play.

Enid said that never in all her years of doing theater had she worked on a play where the cast and crew were so close and invested in telling the story of the play. She said that everyone—men included—was crying backstage. They had developed such a close bond. Knowing that never again would this exact group of people be together like this and telling a true-life story was hard to realize.

That is what is so unique, beautiful, and sad about doing a play. You get a group of people—all from diverse walks of life—together for several months. Then it is over, and everybody moves on.

Finding the words in my heart to say to my cast and crew what doing this play had meant to me was excoriatingly difficult. I wanted to—no, I *needed* to say the right words. I thought for hours and hours. Then, thankfully, I found this poem on the internet. Unfortunately, I could not discover who wrote it as there was no writer credited:

Melina Zaccaria as Anne Frank in The Diary of Anne Frank
(directed by Sondra Learn, February 2014) © Sondra Learn

*Gavin Bailey as Peter van Daan and Melina Zaccaria
as Anne in* The Diary of Anne Frank *(directed by
Sondra Learn, February 2014) © Sondra Learn*

Melina Zaccaria as Anne Frank and Michael Hannigan
as Otto Frank in The Diary of Anne Frank *(directed by*
Sondra Learn, February 2014) © Sondra Learn

The Lives We Never Had

The words were never ours
The situations
and the time
they were different than we were used to
Those lives were never ours
But they were someone's
Once
Maybe

We played their lives upon that stage
Reading their words from a script
Laughing and living
and crying and dying
and acting

And on that stage
We changed
We were no longer the kids that had known nothing
Because we had experienced life
Even if it was not our own
We had grown up
Living out entire lives in a matter of hours
and some died
And learned from their mistakes

And when the time came
We gave something back to the world
So that maybe it could change
As we had
And stop its spinning long enough
To live

We took pictures
Flashing our smiles in every direction

So that the people could see
How much we had changed
And so that we could remember
the people we were for a few hours
So the happiness we felt could never leave us
"Everyone point a camera!"

And many cried,
though it was not in the script,
When we realized it was over
The glitter had faded
and the lives were lived
And people had remembered those
who history had forgotten

Or maybe not
Maybe they were never real
Maybe they had never lived
But we had lived for them
We gave them life

And as we walked
down the stairs for the last time
We remembered
What we would never
Could never
Forget

{Exit Stage Right. Lights Fade.} [111]

Even now, years later I look back fondly on the journey that I took in fulfilling the dream of directing the play *The Diary of Anne Frank*. I did not change the world with that dream, but something happened several months after the play was done that taught me that I did indeed change a tiny bit of the world. I was ushering at the final play of the season. I was talking with a lovely elderly gentleman who, when he discovered I had directed *The Diary of Anne Frank*, said to me, "Thank you for doing this play. It was wonderful." He was teary-eyed and repeated this phrase several times. Even months after we closed, the accolades were still coming in on what an impact we had made doing this play.

Anne wrote many inspirational things and wanted to change the world. I suppose I did change my little part of the world. I feel blessed to have been surrounded by those who wanted to change the world and especially while doing the play. And when you think about it, that is the best way of all to honor the memory of Anne.

YVONNE LESLIE, SALT LAKE CITY, UTAH

THE FIRST TIME I ever laid eyes on Anne Frank was in 1969, when I was in sixth grade in central Oregon. I was in the school library one day, browsing through a rack of paperbacks. What caught my attention was that there were five or six copies of the same book on this rack. On the cover of the book, I saw the young actress Millie Perkins. Millie was the one who had played Anne Frank in the 1959 film *The Diary of Anne Frank* by George Stevens.

The book turned out to be a reprint of Anne Frank's diary, and Millie's face must have been on the cover to promote the movie. I looked at the title, *Anne Frank: The Diary of a Young Girl*. I remember thinking something along the lines of *Oh, it's a diary ... I've never read anyone's diary before*, and that was it. I left the library and didn't really think about the book again, but I did remember Millie's pensive face gazing out at me from the cover and it must have stayed somewhere in the back of my mind. So as you can see, I didn't really "meet" Anne that day. Not properly.

Fast forward two years, and I was now living in a very rural farming community in western Arizona. Although I had developed into an avid reader and budding history buff, I still knew nothing about the Holocaust and the persecution of the Jewish people. I had certainly learned about Hitler, Germany, and the Second World War in history classes, but I never pursued any of it further. Because of my love of reading, I spent a lot of time searching for books. Before the invention of the internet, this was not always an easy task; I didn't really enjoy reading a lot of fiction, so I was always looking for something different. I had access to the small school library, but the nearest public library was some eighty-eight miles away. One afternoon in eighth grade, I was scanning the shelves at the school looking for something interesting to catch my eye—something that I hadn't checked out before, because remember, it was *only* a small library.

Then I saw it! A book written by Ernst Schnabel—*Anne Frank: A Portrait in Courage*. I pulled it off the shelf, and there Anne was, her face drawn in profile in a very interesting way. I saw her, and I wanted to know more. What was courageous about this girl? What was her story? The thought never entered my mind that she might not be alive any longer. I checked out the book and began to read. It took me less than one chapter to discover that not only had Anne died, but that something beyond terrible had happened in the Netherlands (and the rest of Europe) between the years of 1939 and 1945. In Germany, the persecution of the Jewish people began much sooner in the early 1930s.[112]

So many books have now been written about Anne, and with the invention of the internet, it is all there right at our fingertips. Many of us own vast collections of these written works. Mr. Schnabel's book was published in 1958, the year that I was born. Other than her diary (which I still had not discovered at that point), this book was all you could find that was written *about* Anne Frank. Mr. Schnabel's book is an excellent read. It moved me. It haunted me. It made me want to track down a copy of Anne's diary and read her own words, which I very soon did. It also triggered my lifelong interest in the subject of the Holocaust.

After tracking down a copy of Anne's diary, I finally was able to "meet" her. Her words jumped out at me from her first diary entry, where she excitedly tells us about her thirteenth birthday. You can feel her excitement, even though at that point she is not expressing deep thoughts or showing wisdom well beyond her years as she later does.[113]

What she *does* do in those first entries is to write and describe things in a very clear and engaging way, even though she is only talking about friends, school, boys, her family, and her birthday party. She made it seem to come alive right off the page. *Oh, I could read her entries forever,* I thought at the time. *So interesting! I cannot put this down. What happens next?*

Anne's thoughts continued to flow freely in those early entries. I learned that she had a "perfect" older sister in Margot whom she hated to be compared to—a sister who was the *most* beautiful, the *best* scholar, and who had the *nicest* of manners.[114] I learned that Anne was a chatterbox who often irritated her teachers by talking too much in class; yet her parents were not too concerned about her grades as long as she was happy, healthy, and not too sassy. I learned that a boy of *sixteen* (remember, Anne was *only* thirteen) found her to be witty and good company, and he wanted to walk her to school every morning.[115] Most importantly, I learned that even though Anne was always surrounded by friends, she felt that they couldn't really get close; she had never had a "real" friend. Anne had many deeper thoughts that she wanted to share and discuss, but she had not yet found that patient and true confidant.

Anne said that "paper has more patience than people," so Kitty (her diary) would be that friend.[116] Yes, Anne very quickly drew me into her world. I wanted to know more. Even if I had been an adult reading this, instead of being thirteen, she still would have drawn me in just the same. I knew I was going to keep reading . . .

It is 1942 in Amsterdam. If you are Jewish, the Germans say that "you can't do this, and you can't do that." You must wear a yellow star on your clothing. You are branded. You are forced to leave the school that you have always attended. Goodbye to beloved teachers and friends. You are now going to a Jewish school. The teachers try their best to make it a special year for the students, but it is getting harder for teachers and parents to protect the youth from the ugly, terrifying truth.[117] Friends and fellow students who were there one day suddenly do not turn up the next. Have they been arrested, or have they gone into hiding?[118] Who knows? Anne's father, Otto, tells her, "Do not you worry, just enjoy your carefree life while you can." Only three days later (July 5, 1942), her older sister Margot receives a call-up notice ordering her to report to a forced labor work camp. Anne and her family go into hiding the next day.

In the hiding place is where I really started to know Anne as an individual and what made her tick. A writer once said that Anne was "clearly in shock" when she wrote her first entries in hiding, but I am not so sure about that. *Maybe* she was, but *if* she was, she was still very capable of expressing her thoughts and feelings clearly.

Do I have any idea of what it is like to go into hiding? Living with the constant fear of being discovered? I have never experienced anything like that, but Anne writes so well and so expressively that when I read her words, I *do* feel that I know what it is like. That was part of her great talent as a writer. She makes you *feel* it. The fear of every sound outside, the bad food, the stale air, the cramped quarters, personalities clashing, the oppressiveness of never being able to go outside, the awkwardness of growing up, the generation gap, and falling in love.[119] It is all there, and I feel it every time I open her diary. It is not some far-fetched story written in a novel that does not really seem possible. It *was* real, it *all* happened, and she takes us there when we read her words.

She writes so well that I can pick up her diary, open it to any page, and I am right there with Anne. She is a friend. She is familiar. *Oh, how I wish she had lived!* That they had *all* lived. *What if . . . What if . . .?*

Some people talk of Anne as if she were a wise and saintly person. She *was* wise. She was even wise beyond her years, but she was *no* saint. I do not think she would have wanted to be viewed as a saint, because who could possibly live up to that standard. Besides, wouldn't it be a boring life? Anne was anything but boring! As her cousin Buddy Elias once said, "She was a girl, like all other girls, but with a great talent for writing."

That is why I find her so compelling—*she was a real girl.* She was sometimes a flirt, sometimes a brat, sometimes loving, sometimes funny, and sometimes stubborn. She knew her strengths and she knew her faults. She was able to look outside herself, see herself, and be realistic about her flaws. That is something that many people throughout their entire lives are never able to do. She wanted to improve herself and overcome her flaws.

At times because of her youth, she misjudged her parents unfairly. She was especially hard on her mother, Edith. She often did not agree with her parents' advice, opinions, and methods of parenting. We were all teenagers once upon a time. How many of us thought, even at such an early age, that we had it *all* figured out? How could our parents possibly understand or know what is best for us? *Were they ever young?* Most of the time, Anne *did* value her father's opinions, sometimes writing about experiences that he had when he was young. She seemed to understand him much better than she did her mother. She was willing, most of the time, to listen to what he had to say while giving him the benefit of the doubt. *This she could not do for her mother.*

People who knew Edith felt that she was a caring mother who deeply loved her daughters and that she took a great interest in them.[120] While Margot and Edith were similar in many ways, perhaps Anne and Edith's personalities were just too different from each other. Anne once wrote that her mother thought of the three of them as "best friends."[121] Whatever Anne's idea of what a "real" mother was, it was not that. She did not want her mother to be her "best friend." She wanted her to be "a mother," someone that she could look up to as a good example. In one diary entry, she wrote that Edith *was* an example—an example of what *not* to be. Anne felt that her mother was too sarcastic and too quick to judge. The fact that Margot was so close to their mother sometimes made things difficult as Anne always felt that her mother compared her to her "perfect" sister. That was a real source of frustration for Anne. Would her parents ever be able to take her seriously and see her as she wanted to be seen?

After a time, despite all the arguments, hurt feelings, and misunderstandings, Anne *was* able to look back at her past diary entries and admit that she had not always been fair to her mother. She still felt that her mother did not understand her, but she also admitted that *she* did not understand Edith either and had never really tried to.[122]

Here, I want to mention that after Anne, her family, and friends were arrested on August 4, 1944, and later deported to Auschwitz, a woman who was with them in the camp said that Edith, Margot, and Anne were always together.[123] Moreover, that Edith did everything possible to try to help her daughters survive, including going without food so that her girls could have a bit more to eat. Given how she clung to her mother in Birkenau, it would appear that the intense dislike that Anne tells us that she felt for Edith while they were in hiding quickly melted away after their arrest and deportation.[124]

I would like to think that had they both survived the war, Anne, in time, would have found that she did have some measure of love for her mother and that they could have found some common ground.

Anne matured during her time in hiding. She looked back at things that she had written in anger, and realized that she, too, was partly to blame for some of the contention. It is never easy or flattering to look at yourself and see your own faults and failings, but Anne was able to do just that. She knew herself very well, and I admire her a great deal for that. That she was able to learn how to know herself better, to be honest with herself, to admit strengths and flaws, and be able not only to write it all down but also to be able to capture her feelings with such skill is amazing. That she was able to accomplish this at the age of fourteen and fifteen is astounding.

Thinking back to when *I* was fifteen, all I worried about was my wardrobe, high school, popularity, and whether a certain boy liked me—*hmm . . . maybe I was not so very different from Anne at the beginning of her diary!* But life dealt me a much fairer hand than the hand that Anne received. In normal circumstances, and without the war or having to hide, would Anne have developed the same insights into her own personality as quickly? Most likely she eventually would have. Perhaps the intense environment of living confined in hiding brought all this insight to the surface faster than it would have in normal life.[125] It certainly made her emotionally mature sooner. In the hiding place, she had no outside distractions to occupy her mind—only her solitude, fears, and dreams. Too much empty time every day to try to fill as best she could.

Along with the many serious situations, difficulties, and deep thoughts that Anne wrote about while in hiding, she also showed a great flair for humor. Those are the parts of the diary that I love the most. She was able to make even the most everyday things seem interesting. Her descriptions of peeling potatoes, where they each liked to take their weekly bath, snapping peas, the boring and repetitive selection of food available, and the many arguments between Mr. and Mrs. van Pels are perfect examples of her humor.

Her character sketches of the people around her were spot-on and very well written. After the war, surviving members of Mrs. van Pels's family said that Anne had captured and described her *perfectly*. When one of the helpers, Miep Gies, read the diary after the war, she said that it was as if all the eight people in hiding were once more surrounding her. She could hear their voices. Because of Anne's descriptive words, they were once more alive for her.

Moving on, we are there with Anne as she decides that Peter van Pels, the only boy around, maybe was not *so* dull and boring after all. Suddenly he is kind, brave, generous, and interesting in ways that he never was before. She begins to find more reasons to spend time around him, and "lives" for their next encounter. She worries that Margot has feelings for Peter too and does not want her to feel left out.[126] She is determined not to let her parents stand in the way of her "going upstairs" to visit Peter. Because of this determination, she writes a cruel letter to her beloved father that hurts him deeply.[127] She receives her first kiss.[128] She hates that her father uses the word *necking* to describe what is going on between herself and Peter.[129] *Why can't they trust her?* She is determined to "chart her own course and see where it leads her."

Then, the doubts and worries begin to creep in. Does Peter really care for her? Is she throwing herself at him? Is she being too ardent in her affection for him? Should she even be allowing Peter to kiss her? Margot would *never* do that!

After a time, Anne's affection for Peter begins to wane. She is frustrated by his inability to express his feelings. He only wants to cuddle, touch her hair, and be happy in the present moment. Anne wants a deeper connection of their thoughts and feelings that he is not capable of. She admits to herself that in normal life, they would not be together and that she could never marry him. She has already grown beyond him.[130] The challenge of the conquest was over. In her mind, she had built him up into something that she needed but that he simply could never be. In fairness to Anne, she does not want to hurt Peter. She still wants to help him learn to stand on his own and be his own person. Her father was right when he told her that romance in the hiding place was risky because if it did not work out, you still had to face that person every day.[131] There was no getting away from it. Still, she valued their friendship and wanted to be there for Peter as a friend. Because of their fate, we will never know how Peter felt about having to be "just good friends" with Anne.

YVONNE LESLIE, SALT LAKE CITY, UTAH

Anne's attentions to Peter are soon replaced with an urgent desire to rewrite and edit her diary.[132] She decided to use her diary as the basis of a novel that she planned to write after the war about her life in hiding. She started on this at once while keeping up with her regular diary entries. It was through this editing process that I was really able to see the ways in which Anne had matured and grown during her time in hiding. She was dismayed by some of the cruel things she had written about her mother. She was embarrassed by early descriptions of her developing body and sexual matters, saying that she could never write about things like that so freely now. She felt that she truly understood her parents' marriage and that the romantic love that Edith felt for Otto was not returned.[133] She admitted that many of the disagreements between her family and the van Pels family could have been handled better if only her family had been more open and friendly. If they could have seen that their own attitudes and opinions had not always been fair, then life in the annex would have been calmer. She realized that even if the war ended soon, she could never recapture her earlier carefree school days. *She was not the same Anne.* She now truly knew herself, and, as she says in what turned out to be her last diary entry on August 1, 1944, she was conscious of a "purer, deeper and finer" side that she wanted people to see.

Even with all her gained wisdom and self-knowledge, she was still afraid to show the finer Anne to others. How would she be able to do that? Could she? Would she be teased and ridiculed, not taken seriously? How could she make others see that there were actually "two Annes"?[134] She worried that the quiet and serious Anne who thought about God, nature, and self-improvement could become overshadowed by the clowning, annoying, and know-it-all Anne that people had come to expect. *In time, I know she would have succeeded at this.*

* * *

Anne Frank wanted to live. She wanted to help and bring enjoyment to others. She wanted to do her own small part to make the world a better place. She wanted to travel, learn languages, write books. *No, wait*—as she told her friend Bep, who was the youngest of the six helpers, she wanted to marry early and have many children! So many things. *I think she could have done them all had she lived.*

If Anne had survived the war, I do not think that she would agree with what she had written earlier—"that in spite of everything, I still believe that people are truly good at heart." Anne wrote that *before* Westerbork, Auschwitz, and Bergen-Belsen. Maybe *some* people, but not *all* people.[135]

Anne, I am so glad that was able to "meet" you. You taught me, brought a smile to my face, and made me think. You continue to bring me enjoyment and hope every time I read your words, thoughts, and feelings.

Your diary was indeed a gift to the world, but I would *gladly* give up that gift *if only you had been able to survive the war.* You, Margot, your mother, Peter, and countless friends. Life is more important than a book.

I wish you had lived . . .

SIMON RHODES, MELTON
MOWBRAY, UNITED KINGDOM

I DO NOT REMEMBER when I first heard of Anne Frank. I guess I was at school when I read her diary. Perhaps I did not even read it fully then. It was a long time ago, and it seems strange to me now that there was even a time before I had read—or paid attention to—what has since become a favorite book and one that feels central to my life.

I grew up in England, and in my early twenties—sometime in the mid-eighties—I went for a trip to the Netherlands, and to Amsterdam in particular. What a beautiful country and a beautiful historic city!

While on that trip, I noticed the Anne Frank Huis on Prinsengracht where Anne Frank, her parents, sister, and others were in hiding before being betrayed. The trip was not all about going to the Heineken brewery, and we thought that the Anne Frank Huis might be interesting. In those days, it was not necessary to book tickets in advance (thank goodness!), and as there was not much of a queue, if any, we decided to see what it was like. I had no idea what to expect. We climbed the very steep steps that are typical of Dutch houses and went past the open bookcase that was built to hide the entrance to the Secret Annex where Anne, her family, and friends lived for twenty-five months.

The bookcase had been a black-and-white plate in my copy of the diary until that point. But there it was, the simple construction that had kept the families safe and through which they later emerged when arrested by the Gestapo.[136]

We continued to the rooms where Anne, her family, and the others lived. There was the toilet that they all shared. There was the stove on which they heated water. I saw Anne's bedroom with the pictures she loved on the wall. Everything seemed preserved as it had been that fateful day in August 1944.[137]

As I was looking through a window at the horse chestnut tree that Anne had written about, the Westertoren bells of the Westerkerk rang.[138] Anne had written about the tree and the bells as symbols of the freedom that she longed for, and which she would never see again. We had learned at school that six million Jewish people had been killed in the Second World War. This was such a terrible number and too large for me to comprehend—a statistic like so many others. Tears poured down my face as history came to life for me. The six million was *now* no longer a statistic. It was six million individuals *like* Anne.

Sometime later as I was speaking to a group of people about Anne Frank, someone asked me what was so special about her. That was a good question. My reply, after some consideration, was, "Nothing!"

There were plenty of surprised looks in the room. I explained that she had written her diary and was clearly a gifted writer. She seemed gregarious and friendly—one of those people everyone liked. But more than anything else, she was a human being—an innocent human being who was sentenced to death by other human beings. We know nothing about most of the others who perished. Some would have been young, and others would have been old. Some would have been religious, and others would not. Inevitably, some would have been well liked, and others would not. Some would have been intelligent, beautiful, and wealthy. Some would have undoubtedly been criminals and unpleasant to be around. But they were *all* human beings.[139] They were all led to the slaughter in one of the twentieth century's worst genocides.

It took the writings of a teenage girl to help me to realize that. I sincerely hope that others read Anne's diary and come to realize that the dead are more than mere statistics. I will be forever grateful that Anne lived and wrote her diary and short stories.

KIRSI LEHTOLA, HELSINKI, FINLAND

HOW DID I "meet" Anne Frank? I must have been about thirteen years old and still at school when we studied about the Holocaust in our history class. I had watched documents and films about it, so the subject was already familiar to me, and I was deeply interested in what had happened. In our history book, there was a suggested list of different books about the Holocaust, and *Anne Frank: The Diary of a Young Girl* was one of them. I wrote a diary myself at the time, so a diary of another young girl fascinated me immediately.

It was the early 1990s, and a copy of the diary was extremely difficult to get. There was only one copy in our small library, so you had to be quick to get it. From the moment that I read her first words, I began to feel a strong connection with Anne. We were both at the same age, and Anne's words could have easily been mine. We shared many interests, had problems with our mothers, felt a sense of loneliness, and we believed we were outsiders. We had similar thoughts about religion and dreams about the future. I truly felt like Anne was my dearest friend and talking to me from the past.

Later during our history class—by which time I already knew the story well—we watched the movie about Anne.[140] I was so thrilled. I can still remember how we sat in the class, the lights were out, and I could not take my eyes off the TV. After nearly thirty years, I can still remember that day as if it had happened yesterday.

A few years later in 1995, I graduated from high school and my parents gave me a holiday trip as a graduation present. I could choose the destination myself, and it was the easiest decision that I have ever made—Amsterdam! I was nineteen years old, and it would be my first ever solo trip outside Finland. I have made several such trips since, and solo travelling is now one of my greatest loves. Many people were worried how a nineteen-year-old girl could travel to a "sinful" city like

Amsterdam all by herself, and they warned both my mother and me about the city's infamous drug dealers. Although my mother was a bit worried, I couldn't care less. All I ever wanted was to go to Amsterdam and walk in Anne's footsteps!

I couldn't believe that I was there and in Anne's hometown! I wandered around the city and imagined what it would have been like when Anne lived there. My hotel was in the city center, and there were many locations and buildings that were somehow connected with Anne's life. I *knew* that she had walked on those same streets.

But it was the Anne Frank Huis and Museum that would be the highlight of that trip. I visited it three times during the week that I spent in Amsterdam. In 1995 the Huis wasn't as busy as it is today, and you could really take your time and just feel the atmosphere there. Since then I have traveled to Amsterdam several times and have visited the Anne Frank Huis altogether some ten times. Every single time I step into that building, I can feel Anne's presence and spirit. It is a precious experience, and I always want to go there alone. I once traveled to Amsterdam with a good friend, and that was the only time that I *didn't* visit the museum. I feel such a special connection with Anne that I didn't want to share her with anyone.

Amsterdam is one of my favorite cities, and I love to visit it as often as I can. I have developed certain traditions that I have to do each time. In addition to visiting the Anne Frank Huis and Museum, I drop by at the Merwedeplein, where the Frank family lived before going to hiding. It is a beautiful and quiet neighborhood, and I just sit and spend a private moment there. I think about the young Anne living there, playing with her friends, and living a carefree life. I also go to the bookstore just around the corner and buy a new notebook for myself. It is the same store where Anne's diary was bought. It is a silly little tradition, but it means a lot to me.

My dream is to visit all places which were important in Anne's life. Someday I want to go to Bergen-Belsen to pay my respects. I have already visited the Auschwitz concentration camp, and it was such an experience that I can never forget what I saw there. You do not understand just how evil a human being can be until you have been to Auschwitz.[141]

It is believed that Anne stayed at the number 29 barrack in Auschwitz-Birkenau.[142] It was in the women's section of the camp and not very far from the infamous Gate of Death and railroad tracks that brought innocent victims to their last fate. Not far from the number 29 barrack is another barrack where the Nazis took women who were selected to go to gas chambers. There they had to wait, locked inside maybe for days, just to die.

I visited Auschwitz with a guide and a group. The guide gave us a moment just to look around and spend some time alone. Barrack number 29 does not exist anymore, but there are numbers marking the location where each barrack once existed.

I took that tour with a friend of mine, and I told her that I needed to go and see something alone. With a beating heart I approached that spot where the barrack once was, and I had a moment of silence for Anne and her family. I just stood there and imagined watching what was going on at the camp through Anne's eyes. I imagined all the horrors and heartbreak an innocent young girl would have witnessed there. For a moment, I could feel that I was standing side-by-side with Anne. I saw people around her herded to the gas chambers, shot down or clubbed to death in a blink of an eye, and then the black smoke rising from the chimneys of the gas chambers. I said a quiet prayer for Anne and felt that she had found her peace.

*   *   *

I am now nearly thirty years older than Anne Frank was when she died, but I still feel a strong connection. For me she is a very dear childhood friend who is long gone, but who will *always* have a special place in my heart. Her diary gave me support during my teenage years, and she was like a friend during those difficult times. For her sake, I will always try to do my part to fight against anti-Semitism and prejudice, and I will always try to cling to Anne's belief that, "in spite of everything, people are truly good at heart."

PRISCILLA SMITS, HAARLEM, THE NETHERLANDS

"MEETING" ANNE FRANK happened at an early age for me. It was during my childhood in the mid-seventies. I remember it as if it happened yesterday. My mother gave me her copy of *Anne Frank: The Diary of a Young Girl* and told me that I should try to read the book. I did, and it changed my life forever in ways that I cannot describe. Her words spoke to me and took me by the hand.

Since then I have read Anne's diary countless times. She has a wonderful style of writing, and I can relate to her words and what she writes. Because of Anne's diary, I started to try and love writing. It was not just about wanting to write a diary, but wanting to write in general. I understand what she means with "I would become crazy if I could not write" as I have the same feeling.[143] Her diary is a big source of inspiration for me and an important part of my life. I also liked her stories since they are amazing and very nicely written.[144] You cannot help but think about *"What if . . .?"*

The copy of Anne's diary that my mom gave me is now filled with autographs of many people related to Anne, to those mentioned in her diary, and to others who were part of her life. I have also included autographs of those connected to the Anne Frank Huis and Museum.

In addition, I have discovered lots of books and writers through reading Anne's diary, such as the Joop ter Heul stories by Cissy van Marxveldt.[145]

Anne's diary was also the start of a lifelong interest in wanting to know more about Anne Frank, her sister, parents, and friends. I wanted to know more about the van Pels family and Fritz Pfeffer. They each had a life and a story before they went into hiding, as too the helpers and everyone else connected to Anne's diary.[146] This resulted in my starting an ever-growing collection with all kinds of items. No, I do not have the original first edition pressing of Anne Frank's diary. I have had it in my hands several times, but financially speaking, it is impossible for me to buy—at least, it has been so far.[147] Besides my interest in Anne and her diary, I have also had a lifelong interest in books and collections associated with the Second World War.

My late parents were always incredibly supportive of my interest in Anne and her diary. They both helped and encouraged me to read the diary and then to build my collection on everything associated with Anne Frank. Everywhere they went they looked for items connected to Anne. I am very thankful that they did.

I have been to the Anne Frank Huis and Museum whenever possible—yearly, I would say. I have gotten to know and then befriend the people from the organization. They allowed my mom and me to visit parts of the museum that are not usually open to the public—such as the kitchen and office space of Otto Frank. This was an incredibly special moment for both my mom and me. I have seen the changes and the exhibitions. I think the recent changes have been very positive and make the people and the history of the Secret Annex come alive.

I have been to several events related to Anne Frank's diary throughout the years. I was at the unveiling of Anne's statue at the Merwedeplein.[148] This was really a surprise. I found out just in time, on the same day, and went at the last second. I was right on time. This was great to attend as Anne's childhood friend Jaqueline van Maarsen gave a speech and the mayor of Amsterdam at that time, Job Cohen, was also present. I was able to meet and thank him for his presence.

I have met several people who once knew Anne, such as Ms. van Maarsen, whom I have now met several times on various occasions. Once she included me during a speech that she was giving. This was a big honor for me.

A very moving experience was when I got to meet another of Anne's childhood and school friends, Hanneli Goslar. This was an incredibly special and emotional meeting. I had tried for years to meet her without success. Now I was finally given the chance! This was at a special event for the performance of *Anne* in the Amsterdam Theater.[149] I asked for this meeting at the organization and met her backstage. I met the crew of *Anne*, and the actress who played Anne on stage signed my program book.

Hanneli and I talked about how the Holocaust must never happen again and that it was up to us and my generation to make sure it could never happen again. She signed my copy of Anne's diary and added her name in Hebrew. I had my photo taken with her. Nanette Blitz-Konig and Jaqueline van Maarsen were also present, but as they were very busy talking, I did not want to bother them.[150] I can still hardly believe that it happened. This was also my feeling afterward—total disbelief and a dream come true.

These same feelings I also got when I met Buddy Elias—Anne and Margot's cousin.[151] During an event several years ago, Buddy Elias was invited as well, and I had the chance to meet him. This was just a short meeting as it was busy and there were lots of people around him. It was still very special. I was so very shy and nervous. I hardly dared to talk to him. This does not happen to me often, but it was such an honor to me. Buddy was exceedingly kind to me and friendly; he took time for me and signed my copy of Anne's diary. I was also lucky enough to have a photo taken with him. I told him that it was really a big honor for me to meet him, and I thanked him for his time.

After Buddy died in 2015, I sent a mourning card and got a thank-you card back.[152]

During the opening of the exhibition on the helpers who protected the Franks, the van Pels family, and Fritz Pfeffer during the days of hiding at what is now known as the Anne Frank Huis, I met Joop van Wijk. Joop is the son of one of the helpers, Bep Voskuijl. It was a very nice meeting, and he took the time to sign my copy of Anne's diary. I had my photo taken with him as well. I have his book, which I strongly recommend.[153] It is a wonderfully written book, and it is so important that all stories from this era be told and known. We must never forget what happened during the war.

I also wrote to Miep Gies after the publication of a book about her and Jan Gies.[154] I got a very nice letter back from her.

When Miep Gies passed away in early 2010, my mom and I went to say goodbye.[155] I will never forget it as it was a quiet journey with lots of snow. But we got there, and I was able to say goodbye and thank her for everything she had done and for saving Anne's diary. We also got to meet her granddaughter and had a short conversation with her. I thanked her for her time, and I got a thank-you card because of our visit.

About two years ago, I went to the Franks' former family home at the Merwedeplein. Unfortunately, we were not allowed to take photos [of the inside] at that time. Out of respect, I did not take any photos. *But* I do have photos from the window where the only existing film of Anne was taken.[156] I could not believe that I was walking around in the house at that moment. I cannot describe my feelings when I walked there—being at the place where all the people who Anne wrote about had once walked, talked, and lived. I hope to visit the house again sometime soon.

Over the years, I have also been to readings, exhibitions, musicals, and theatrical performances—you name it! There has been one exception in recent years—a [play] called *Achter het huis* which my intuition told me not to go to. Based on what I heard about it—the themes had nothing to do with the diary—I decided not to go.

I have also visited both schools that Anne and her sister Margot attended. It was great to be able to find and visit them. I have only seen them on the outside and have not been inside. The now renamed 6e Montessorischool Anne Frank has Anne's words all over the outside of the building.[157] The former Jewish Lyceum that Anne and Margot attended now has no mention of them but, instead, references what happened there during the Second World War.[158] The idea of Anne and Margot having been there together with their friends over the course of the year before they went into hiding was a touching moment as we now know their eventual fate.

At home, I have a cupboard filled with my Anne Frank memorabilia. I call it "Anne's cupboard." When I am not feeling well or am sad, I sit down there and let my feelings go. It always helps.

Whenever I visit the Anne Frank Huis, I feel that Anne is very close, watching us, and listening to us.

Priscilla Smits and Buddy Elias (Anne Frank's cousin) © Priscilla Smits

Priscilla Smits and Jacqueline (Jacque) van Maarsen. This photo was taken at the unveiling of the statue to Anne on the Merwedeplein (July 9, 2005) © Priscilla Smits

Jacqueline (Jacque) van Maarsen (left), Nanette (Nanny) Blitz-Konig (center), and Hanneli (Hannah) Goslar (right). This photo was taken at a question and answer session before the performance of the new play Anne *(de Winter and Durlacher) in Amsterdam on June 12, 2014 (Anne Frank's 75th birthday) © Priscilla Smits*

*Priscilla Smits with Hanneli (Hannah) Goslar. This photo was
taken after the performance of* Anne © Priscilla Smits

I *do* wish that Margot's diary could have been saved as well. I sure would have liked to read her words and thoughts! But most of all, and as Miep Gies once said, I wish that Anne, her family, and *all* the eight people hiding could have been saved. *Even*, if it would have meant the loss of the diary or the Anne Frank Huis. But as that is not the way that it happened, I keep visiting the Anne Frank Huis and collect everything related to Anne. I continue with my growing collection and Anne Frank and her diary will *always* be a big and important part of my life.

FR. JOHN NEIMAN, CHESTER, WEST VIRGINIA

I FIRST "MET" ANNE Frank in the fall of 1963. I was a fifth-grade student at Meadow Oaks School in Calabasas, California. In 1963, Calabasas was in the middle of nowhere, and it was long before the Kardashians lived there! Meadow Oaks was a new school, and I was really having a hard time. I had absolutely *no* athletic skills, and thus, I was awful at every sport that I tried. I was a charter member of a very exclusive club known as the ARJ (Athletic Rejects for Jesus).

One day in English class, our teacher put a table full of books in the middle of the class and then called us to go up row-by-row and pick a book to read. We were then to write a report. My row was the last to go up, so most of the books had already been taken. My eyes fell on a copy of *Anne Frank: The Diary of a Young Girl*, and I picked this one, read that it was about the Second World War, and brought it back to my desk.

Since first grade I had been fascinated with history. Because I did not play sports, I had a lot of time to read, and I became an avid reader. I was especially drawn to history. I had yet to read anything about the Holocaust. In the 1960s there was not a lot of material about the Holocaust available to the public. I already knew something about the Second World War from my father, Colonel Robert M. Neiman, USMC (United States Marine Corps). He had fought in the Pacific Theater of the war and was highly decorated. In addition, my parents' closest friends included someone who had been a prisoner of the Japanese in the Philippines, another who had been a member of the Danish Resistance, and a third who was a Hungarian Jewish man who had lost his entire family at Auschwitz.

I found Anne's diary to be fascinating. In fact, I could not put it down. I did not understand everything, but I found myself very moved and wanting to know more. I still remember when I read those horrible words in the epilogue for the first time: "In March 1945, Anne died in Bergen-Belsen. . ."

As part of trying to find out more about Anne, I discovered Ernst Schnabel's book: *Anne Frank: A Portrait in Courage* as well as a *LIFE* magazine article from August 18, 1958.

Not long after I first read Anne's diary, the George Stevens movie was on television, and my parents let me stay up past my bedtime to watch it.

Over the course of the next few years, I read every book that I could find on the Holocaust. I remember having frequent nightmares, and my parents told me that I could no longer read any more of "those" books. But each time, I begged to read more, and they would always give in.

I felt very close to Anne and to the others in hiding with her. I knew her father was alive, but it never occurred to me to write to him. I continued to soak up whatever material that I could find, and I felt more and more drawn into that very dark chapter in history. I also felt drawn into the whole experience of the Nazi occupation of the Netherlands.[159]

Fast forward to my senior year in college. I was attending Hardin-Simmons University, a Southern Baptist school in Abilene, Texas. I had seen something about Anne in a magazine, and I just decided that I wanted to write to Otto Frank. I wanted to let him know how much Anne's diary had impacted my life and to tell him that not a day went by when I did not think about Anne. In the fall of 1974, 1 wrote my letter and sent it off to Buchenstrasse 12 in Birsfelden, Switzerland.[160]

Soon after, I received a reply! I was so excited, and I could hardly open the letter. I really was not expecting a reply. I had just wanted Otto to know how much Anne had touched my life. I soon learned that Otto received (and continued to receive) thousands of letters and that he answered each one. I must have read his letter fifty times! It was wonderful, and I could tell from the words that he wrote that he must be a kind, good-hearted, and friendly person.

I quickly wrote back. In his next letter, Otto kindly thanked me but said that he was not able to keep up a correspondence because he received so many letters.[161] I wrote back and told him not to be concerned. I would continue to write to him, but he did not need to answer; however, he *did* answer every single letter that I wrote! Otto Frank was a hero to me, and it was such a wonderful experience to be able to have some correspondence with one of my heroes.

In one of his letters, Otto invited me to come to visit him and Fritzi in Birsfelden if I ever found myself in Europe. Once I read *that* letter, I decided to "find" myself in Europe as soon as possible.

My first opportunity came in May 1976. I went to Amsterdam first and went to the Anne Frank Huis. I have never really been able to put into words what it *actually* meant to me to walk through the *achterhuis* (the Secret Annex). I think that I was in a daze, and I *know* I could think of nothing else for days. When I left, I proudly told the lady helping me in the bookstore that I was on my way to meet Otto Frank.

I met Otto and Fritzi for the first time on June 4, 1976, in their beautiful home in Birsfelden. I hardly knew what to say as I was so nervous. Within a few moments, Otto had put me quickly at ease. He was so warm, welcoming, and kind. After being with him for fifteen minutes, I felt as if I had known him all my life! We talked for what seemed like only an hour, but which was more like three.

After hearing about Anne, the diary, and his life since the war, I asked him if he would tell me about his time at Auschwitz. Otto told me that he never talks about his experiences in the camps. He always refers people to the library to get information there. My heart sank because I felt as if I had offended him.

He paused for a moment of silence and then said, "Because you love Anne so much, I will tell you." Suddenly, I felt like I was ten feet tall! He spent the next hour telling me about their arrest, their month in Westerbork, that horrible three-day journey in the cattle cars, and then Auschwitz. He told me about seeing Edith, Margot, and Anne for the last time, and then the indescribable months of hunger, beatings, humiliation, and fear.

Otto also related the story of how he could no longer go on after weeks of slave labor and terrible beatings at the hand of a particularly vicious *Kapo*.[162] A prisoner doctor arranged to have Otto taken to the infirmary block. It was there in mid-January 1945 that Otto tried to convince Peter van Pels to hide in the hospital and not go on what became known as the Death March. Peter's father, Hermann van Pels, had been gassed at the beginning of October 1944. Peter had a good work detail at Auschwitz and often brought extra food that he was able to obtain to the starving Otto.[163]

Peter told Otto that he was still young and strong and that he would be able to manage the march. Peter was one of 58,000 prisoners who were then marched out of Auschwitz in January 1945. Thousands perished along the way. Peter made it to the Mauthausen concentration camp in Austria, where he then died on May 5, 1945, the day the Americans liberated the camp.[164] When Otto was relating all this to me, it was the one time that he came close to crying. His eyes teared up, but he was somehow able to hold back the tears.

His eyes lit up when he told me about how Auschwitz was liberated by the Russians on January 27, 1945, and then about his long six-month journey back to Amsterdam.[165] He arrived back in Amsterdam on June 3, 1945, and went to find Miep and Jan Gies.[166] The very next day, June 4, he went back to work at Prinsengracht 263.

In mid-July 1945, Otto found out the terrible news that his children would not be coming back.[167] He already knew that Edith had died in Birkenau just three weeks before the liberation.

After Otto had related all this to me, the three of us just sat in silence for several minutes. Then Fritzi told me her story. She told me about fleeing Austria, coming to Amsterdam, going into hiding, her betrayal, and then her deportation to Auschwitz. She told me the incredible story of how she escaped the gas chamber *twice* in one day and then her liberation by the Russians in January 1945.[168]

We were all exhausted by this point. After Otto said we should not talk about such things anymore, we went outside and sat down on the patio. Otto and Fritzi were extremely interested to know all about me. After another long talk . . .!

Otto took a brief nap, and then we went for a walk while Fritzi cooked dinner. It is still hard for me to describe how much it meant to me to be with Otto Frank and how humbled and honored I felt that he had shared memories with me that he very rarely shared. The time that I spent with Otto and Fritzi that June day was imprinted on my soul, and I am so grateful that I had the chance to meet them both and to spend so much time with them. I feel that I had indeed "met" Anne and that she would always be with me.

After a most delicious dinner, Otto called me into his office. He took something out of a drawer and put it in front of me. It was Anne's diary and one of the ledger books in which she had continued her diary. I could hardly believe it! I just stared at it for a few minutes until Otto finally said, "Do not you want to look at it?" I spent the next hour looking at it.[169]

I did not want to leave, but I soon realized that I had been there all day and well into the night. Fritzi called me a taxi, and I said a reluctant goodbye.

During the years following my visit, we stayed connected by mail and by phone—I used to call Otto once a month. From Otto's letters, I could tell that he felt as close to me as I did to him.

I also had the opportunity to speak in several schools, to several civic organizations, and synagogues about my interest in Anne's diary and my day with Otto and Fritzi.

I would go on to "meet" Anne again many times after my day in Basel as I had the opportunity to meet so many wonderful people who wanted to show their affection for her. It was especially meaningful to be able to talk to a cast performing the play and then to sit in the audience to watch the performance. I always had the cast and crew sign a program that I would then send to Otto.

Over the course of the next few years, I got involved with the Holocaust Education Committee of the B'nai B'rith in Los Angeles.[170] I had the honor of meeting and working with many Jewish Holocaust survivors. Many became my dearest friends, and I found these beautiful people, who had suffered so much, to be full of life, love, and compassion. They were not bitter or angry, but rather, they hoped that they could make the world a better place. They dreamed of a world where there would be no more holocausts. They were like shining lights to me. By this time, I had become Roman Catholic and was seriously thinking about the priesthood. These dear friends taught me by their example what it *really* meant to be a good Christian.

FR. JOHN NEIMAN, CHESTER, WEST VIRGINIA

I "met" Anne in each of these survivors. It was not only through the unimaginable suffering that they had endured, but I was impressed by their courageous optimism and good hearts. Anne wanted so much to do good and bring joy to people—even to those she did not know. She refused to surrender her hopes and dreams in the darkest circumstances.

In June 1981 1 attended the World Gathering of Jewish Holocaust Survivors in Jerusalem.[171] It was an experience that is firmly implanted in my heart. It does not seem possible that so much pain and so much love could exist side-by-side. Each of those survivors, as Otto and Fritzi had done earlier (and Anne to a degree as she did survive the horrors of Auschwitz), showed me how the power of the human spirit, as created by God, could survive even Auschwitz and Bergen-Belsen.

In April 1983, 1 attended the American Gathering of Jewish Holocaust Survivors in Washington, DC. It was there that I met Eva Mozes Kor, who as a ten-year-old girl, had suffered at the hands of Dr. Mengele along with her twin sister Miriam.

*   *   *

My second visit with Otto and Fritzi was in London on January 3, 1979, at the home of Eva Schloss, Fritzi's daughter. I was flying over from Dublin, and due to inclement weather, I did not arrive until the evening. It was this visit that changed my life forever. I was talking to Otto about how much Anne still meant to me, and suddenly, he stopped me in midsentence. He said, "It is very moving to me that you love Anne, but if you really want to honor Anne's memory and the memory of all those who died in the Holocaust, you have to do what Anne wanted to do . . . you must live your life doing good for other people."

It was at that moment that I knew that for me to fulfill those words, I would become a Roman Catholic priest. God surely used Anne and Otto to lead me to the priesthood.

When I was ordained a priest on February 1, 1986, there were fifty Holocaust survivor friends in the congregation. Also present were Miep and Jan Gies, who had traveled all the way from Amsterdam to celebrate this day with me. I would also like to think that Anne and Otto were very much present with me as I became a priest. I owe so much of who I am to them, and every day they continue to inspire and encourage me to do good for other people. After the life-changing visit with Otto and Fritzi in London, I continued my involvement in Holocaust education and speaking in schools.

In May 1980, 1 had the chance to visit Otto one last time. He was very weak, but he insisted on seeing me. We had a very short yet wonderful visit. I knew it would be the last time I would ever see him, and I held each moment that we spent together close to my heart. Fritzi and I spent several hours talking that day. She, of course, was terribly worried about Otto. I assured her of my constant prayers and loyal friendship. During my short visit with Otto, Fritzi brought out some finger sandwiches that Otto insisted were "too thick" and which Fritzi insisted were nice and thin. Even in his weakened state, Otto was always ready to lighten the mood and make us laugh.

When I said goodbye, Otto told me that he considered me one of his closest friends. It was one of the most moving and tender moments of my life. He looked at me with such affection, and then it was time to say goodbye to my mentor and hero.

Otto died on August 19, 1980. I am so grateful that I had this one last visit. Fritzi and I became great friends, and I made many visits to see her in the 1980s and 1990s. She had a deep sense of humor (as did Otto) and a heart full of compassion and goodness. Every time that I came to see her, she always planned a day when we would do something Catholic (such as visiting a church, a monastery, or a pilgrimage site).

She confessed that she was an avid fan of the American television show *Dallas*. She was also very critical of the way that the Swiss spoke German. She took me to the art museum in Basel and lamented how Modern art was "terrible." On one of my visits, Fritzi told me about going to the trial of the person who had betrayed her and family to the Gestapo. Because this person had also happened to save a famous opera singer, she was acquitted and went free. I could see all the pain, anguish, and suffering of those years on her face as she was relating all this to me.

I also got up the nerve to ask Fritzi if Otto had ever discussed his relationship with Edith. She assured me, "Otto loved Edith very, very much, but he loved me more." Fritzi and Otto had spent twenty-seven beautiful years together as husband and wife. After all the suffering and loss that they had endured, they found a new life together. Fritzi proudly told me that Otto answered every single letter he received. He dictated the answer while Fritzi dutifully typed the letter. Fritzi was my dear friend, and she lived to see her grandchildren and great-grandchildren. She died in October 1998. I "met" Anne Frank many times through Fritzi.

I also "met" Anne in Miep and Jan Gies. Fearless, strong, and good-hearted, Miep risked her life every day to hide the Franks. Along with the other brave helpers, they remind all of us that there are causes for which it is worth risking our lives. They also remind us, as Miep always said, that "everyone can shine a light in the darkest place."

Even though I never had the opportunity to meet Bep Voskuijl, I did exchange several letters with her, and I certainly "met" Anne when I encountered her goodness and self-sacrifice.

*   *   *

Anne wrote in her diary that she wanted to go on living after her death.[172] Even with her dreams and vivid imagination, I do not think she could have begun to realize how powerfully that wish would be fulfilled. Anne Frank is still very much with us, and she is, indeed, one of those great lights who can lead us out of the darkness.

Otto and Fritzi Frank, June 4, 1976, Birsfelden,
Basel, Switzerland © Fr. John Neiman

Otto Frank with Fr. John Neiman, London,
January 3, 1979 © Fr. John Neiman

Otto and Fritzi Frank, London, January 3, 1979 © Fr. John Neiman

Otto Frank and Bep Voskuijl © Fr. John Neiman

Otto and Fritzi Frank © Fr. John Neiman

Miep and Jan Gies, Oliver Elias (Buddy Elias's son), and
Fritzi Frank, Birsfelden, July 1981 © Fr. John Neiman

Miep and Jan Gies in Anne's room in the Secret Annex,
Prinsengracht 263, Amsterdam © Fr. John Neiman

RYAN COOPER, CAPE COD, MASSACHUSETTS

A WELL-KNOWN HOLOCAUST SURVIVOR once said that if you want to know about the Holocaust, you ought to read the diary of Anne Frank; indeed, to many, their first introduction to the Holocaust *is* Anne Frank. She is the icon, the one young girl who stands for the millions who were murdered by the Nazis.

It was not until I was in my twenties that Anne Frank became part of my life. Beforehand, I knew nothing about her nor the hiding of the Frank family from the Nazis. As a Jehovah's Witness, I was familiar with the Holocaust as Jehovah's Witnesses were persecuted and imprisoned during the Second World War for not pledging allegiance to Hitler.[173] As to Anne Frank, though, I was ignorant.

At that time, the only world that I knew revolved around Jehovah's Witnesses. Witnesses were admonished to shun the outside world. Education beyond high school was deemed unhealthy to one's spirituality, and association with people outside the sect was frowned upon.[174] But after my mother's death and the breakup of my engagement, I slowly drifted away from the Witnesses. I ceased going to meetings and those one-time brothers left me as one fallen from the faith. In this void and period of despondency, Anne Frank became part of my life.

It was late one night while searching the *TV Guide* for something to pass the remaining hours of the day, that my eyes fell upon the film, *The Diary of Anne Frank*. That then led me to read *The Diary of a Young Girl*, which led me to seek out other material about Anne Frank. One was a magazine article which mentioned the countless letters that Otto Frank had received and noted that he answered each one.

After the publication of Anne Frank's diary, Otto Frank began to receive letters from mostly young people who had been inspired by Anne's words. As Mr. Frank saw the hope for humanity through the youth, he made it a point to answer every letter. A flame had been lit, and I felt the need to reach out to him as well.

I wrote my first letter to Mr. Frank in December of 1972. His reply the next month told me that this man was very special. He wrote that he was extremely impressed with the honesty in which I expressed the circumstances which led me to write to him, and he invited me to continue our correspondence.[175]

I knew that this was a man I had to meet, and within months, I was on my way to visit him in Basel. Here I found a man who could have become closed off and bitter for the loss of his family. Instead, I found Mr. Frank to be warm and generous as he opened his home and heart to me. We bonded almost immediately. Mr. Frank was very generous with what he could give, but when talking of his lost children, and especially Anne, he could not take too much. Several times when looking at Anne's photograph album or through a box of images, he would quickly flip through them, his eyes unable to linger for long on the faces of his lost children.

Otto Frank rarely spoke about himself, for in his mind, he was not important. It was *Anne* and her legacy, the *diary*, which were more important to him. If through Anne, he could bring some goodness to the world, then that was what mattered the most; indeed, it was only *after* his death that I ever learned much about his life before going into hiding.[176]

During that week in 1973 that I spent with Otto and his wife Fritzi, he shared with me the things he usually showed to visitors—Anne's photobook and other things. But when I asked if I could see Anne's diary, he replied that he had a facsimile he could show me. As we sat together with the copy, I asked if I could see the original, as it was a dream of mine to hold it. His expression seemed to suggest that no one had dared asked this before. He paused for a moment, tilting his head a bit, before finally answering "Yes!" Fritzi jumped in, "Otto can take you to the bank, and you can see it there." But Otto decided that he would bring the diary home so I could see it in a more comfortable setting.[177]

The next evening after we shared a meal prepared by Fritzi, Otto led me to his study, where Anne's diary lay on his desk. He stopped in the doorway and, taking my arm, said, "Now, I leave you alone with Anna's diary." I was stunned, and before I could say anything, he had

"MEETING" ANNE FRANK: AN ANTHOLOGY

disappeared. Not only had Otto let me *see* Anne's original diary, but he had left me *alone* with it! It actually upset Fritzi. As I sat down at the desk, I could hear her arguing with him in German. Otto answered her in English, "But he can't read it!"

There was a reason that the original was kept secret. Much of it had never been published. When Anne was rewriting her diary for possible publication after the war, she edited out significant portions as being too personal. Otto had used Anne's revised copy but reinstalled some of the entries that Anne had cut. I realized the complete trust Otto had in me and that he *knew* that I felt the spirit of Anne. I *knew* that he believed that his daughter's written testament of the Holocaust was safe in my hands.

All was quiet now as I slowly began my journey through Anne's diary, starting with the iconic red-and-white checkered album that had been her chosen birthday present from her father. Of course, I could not read the Dutch entries for the most part, but there was the spirit of Anne within the pages. There were of course the well-known photographs that Anne had inserted with little captions. Of particular interest was Anne's little sketch of a pert skating outfit. She had written a fantasy of skating with her cousin, Bernhard (Buddy) Elias, who would become a well-known skating star, actor, and later, a close friend of mine.

Otto never came into the study, and I had all the time that I wanted. Finally, I gathered up the three volumes which made up Anne's original diary and carried them into the living room where Otto and Fritzi were relaxing. I knelt with Otto, and again opened the red-and-white checkered album. At that moment, Fritzi took a photograph of us, as she knew that it was a special occasion.

Of all the memorable events that I experienced in my relationship with Otto Frank, this will always stand out as the most meaningful of my life.

I spent that summer in Amsterdam, where I met Miep and Jan Gies and spent many moments at their flat, where Miep shared her experiences as well as precious mementos given to her by the residents of Prinsengracht 263. Otto and Fritzi came to the city, where we again shared each other's company.

Toward the end of my time in Amsterdam, I visited Rootje (Rosa) de Winter, who was imprisoned with her daughter Judith in Kamp Westerbork. They shared the same cattle car with the Franks when they were transported to Auschwitz. Rosa remarked about Anne that she seemed happy despite the circumstances.[178] I recall her mentioning Anne's deep dark eyes and her long hair, which would soon be cut off. Anne had a presence that you could not forget. Rosa described being with Edith Frank when she died, her mind gone, saving crumbs for her children.[179] Rosa published her account right after the war—possibly, the first account by a Holocaust survivor.

Over the rest of the decade, I returned to Europe twice to see my "family away from home." Otto and Fritzi were always there to welcome me. We were close friends enjoying each other's company with excursions to the mountains, a pub, or movie. So we did not focus on Anne or the Holocaust all the time. Otto said to me that he did enjoy life as it was presented to him and did not think about the horrible past all the time. "Pim is een grote optimist," Anne wrote of her father, and indeed I found that despite all that he suffered, he continued to be optimistic.[180]

In 1977, I made what would be the last visit to see Miep and Otto and Fritzi. At Miep's home in Amsterdam, I phoned Otto and Fritzi. After I hung up, I turned to Miep and asked how Otto was . . . really? "He gets very tired these days. He's a very old man now," she said. Then she added, "I think it will come very fast."

In Basel, things were not well—Fritzi's sister was dying of cancer and Otto's sister Leni was in the hospital, having broken her breastbone. Fritzi was very distraught, but she hid it well. Despite the anguish, they managed to make my visit pleasant. Several times I would be alone in Otto's house as they went to the hospital. There I would revisit Anne through the pages of her photograph album and record my thoughts in my journal. During that visit, Otto took me up to the attic, where he had never taken anyone before. Here was the Frank family history through their personal possessions. From a box full of photos, Otto gave me an image of Anne that had been cut from one of the family albums. I took this with me as a remembrance of my last visit.

Otto Frank died August 19, 1980. Following his passing, I felt that my special relationship was at an end. All my letters and memorabilia were tucked away, seemingly forgotten. But years later, a carpenter was constructing a library for me and noted the books that I had on Anne Frank. He asked me why I was interested. When I told him that I had been a close friend of Anne's father, he asked if he could share this with his wife, who was a middle-school teacher. I agreed, and shortly after, she called and asked if I would speak about Anne Frank to her class. That was the beginning of a rebirth.

From then, I began speaking to audiences at schools, libraries, and synagogues. Speaking about Anne and my relationship with her father always filled me with warmth. That *somehow*, I was fulfilling that admonition that years before Otto had spoken to me about—namely, that Anne wished to work for mankind. *If* through my words I was able to move *one* person, then I felt a sense of success; indeed, it has happened.

I began this odyssey alone years ago, but now I have a family beyond just my siblings who were also drawn to Anne Frank and who found a closeness to her through knowing her father. A few I was introduced to by Otto and Fritzi, while others like Cara Wilson-Granat and Fr. John Neiman became family later.

In 2009, Father John and I met in Amsterdam for a very special event. We were honored to be invited to Miep's 100th birthday party, which was a private affair with the family. I had brought with me a special birthday card signed by all the students at a school where I spoke each year. It was a wonderful opportunity to see Miep after many years.

During that trip we also had the privilege of going up to the attic and loft of the Secret Annex. That experience was like going back in time. There was an old bedstead there along with a stove and trunks. They looked left as they had been in 1944. No tourists came up here, and even some staff had never stepped foot in this sacred place—the space that Anne so often wrote about. It had been her sanctuary from the others and the place where she felt the blossoming of young love.

Father John and I also went to the Franks' apartment on the Merwedeplein, the first for both of us. The apartment was being occupied by a writer from Chad, who had been advised beforehand that we may go up.[181] He invited us inside. There was a steep winding set of stairs, and I thought of Helmuth "Hello" Silberberg meeting Anne at the same spot.[182] I could see Anne with her hair smartly brushed and trying to look as attractive as possible.

We were allowed free reign to explore this spacious apartment. Anne's room was set up as it was when she lived there. Next to a window which looked out over the central courtyard, a photograph of Anne writing at her desk rested on top of an exact copy of the same desk. The original was given to Miep by Otto.

* * *

Today only a few childhood friends remain who ever knew Anne Frank personally. Some use that unique position to carry on Anne's legacy so that it will never be forgotten. In not too many years, they will be gone. Those of us who were blessed to have known her father will carry that legacy on.

Today, a large portrait of Otto Frank hangs in my library. It used to hang in Otto's home after his death. Fritzi would look at it and remember the man whom she loved. I look at it, and I, too, remember the man whom I was blessed to have known—the father of Anne Frank.

Otto Frank and Ryan Cooper with Anne's diary, 1973 © Ryan Cooper

Otto and Fritzi Frank, 1973 © Ryan Cooper

*Barbara Goldstein (a friend of Otto and Fritzi), Otto Frank, and
Ryan Cooper prior to Otto and Fritzi sailing from Amsterdam
on their Norwegian cruise, 1973 © Ryan Cooper*

Otto and Fritzi Frank, Basel, 1977 © Ryan Cooper

Eva Schloss (Anne Frank's stepsister); this photo was taken with Otto's Leica camera that he used to photograph Anne and Margot © Ryan Cooper

Ryan Cooper and Fr. John Neiman in Anne's room at Merwedeplein 37, Amsterdam © Ryan Cooper

Ryan Cooper and Miep Gies at Miep's 100th birthday,
February 15, 2009 © Ryan Cooper

Ryan Cooper in the attic of the Secret Annex,
Prinsengracht 263, Amsterdam © Ryan Cooper

COLLEEN SNYMAN, ASH, UNITED KINGDOM

A VORACIOUS READER RIGHT from the get-go, I was constantly on the lookout for the next adventure or knowledge between the pages of a book—the fatter the better! I spent many evenings and nights devouring page upon page. Days were not spared either. I can remember how weekends spent in the African bush or at home in pajamas allowed me ample hours to escape to other worlds. Sometimes I would inhabit three worlds in one weekend!

This did, of course, all mean that I got through my school library's age-prescribed material in about three months, that I was not allowed to move on to the older books until the following year, until a new book appeared, or until I begged hard enough to go to our public library, which was in a dodgy part of town.

When I started school at six years old, I was already able to read and read well. I raced through easy readers and slim books and then on to storybooks by the age of seven and even bigger storybooks later that same year—works that would normally be reserved for children who were ten years and older. It put me in a precarious position with our librarian, Mrs. Lovett, who did not fully believe that it was possible; however, she kept an eye on me and soon concluded that she could trust in my abilities. She gave me permission to take books out of *any* section of the library and books suitable for *any* age! What a treat!

I was nearly nine years old when I came upon the biography and autobiography section near the back corner of the school library. Peeping out from between some yet-to-become dog-eared books was a pale face with dark hair and big dark eyes on the spine of a delicious-smelling paperback. To this day, I can remember how the plastic-wrapped cover felt in my hands, the pages fanning easily between my fingers. Most of all, though, I was captivated by this young girl who had her name on a book. It blew me away! I also had a diary and home time could not come soon enough. These days, it is not lost on me just how lucky I was to be able to look forward to going to the library whenever I wanted and then be able to go home afterward to read in peace and quiet.

Approaching the counter to check the book out with my new privileges, Mrs. Lovett spied what I was holding, and she did not seem pleased. I was told that I was not old enough to read the book and that I had to put it back.[183]

This all felt like a real blow for a second or two, but I returned the book as requested. But I did not pick up anything else, which was a purposeful move. Mrs. Lovett left early on a Thursday so she would not be there for our big break. This was when I returned and spent forty minutes poring over Anne Frank's words until five minutes before the lesson bell rang. I then dashed to the counter and declared myself in a rush. The library monitors, who were up to their elbows in returns and who had the same need to return to class, told me to just stamp my card and go! Talk about having plans come together!

Both Thursday afternoon and Friday, plus an excess of homework, came and went without my being able to get any reading done. Saturday, however, turned into a day of reading just over one hundred pages of some laughter, many tears, fear, and shock. Unable to digest any more, and not really understanding a lot of what was going on, I spoke to my parents and asked about being Jewish.

We talked for ages, and they explained a lot of the history and culture. Of course, we discussed the Second World War. My grandpa fought in the war and was stationed in both North Africa and, later, Italy.[184] All at once, the fact that he was alive at the same time as Anne made a connection in my then eight-year-and-ten-month-old brain that has endured. It was a need to know more, to ask questions, to find out about others who had been where Anne was. I needed to find other helpers who had been just as brave as the Frank family's helpers had been—*anything*, as I was hungry to learn.

Late 1991, and nearly fifty years after the Frank family went into hiding in Amsterdam, I turned the last page of Anne's diary. It had been an intense read, but I felt such a connection to her, feeling as I did as if she had written those words to *me*.

We happened to be learning about different religions and tolerance the following term (a new school year had begun) and had two excursions planned. By now, I was nine, and I had English friends, Afrikaans friends, Zulu and Xhosa friends, Italian friends, Canadian friends, Christian friends, Muslim friends, Catholic friends, Hindu friends, and Hare Krishna friends. Differences were not an issue for us. We were just friends, end of story. Out in the wider world, of course, we were still living in South Africa under the former apartheid regime. This was a regime which looked to divide citizens—and by force, if necessary.

I could see the parallels to Anne's life, but it felt different, and I did not know why. We coped, and life just went on. I never felt scared of where I was, scared to go out, or scared that someone might take me away.

Our first school excursion took us to a synagogue in Durban, our closest big city. I was so excited, and I had millions of questions. Although "my friend Anne" had taught me so much, I still wanted to know more. We arrived just before noon. The girls went to one side, and the boys to the other. We were given scarves to cover our hair and were taken upstairs to where the women sat.[185] Honestly, I cannot remember a single word that the rabbi said as I was just enthralled by the building and everything in it. We could ask a single question each, but it never came around to my turn as my surname comes near the end of the alphabet. As it was now past lunch, that was that! I never got to ask what I had wanted to know. Basically, my question would have been, "Why were so many people mean to Jewish people?"

For her thirteenth birthday, Anne received her beloved red-and-white checkered diary, calling it "maybe one of my nicest presents."[186] I too received a diary for my thirteenth birthday. My parents had seen me reading Anne's over and over, and so got me one of my own. It was blue with white swirls and cloudlike in a way. I loved it and began to write even before the end of my birthday!

I quickly found that I was not writing anything interesting, and I would often feel frustrated at the silly things that I wrote. As a result, I left the diary for nearly a year and came back to it a few months before I turned fourteen. Much happier with how and what I was writing, I got used to making entries twice weekly, sometimes more. I still have all my diaries and letters from friends in tins and boxes!

In my final year at school, I was extremely ill, and I nearly died from two brain hemorrhages. There was a period when I was unable to speak or move. It was scary to say the very least. One of the days, and while I lay awake with only my own thoughts and searing pain to keep me company, I thought to myself that this was torture and wished for it to be done. Suddenly, my thoughts turned to the Frank family and how they would have been doing (almost) the same as what I was doing—being still and quiet. It made everything a little more bearable. *Unlike* Anne, I got to finish school and return to a normal life. Every single day I am grateful for this. Her words, "Where there's hope, there's life. It fills us with fresh courage and makes us strong again."[187] This kept me going on many a difficult day.

Over the years, I have read and reread Anne's diary, along with other texts and books by various authors, always returning to the original. There is something incredibly humbling knowing about a young girl who had led a relatively normal life until things became so unsafe for her family that they had to hide away and then deny Anne nearly everything she had known until that point. Humbling, too, that by the grace and kindness of others who put themselves at risk, Anne, her family, and friends were kept safe.

The emotional turmoil that all those hiding in the Secret Annex surely felt and how it must have affected Anne as she grew up have been things that I have tried to comprehend my whole life.[188] Honestly, I do not think I will ever come close; however, "meeting" Anne in an almost clandestine manner has changed the way that I view the world and my own life. I am a much more determined person and can get myself through tougher days without moaning. Moaning just seems pointless. I am safe and free, so why moan?

I have always loved trees and nature, and I always feel more at home when out in the wild, especially after growing up in Africa. I spent hours wandering around the patch of bush at the bottom of our garden, often taking my book and sitting on a fallen tree that served as a wonderful place to nestle down and be quiet. When Anne wrote of her horse chestnut tree, I was so happy. I, too, had a tree. It was my favorite place in the world to sit and read, and it took me to a place nobody else had and one that felt special. I really felt close to Anne when I sat there and read. When we moved away from South Africa, I was so sad to have to bid my tree farewell. I promised her that I would be back one day.

*   *   *

Recently, for my thirty-seventh birthday, I was given a new copy of Anne's diary as my old one was now really fragile, well-thumbed, and in several pieces.

Giddy with excitement, I settled down with coffee and some biscuits and intended to read only fifty pages. *Intended* is a strong word. Waking the following morning with crumbs in my hair and cold coffee, I discovered my book was closed and with the bookmark on top. That is usually my signal to myself that the book is finished and to move on.

A brief sinking feeling in my stomach made me resolute. I would have to read it again and stay awake this time! So now, I am two weeks in and halfway through the book again. It reminds me of when I was a kid—I would read about something and then need to know *everything* about that subject. My scrapbooks are my evidence. As Anne had once done, my scrapbooks also hold pictures of my favorite movie stars and the clothes that I liked. Did we not all do this?

This time around, however, I have started something new. Once again inspired by the sheer willpower of the families in hiding, I have revived my meditation practice and have begun a daily meditation in which I reflect on the day and how I handled things. I wonder whether there is anything that I could have done better or changed my attitude toward anything that I found unpleasant. Anne spent a lot of time in self-reflection, which was admirable considering her age and circumstances. If everyone could take a *tiny* part of that and apply it to their day, then I think we would have a much happier world.

Our world is surely the poorer for having lost Anne Frank, but hopefully her legacy will endure a very long time and continue to inspire, encourage, and enthrall generations to come. The power that her words hold is immense. Personally, I now live a quite different life after having read her words, and I feel absolutely privileged to have "met" her through her diary. We have "met" many times now and at various stages in my life. She has been relevant in them all, despite her not ageing along with me. Forever fifteen years old, Anne will be with me until it is my time to leave this mortal earth. We "met" through a shared appreciation of books—just the way she would have loved.

AMANDA TOMKINS, CHICHESTER, UNITED KINGDOM

I VAGUELY REMEMBER HEARING about Anne Frank during my childhood. I knew that she was a girl of importance, but at an early age, I didn't know what until my high-school days.

At high school, I learned a bit more about her. Fast forward to 2019, and after years of wanting to read her famous diary, I picked it up and realized how alike we *both* were in terms of our teenage emotions, how we *both* had fights with our mothers, and how we *both* argued and occasionally fought with our siblings. And we *both* like to write.

Now the other similarity between us is that we both started a diary when we were aged thirteen. But it was not until the end of 2018 that I finally started to write my own letters to Anne—something that I still do to this day. I tell her my feelings, my life, and my problems. I tell her everything and I feel—as Anne did with Kitty—that Anne has become my own best friend. A best friend was something else I have also never had.

Just like Anne, I often start my letters off with a simple *Lieve Anne* (Dear Anne) just to make my letters to her more homey. It has now become such a big part of my life writing to her that I cannot bear to think what I would do if I *did not* write to her. I sense that she understands the anger, joy, or sadness that I feel when I write. I feel happy that I have been able to talk to her through my diary entry for that day. I have even started to learn Dutch so that I can read her diary in the original and get a true sense of how she wrote it in her own language.

I even decided to write my own stories on Anne and her point of view based on her time in Auschwitz-Birkenau or Bergen-Belsen. I have read every surviving account of people's time in both camps to get a sense of the horror, and this has allowed me to be able to write out my version of Anne's last seven months. I even wrote about Anne surviving

Bergen-Belsen and how she might have felt during the liberation of the camp in April 1945.[189]

I would become a child, teenager, and adult in terms of how I loved devouring anything about the Second World War—especially the Holocaust. I would read any book that I could on Anne, including even books that I had read before—just so that I could read the same information again about her and the other seven hiders in the Secret Annex.

Even now, many years after her death, I feel a sorrow in my heart that we lost such a great person. I feel that Anne would have told her story during her life and, as her friend Hanneli once said, "she would have loved the fame." I agree that she would have, and I hope that one day I will be able to go to Amsterdam, Auschwitz-Birkenau, and Bergen-Belsen so that I can pay my respects to such a wonderful girl, to her family, and to her helpers.

I thought that I would share with you one of my letters to Anne's *Kitty* based on what I think Anne *might* have written if she had been able to find paper and ink at Bergen-Belsen:

Bergen-Belsen, February (?), 1945

Lieve Kitty,

It's been 5040 hours . . .

I'm sorry for my terrible writing, but paper and pencils are hard to come by here.

It's been a total of seven months—seven months of hell, pain, hunger, sickness, and death. The month, I think, is February, but I couldn't tell you what date it is. I lost track months ago. At first, while in Auschwitz, we kept track of the days and months, but soon we all became so hungry and confused that we just gave up trying to remember.

Back in Poland at Auschwitz, I tried to be the helpful one, the one who gave bread rations to people, sang songs, talked. But then things changed, and I caught Krätze.[190] I got put into a Krätzeblock.[191] And because of my scabies, I couldn't go with the others into Czechoslovakia to a munitions factory. In fact, my mother and sister wouldn't go without me, so we stayed. I was shocked, pleased, yet still fearful. They should have gone, and they would still be relatively healthy. But sadly, my dear mother is dead, and my sister is dying. Margot came with me to the Krätzeblock and caught the disease too. Our mother tried to give us all the bread she could by digging a hole underneath the wooden barracks with the help from another inmate. It worked for a while.

Then one day, at 5.00 a.m., those who could, got called to Appell to be chosen to go on another cattle car to another unknown destination.[192] We stood in line, and although scared, my sister and I remained stoic. We had no emotions left, if any. The guards walked down the line, shouting "Gesund!" for any who were healthy. Or "Krätzeblock!" which meant a certain death if you ended up back there. Unfortunately (or fortunately), we got picked to go on this new transportation. I was relieved to be leaving hell, but not without mother. I couldn't do anything about it. So we went about our day of hard labor and sickness. We had very little food and very little water.

The next day we got shouted at again—"Raus!" "Schneller!" We were tired, hungry, ill, and exhausted, but still we got up and dragged our feet to the line to be counted. Then three hours after being in desperate need to go to the latrine, we got pushed onto a cattle car to go to our new destination. Though cold, half-naked, and hungry, we were alive. The people whom my sister and I had befriended both here and in Westerbork were all glad that we were away from the hellhole.

After three days of nearly no food, sanitation, or water we arrived, and we were very happy to be somewhere different. But we quickly realized, after being pushed through the mud to our new accommodation, that here at Bergen-Belsen, conditions were just as bad, if not worse, than they'd been at Auschwitz.[193] They had no running water—the SS guards liked to play tricks on us by turning it off—and hardly any food or basic sanitation needs. We got placed into makeshift tents which, after four days in the freezing cold, wind, and rain, blew down and fell due to the force of the weather. We managed to find refuge in some wooden barracks. We were thin, diseased, and starving, but alive!

A few weeks after arriving, we met up with Mrs. van Pels, who had been put into a different barrack than us at Auschwitz and who had obviously arrived on the same train here. She told me that my mother hadn't come with her. I knew that meant death.

She then told me in the middle of the night a day later that my old friend, Hanneli, was asking for me and I was relieved.[194] After a tearful meeting and sobbing to Hanneli that my parents were dead and that my sister was sick, I told her that we were all so hungry, freezing, and ill. She then told me that she had a package she could throw over the fence between us. After trying to catch it, everything got stolen from my arms by another girl. But luckily the next day I caught another one. It contained socks, Knackerbröt, and gloves! Oh, what luck!

We said our goodbyes and parted ways by telling each other we would talk again the next night. But that never happened as they moved our group to a new part of the camp. We had a few people from Auschwitz that had moved with us, and one who was a nurse.

This is where it all gets difficult. You see, I'm dying, Kitty, and I know I have typhus. I couldn't stand the lice anymore, so I ripped off all my clothes and grabbed a thin horse blanket. I was standing there in front of my friend who found me wandering trying to get back to Margot. She later clothed me and gave me some of her bread ration.

Which brings me to here and now. All that was yesterday. Oh, Kitty! My sister is dead! She's gone, Kitty. The damn Nazis took her. We'd both been shitting the bed, and we both had high fever. Early this morning, I awoke to the sound of birds. Oh, it was such a wonderful sound! I tried to wake Margot, but I shoved her, and she gasped and fell. I immediately tried to get her up, but she'd died—from shock, I think. Now I'm wondering how I'm going to go on. But I must, Kitty—for Margot's sake, for mother's, and for father's. Although I'm ill, I don't want to be known as A-25102.[195]

My name is FRANK, ANNE FRANK! And I will survive and live to tell my tale of war!

ANNE TALVAZ, PARIS, FRANCE

Growing (up) with Anne Frank 1975-1992

I CAME TO ANNE Frank through Auschwitz and Belsen. Europe was celebrating the thirtieth anniversary of the end of the Second World War, and I was eleven years old. The spring of that year was unfolding into the first of the hot summers no one had yet thought to connect with climate change. I had taken advantage of my mother's more relaxed attitude to bedtime toward the end of the school year, and I was watching a documentary on the final year of the war.

All that I knew of the Second World War and of war in general were the stories I had heard from my parents who, in 1945, had been my age. In the main, the older generation kept quiet, for whatever reason. I was also vaguely aware that the Germans had not been nice to the Jews.

There were no words for what I saw on the screen that night. Forty-five years on, there are still are no words. Millions of words, hundreds of thousands of which I have read, have been written on the subject, and still the words somehow elude many of us.[196] I went to bed that night with a wild fantasy in which I was a giant being of light throwing open the gates of the camps before they had been able to do their evil work. But when that dark elation subsided, the residue proved impossible to deal with, as if it had been baked into my brain. Images rose in my mind that would not dissolve. I began to close my door and curtains hermetically at night to avoid the beams of light that reminded me of evil eyes or searchlights—I was not sure which. Instead of ghosts and fiends, camp inmates with terrible eyes began to haunt dark corners. And finally, I became a concentration-camp ghoul.

In those days, there was no internet, and my covert research was limited to the entries in the family dictionaries, the school library's reference works, and the odd mention in a work of fiction. Holocaust education for young people was not a concern in those days, and I was limited to adult works. I developed a curious attitude, refusing to look at photographs but seeking words, words, always words. Sometimes, I unexpectedly struck lucky. In one educational monthly magazine for kids, I found a graphic short story about Anne Frank, with the magic word *Belsen* in the last paragraph. It was also a good yarn with an interesting heroine. Bizarrely, though, there was no emphasis on the fact that Anne's diary might be available to read.

The summer holidays passed, with self-tormenting peeps into various books in the public library. Then it was back to school and Saturday afternoon trips to the supermarket with my mother and sister. Like most of its kind, the local supermarket sold a selection of paperbacks. The book with the enlarged black-and-white photograph of Anne on the cover and the accompanying quotation—"I wish I could always look like this photo. Then I might make it to Holywood [sic]"—might have been waiting just for me.[197]

All through the day, I read. It was a strange experience. In the outside world, all Anne and I shared was a first name. She was attractive, outgoing, cheerful, popular. I was intellectually precocious, fat, indifferent to my appearance, and given to mood swings that in adulthood would morph into full-blown chronic depression. It is a mercy, I think, that we did not know each other in those days, and that she was not in a position to include me in the descriptions of her classmates.[198] The idea that I might be a Hollywood actress or marry was also beyond me.

After Anne went into hiding, though, her tastes and mine began to coincide. She was interested in royalty and made family trees—so did I. She loved history and mythology—so did I. She loved nature—so did I. She cast a jaundiced eye on the adults around her—so did I, although I had nowhere near the same ability to put it into words (again) that she had.

And what a storyteller. What a world-class storyteller. I finished reading the book that evening in the living room. My parents had gone out and left us with a babysitter. Intrigued by my intermittent chuckling, she finally asked me what I was reading. When I told her, she exclaimed, "But that's such a sad book."

ANNE TALVAZ, PARIS, FRANCE   ~233~

Was it? Anne did indeed tell of sad events. Perhaps my previous Holocaust reading had hardened me to the cruel facts she related—I do not know. But what stood out was the wit, the needle-sharp portraits, the flawless dialogue, and the sense of comic timing. The description of the potato peelers' thoughts, the cat peeing in the attic, the strawberry preserving, the German soldier shooting his officer for treason all had me laughing out loud.[199]

And then there was the sheer wizardry of her use of words.

To my amazement and delight, our French teacher decided to set Anne's diary for the spring term's reading. It turned out to be disappointing, though. He was in his early twenties, of the (then) new school of teachers who believed in verbal self-expression—the more of it the better. Most of the lessons on Anne turned out to be class chats I cannot even remember; I must have tuned out. I only recall one question, "What do you think Anne was like?" I could not have answered the question for love or money. I had found her to be exactly what she called herself—"a bundle of contradictions."[200] Somehow the Anne I had sensed—*my* Anne—never surfaced in all those hours. One consequence, though, was that I carried her diary in my satchel throughout the spring term and read it incessantly on the school bus. It stayed there during the whole summer term, too, and ultimately the cover came off. No matter: I mended it with cardboard and read on—over and over again through the record temperatures of the summer of 1976.

Little information was available about Anne as people had not yet begun to speak up very much. After all, she would have been only forty-seven and getting on with her life much as my parents, uncles, aunts and other surviving contemporaries were doing. It did not occur to me that Miep was only in her sixties and "Elli" in her fifties.[201] I found out Anne's father was still alive from a news item—the German government had been trying to secure the early release of three former SS men serving life sentences, and Otto Frank had spoken up against it. Still, I did not feel I could write to him. What would there have been to say? So many people had been deeply stirred by his daughter's diary. And what could my own comparatively minor troubles possibly mean to a man who had lost so many loved ones to the camps? Later, having read his correspondence with Cara Wilson, I realized that this had been a man with a big heart, bigger than that of anyone I had ever met. Since then, I have always regretted not getting in touch.[202]

The school year of 1976–77 was a nightmare. I had always been a target for some bullying, but during that year, I experienced peak hate. Anne receded into the background as I carried on trying to survive. It was just as well, as probably she would have sided with my tormentors. Looking back, I can see we were all just thirteen years old and finding life difficult. I do not bear the kids any grudges; I have even had apologies from two of them after reconnecting on social media and, though very touched, did not truly need it. The ones I shall loathe to my dying day are the handful of adults who stood on the sidelines, saw what was happening, and who either ignored the situation or encouraged it. I see no reason to change my mind. The older I grow, the more I realize that they knew what they were doing.

Something, though, was at work inside me. Up to then humor had not been a big part of my life, but gradually, laughter became important. I was also beginning to get the notion that I wanted to write, or "be a writer," and that somehow comedy was more important than tragedy. Tragedy was easy—anyone could write of sadness or be sad—whereas people needed laughter, and it was not that easy to produce from everyday material. The funny side of things suddenly became important. I started to make jokes now and then. People laughed, but this time, the laughter was appreciative. Bullying became a thing of the past. I began to make friends again.

Around the same time, I also began my own diary—and on paper the words did flow.

Anne did not come into any of these events, not consciously, but how can she *not* have been lurking in the background?

The following year, several opportunities came my way that helped me reconnect with Anne. The 1959 Millie Perkins film was shown on TV, and I found a copy of Ernst Schnabel's book in an English bookshop.[203] Although delighted by this acquisition and its wealth of new information, I carefully tore out the pages on Belsen after a single quick reading, as by now I was shying away from anything, even in words, that might trigger the horror flick lurking inside my head. We lived in Belgium, and Dutch was among the available language options at school. After studying it for a year, I was able to read Anne's diary in the original. As I still knew the French by heart, it was not difficult—it helped that Dutch is easy to read—and I was now as close to Anne as I was ever likely to get.

My parents also organized a family trip to Amsterdam, during which we visited the Anne Frank Huis. It was not an entirely happy occasion. One of the things to which I was not able to relate in the diary was Anne's relationship with her parents. I would have loved to have parents like Otto and Edith Frank, and a sister like Margot. My own folks were basically decent people and loved me, but they were frequently unkind in ways that would not have occurred to the Franks. Come to think of it, with their outbursts of temper and temperament, they had more in common with the van Pelses. No wonder Peter was so shy and lacked confidence. But I am glad that I went. The museum was fairly quiet that day, it was also filled with daylight, and there was the physical and mental space to walk and feel where Anne had once walked and felt. I stared at the pictures on her walls and thought. I also took a quick look at the foot of the staircase to the attic in case a stray bean had remained there. I wonder how many of us have done that.

And then, once more, Anne faded into the background. This time it would be for almost ten years. It was a busy time as I fell in love with literature and began to write poetry. University was also beckoning in France. At the same time, I developed glandular fever, became exhausted, fought back, and then had a full-scale nervous breakdown at the age of nineteen. Then I began to write poetry in earnest.

I did go and see the play and noted the deaths of Otto Frank and Victor Kugler.[204] All my clippings were stored in the play program. There was also a 1981 item on the discovery of some personal belongings and photos of the Franks handed in by an anonymous donor in Hamburg and about the future use of childhood letters of Anne's to determine the authenticity of the diary. But it was not until I was fully adult and about to complete my postgrad training as a translator that I found the

Critical Edition of the diaries in Dutch in a beautiful blue jacket—*The Diaries of Anne Frank*—and Miep's memoir. The second wave of Anne Frank publications had begun.

The *Critical Edition* was a fascinating read. I learned, with some sadness, that Bep Voskuijl had died and, with much irritation, that some of Anne's writings had been censored in this so-called *Definitive Edition*.[205] Otto Frank was dead, and I could not see what the problem might have been. To this day, I still do not see what it was. The process by which Anne revised her diary, though, was fascinating, especially the early entries. One of the Anne Frank deniers' arguments was that no thirteen-year-old could have written them. It was a real-life Agatha Christie story, with the person key to the events speaking in the first person and justice done at the end.

Again, real life stepped in. I got my first job, married, moved back to Belgium with my husband, and became a freelance translator. I remain as such to this day. It was a glorious time. My first poems appeared in magazines and attracted favorable notice. I was also once more able to visit Dutch-language bookshops and found Jacqueline van Maarsen's first memoir, with its fascinating teen's eye view of Anne, description of Anne's former Merwedeplein home—which Jacqueline had been able to visit—and anger at Eva Schloss's claims of friendship with Anne.[206] The latter gave a whole new dimension to the story. I was able to rent the TV film *The Attic*, based on Miep's book, and record the version of the play with Melissa Gilbert on our brand-new VHS player.[207] Finally, we made a day trip to Amsterdam, which was a happy one as it involved a visit to a major Van Gogh exhibition, a canal boat trip, a paper cornet of fries with peanut sauce by the Prinsengracht, and of course, a visit to the Secret Annex—which I don't remember.

No more do I remember my next visit to the Annex on a solo trip that I made a couple of years later—a trip that was almost entirely devoted to Anne Frank. My hotel was on Jan Luykenstraat, where Anne had once been to the dentist. It made sense to walk from there, and along a canal with a name I do not think I ever knew, to Jozef Israëlskade where once a kindly waterman had plied his trade. I walked past Geleenstraat 1 (still called *Oase*, but a now a Middle Eastern snack shop), Niersstraat 41 (the Montessorischool Anne Frank with its awful facade covered in Anne's writing but mostly reminiscent of graffiti), and finally came to Merwedeplein 37, which still bore its original number plate.[208] While searching the Yellow Pages, I had also found a bookshop with an address on Rooseveltlaan, which did indeed turn out to be "the bookshop on the corner."[209]

The window did not contain a single work on Anne Frank. In fact, except for the school, there were no references to Anne Frank anywhere. Nothing—apart from the trees at the center of Merwedeplein that had had sixty years in which to grow—appeared to have changed since Anne's day. It was also, I noted, a very Jewish neighborhood, with many kosher businesses, as if somehow the neighborhood's original landscape had reconstituted itself after the appalling pyroclastic surge of the forties. At the time, I wondered, but I now know that observant Jews need to live within walking distance of a synagogue. That, too, must have been a factor in the Franks' choice of domicile.

Such discretion could only be deliberate, I thought. It took an effort of will in order to walk into the bookshop and ask for a new book on Anne I had read about—one that was lavishly illustrated and with many yet unpublished photographs. The saleslady smiled and pulled it off a shelf behind the counter. Clearly, whatever the neighborhood policy, the bookshop owners were well prepared for Anne pilgrims. I walked back to the garden on Merwedeplein. There were empty benches under spreading trees, the perfect spot to sit and read and think. I mostly did the latter. It occurred to me that fifty years was not that long a time and that many of the original residents probably still lived here—some with cruel memories, others with memories of their cruel deeds.[210]

Since then, the last witnesses have passed into great old age; indeed, it is amazing that both Anne's best friends should have done so.[211] There are two full-length biographies, many documentaries and films, with the latest a German feature that for the first time explores Anne's German roots and her birth country's responsibility for her fate. There is fascinating late testimony to facts and events that could not be revealed earlier. There are now multiple versions of Anne's diary, including the one she herself intended to publish. There are books about Anne and books about books about Anne. And she is now abundantly memorialized in the area she knew as home.[212] As for the Secret Annex, which I visited again in 2006, it is now tourist hell.

Finally, that entire Anne Frank galaxy is only a mouse click away. Do I wish I could have accessed it in childhood? Yes. But would I have grown up in quite the same way? I do not think so. Anne taught me some of the most important life lessons, she showed me the way to writing, and she taught me to laugh. In the process she helped me come to terms with the world as it was. I also like to think that I owe her and her story some of my ferocious loathing for racism and discrimination. Importantly, all of it came gradually and at the proper time.

Rest in peace, Anne. And thank you from the bottom of my heart.

ANNE TALVAZ, PARIS, FRANCE

PART V

Playing Anne

An Interview with Miranda Antoinette Troutt

M IRANDA ANTOINETTE TROUTT played Anne Frank in *The Diary of Anne Frank*, as directed by Janet Allen in April 2019 for the Seattle Children's Theatre, Seattle.[213] This production was performed in conjunction with the Indiana Repertory Theatre, Indianapolis. Miranda was cast as Anne in both Indianapolis and Seattle.[214]

I sent Miranda the following interview questions in January 2020, and she graciously agreed to answer them based on her time playing Anne Frank. My questions and her answers are as follows:

1. *How did you become involved in playing this iconic role? Was the part of Anne Frank a dream role for you and one that you had always wanted to play?*

I was "called in" by Seattle Children's Theatre—many theaters will request specific actors to be at auditions or callbacks for a show. I had worked with them before, playing Lucy in *The Lion, the Witch and the Wardrobe*. This was a bit of a unique casting process since the show was a coproduction with the Indiana Repertory Theatre. This entailed casting half the actors from Indiana and half from Seattle and flying our director [Janet Allen] out here to see the Seattle folks. I felt really honored and excited to be specifically asked by SCT to audition for this role. They gave me the script, saying that they really wanted this director to see me and for me to be well prepared. I felt very supported and like they were really rooting for me to be cast, which was an amazing feeling reflecting not just my standing with the company but also my standing as an actor in whom folks had the confidence to play such an inspiring historical figure.

Anne was a bit of an under-the-radar dream role. I had done the play in high school, playing Margot, her older sister, and had an incredible experience. Since I played one of the girls when I was age-appropriate, it almost felt like I had aged out of those roles and didn't expect to have this opportunity. But I am so grateful that I did—sometimes being a very short and petite actor has its advantages! Oddly enough, I do really think that at that age I was much more like the rule-following and book-smart older sister, whereas *now* I relate much more to Anne!

2. *Before playing Anne, how familiar were you already with the story of her life, her time in the Secret Annex, and what happened after everyone's arrest on August 4, 1944? How did you prepare for the role, and have you continued to walk with Anne since?*

As mentioned above, I had done the show in high school, but it was an older version, before the diary was republished in full after Otto Frank's passing.[215] I really relearned a lot of the more intimate details of Anne's life and personality through our recent production at both the Indiana Rep and Seattle Children's. I must admit that this was the first time I had read her diary, and this was probably the most essential part of my prep because I felt her words and could connect with her personal journey—even the parts we *don't* see in the play. I felt it was the only way that I could truly honor her as the real person she is, which is a different feeling than playing a made-up character. There's a responsibility there to honor her and to honor what she means to the thousands of people whom she inspires worldwide.

We also had incredible support preparing for this show not just through comprehensive dramaturgical packets but also through a trip to a museum exhibit featuring Anne and a visit to one of the seedlings cut from the tree she watched out her window.[216] Our rabbi-in-residence answered questions and helped us connect with Jewish history and traditions, led talkbacks, and invited us to share some readings at his synagogue. Our experience built a real sense of community beyond just our cast, a lasting connection to the larger history of Anne and her family, and a very grounded sense of purpose in why we needed to tell this story now.

"MEETING" ANNE FRANK: AN ANTHOLOGY

I live every day with the gratitude of what I learned from Anne about hope, being oneself, expression, moods, and more. There were two big topics that I became very passionate about discussing in talkbacks and that stick with me now. One of these was that we have to remember that this awful time in history that resulted in unimaginable death and suffering did not *begin* that way. Instead, it began with suspicion and "othering," with something as seemingly harmless as name-calling.

We need to work for a more compassionate world in our everyday lives. It's a small but attainable thing that we can do as individuals. Yet it can have a huge impact on our world. I think a lot about how I can put compassion and community-building into the world.

The other thing that I was so grateful to Anne for was how she talked about her changing body. I felt so empowered that I got to speak her shame-free words of discovery about her sexuality and the discomfort and joy of becoming a woman to audiences of young folks probably going through the same thing. I wished that I had heard her words when I was her age, because I felt awful and embarrassed and like I couldn't really embrace the changes of my body growing up around me. Having the confidence, compassion, and no-nonsense and no-shame wherewithal to talk about that stuff is inspiring in my everyday life. It makes for a more sex-positive and communication-positive world.

3. *You used Wendy Kesselman's "newly adapted" version from 1997 of the original 1955 play, The Diary of Anne Frank, by Frances Goodrich and Albert Hackett. Why did the director, Janet Allen, decide to use this updated adaptation as opposed to using the original script of the play? Did you talk a lot about the differences between the two versions?*

We did talk a bit about the differences, and the reason we did the updated version was that it included more of the rough-and-tumble parts that make Anne a real person. It also honors what she *really* felt and believed, and who she was without censorship. She was a brilliant writer and absolutely worthy of all the love and admiration she gets, but she also fought with her mother and had some really low and dark feelings. The more real these characters are, the better. It puts faces to the millions who died in an almost incomprehensibly large-scale tragedy.

The Wendy Kesselman version gave the characters more dimension, which gives the audience more to connect to. We also talked about why we chose this version regarding the end. The original version ends with the sounds of the Gestapo breaking down doors to get to the Annex, whereas this version has the SS actually *entering* the house and physically separating the families. It also ends with a monologue by Otto Frank years later, giving an account of the deaths of his loved ones. It was a very hard ending. But it was important, especially for young audiences, that the story not be sugar-coated. The facts of how they were taken from their hiding place and how they died are there, and we cannot ignore them. This was a key telling of the story, not just for the fate of those in the Secret Annex, but for the countless thousands whose stories were the same. It was an ending that did not let people forget that Anne's story is *not* unique.

4. *Did you talk about difficult issues such as Anne's relationship with her mother and her jealousy toward Margot? How do you think our impressions of Anne would change if we had the legacy of Margot's diary or could interview her mother today?*

We did, and we were actually fortunate to have some information about Margot's lost diary and other documents.[217] There are some really lovely bits in Anne's diary which do speak to her relationship with both her mother and her sister. We know that her relationship with both improved in the later parts of their lives.

I get the feeling that some might idolize or make Anne out to be a martyr. Yet I think that knowing the challenges she faced with relationships and that she *did* make mistakes can only improve anyone's connection to her by turning her into a real person with faults and complex feelings.

A saint is beyond us and is easy to think of as having a separate history from our own. But the key to learning about this time in our history is to remember that the Holocaust is part of us, that these were lives and *not* anonymous numbers, that anti-Semitism is something we are still living with the repercussions of today, and that we need to learn from this fact in regards to all forms of prejudice.

5. *How did you as Anne and Ryan Artzberger as Otto decide to approach the much-loved father-daughter relationship? Was this something that you both discussed at length with Janet? Do you think that Anne and her father would have continued to understand one another if they had both survived the war?*

It was not a huge point of discussion as we really just felt it out through the process. We had a great deal of textual reference going in—from facts in her diary, to interviews with Otto, to the script, and more. I think we just knew what that relationship meant, and there it was—it just happened. I enjoy dramaturgy and table work and chats with the director and fellow actors, but I'm never thinking about that on stage. It's great to have that info and then just trust that you know it, see what has absorbed, and then how it affects you. This was a very intense show and process, so as actors we developed a strong bond pretty quickly. Everyone in that room was so kind, supportive, and hard-working, so it was easy to find the kind of comfort and kinship we needed.

When we weren't in rehearsal or performance, we were all very silly. That was important. Ryan, Hannah (Margot), Betsy (Edith Frank), and I would be goofballs in places, telling our inside-jokes up to the minute before we went on stage. That tiny and lighthearted personal history we created for ourselves was really important to playing a family with their own history on stage. I think that had they all survived, Anne and her family would have absolutely remained close. As I said in response to your previous question, we know that Anne and her mother were much closer at the end of their lives than they were during their time in hiding.

6. *With my "Meeting" Anne Frank book, I invited my contributors to describe how they first "met" Anne and how they were*

then inspired to go on a journey with her. For some, this meant literally making pilgrimages to many of the places associated with her life and tragic end. When Melina Zaccaria approached this role—and her response can be seen earlier in this anthology—she refers to how "chipping away at what is Melina and finding what is Anne" was important to her. Was this something that you felt that you needed to do in terms of finding the best way to play Anne?

My approach to a great deal of my acting work is to feel what I have in common with a character. Then those common traits are dialed up or down to create the character that uniquely stems from me. I'm never going to entirely erase myself—that just isn't what the art form means to me. I transform, adapt, and bring life to a *character* through the lens of *Miranda*, the *actor*. If there is a big opposite in a character's personality or situation, I use a lot of imagination and find similar *tiny* moments in my life to build off of to imagine what a *bigger* version of that feeling or situation would be. From there, it's all about living as truthfully as one can in the moment—a real experience in imagined circumstances. Connection to the other actors and the characters is crucial and makes performances different every time.

7. *Do you think that if Anne Frank had survived, she would have still believed that "in spite of everything, people are truly good at heart"? Some of us who have been writing for this book—as well as David Gillham in Annelies, his recent fictional account of how Anne would have behaved had she survived—feel that Anne would have modified an opinion that she wrote before her arrest, before her transportation to Westerbork in the Netherlands, and before her subsequent transportation to Auschwitz-Birkenau and Bergen-Belsen. How do you think Anne would have felt about much of the chaos in the world today? With respect to her opinions, do you view Anne as a historical forerunner of, say, an activist such as Greta Thunberg or as someone who, while she would have certainly thought*

as richly as Greta, would have allowed herself to be easily distracted by the richness of life? Anne, in her diary, speaks several times to the existence of "two Annes," with one Anne who was silly and frivolous and one who was deeper and more sensitive. Would you agree that this speaks to Anne's ability to define a positive and progressive identity for herself, but also to her willingness to have fun?

I do think that. She wrote what she did knowing the horror of the world, and I don't believe that she said it lightly. She was not naive enough to say that when it wasn't her in the camp and then to change her mind just because she had to personally face the reality of the horror herself. Just as we all fluctuate in our opinions and moods day-to-day—and we know from her writings that Anne did too—I'm sure she would have found herself too angry or in too deep of despair some days to admit it consciously. Yet at the core of her being, I think she could not have felt anything else.

Anne knew the complexities of people—she was wise enough to recognize it and try to deconstruct it in herself. I believe that she would be able to recognize a hateful, evil person as being *built* and that just because they might be beyond goodness or redemption *now*, did *not* mean that they *never* were. But that also does *not* mean she would forgive them or have faith that they would change, and I believe she is justified in that. She had a faith in humanity that someday we could do better and remain connected to that spark of goodness. And *that* is what we should forever strive for.

I'm sure she'd be disappointed, even angry, at many of the things she would see around us today. She might want to give up after the horror she'd been through as well. I believe that she would have to live with some amount of numbing from that ordeal and that she would still be struggling with some forms of depression to this day if she had been lucky enough to have survived the horrors of Auschwitz and Bergen-Belsen. But I believe she would be grateful for her survival and strong-willed. I believe she would still be outspoken, that she would be proud of those who are still working to change our world for the better, and that she would continue to have some of the awe-inspiring hope of her youth.

8. *Melina Zaccaria said in an interview to Gary Smith of the Hamilton Spectator that Anne does not know her end when she is writing her diary. As a result, she expresses a lot of hope in her entries as well as despair over what would have probably seemed completely trivial if she had survived and become the writer or journalist that she dreamt of becoming. Do you think Anne would have published the same diary as her father chose to do on his daughter's behalf and as a way of keeping her alive in his mind?*

She was always editing and tweaking bits of her diary to ready it for publication. I'm sure she would have looked back and seen some of it as a bit silly but that she would respect and find the value in a lot of what her younger self had thought and said.

I think she would have kept much more of her diary than her father did. She was *not* shy, and she was *not* ashamed or afraid. I think she would have been open about her relationship with her mother, with her sexual discovery, and with her dark feelings, and she would have wanted to talk about those things. She might have made some edits for professionalism or gone back and given some retrospect or more context to some entries, but I believe she would have kept the integrity of the writing. She would have been ahead of her time and done a great deal for young and female writers.

9. *Ultimately, Anne Frank is sadly frozen in historical time and did not live to see what could have been her ninetieth birthday in 2019. She is famous for having died young and so tragically and for leaving behind such a moving testimony in her diary to a time of unprecedented madness and prejudice in history. Yet if we were to liberate Anne from this bizarre definition of the word fame, we would have to make her seem ordinary, take away her symbolism, and reduce her to one of the statistical*

1,500,000 children who also died during the Holocaust. Does this seem fair to you, or should we continue to impose on Anne her status as an iconic symbol of historical genocide? Anne certainly thought that she was special and enamored by all— one of the popular girls in school—but this was also fairly typical behavior for a teenage girl who was trying to be popular. Do you think that she would like all this attention now?

I think we need to remove her from "fame" in order *not* to make her a number but to make her real. In doing so, we can free those countless others who died in the war, and whose stories we don't know, from becoming anonymous numbers. Instead, we can think of them as individuals with names—as the teenage *Anne Frank* who had trouble with her mother, as the older teenage boy *Peter van Pels* who brought a beloved pet cat with him to the Secret Annex, or as the dentist *Fritz Pfeffer* who had a distant lover and a son.

I think that Anne Frank would be overwhelmed by the attention she gets now and would probably feel a great deal of pressure and expectation put upon her. Although she *wanted* to share this story, she imagined a far different set of circumstances. She did not expect to be taken to a camp and to die young.[218] It's very hard to conceptualize how she'd feel because she never thought about this particular situation—and neither did I as I played her. But I believe that she would have grown to be proud of the inspiration she brings, feel a bit misrepresented or misunderstood to some small degree—because as a strong-willed opinionated writer, how couldn't she—and that she would have come to appreciate her role in helping people to understand the Holocaust. Most of all, she would want to be seen as an individual, as a human being.

10. *Lastly, what did you most take away from playing Anne Frank and do you feel as if you truly "met" her by playing her in this play?*

I learned so much from Anne personally about history and about how I want to walk through the world and make it better, all of which

I feel like I have touched on in answering these questions. But I also gained so much from seeing how the show affected others, feeling their gratitude, and how they wanted to add their perceptions and love of Anne to my own.

It was an honor to hear that I could bring a new side of Anne to the stage for people who had "known" her their whole lives. It also really solidified the fact that our work as theater artists is important. Our role as storyteller is imperative to the human condition. Some of the most meaningful moments in this process were the postshow talks and also the letters we received.[219]

We had many students reaching out to say that they didn't really understand this part of history until they saw live people living it, and they felt that they really got to know the people whose lives are represented by numbers in their textbooks.

We changed people, and I really think we gave some people out there an experience that will help them put more love into the world. I do feel like I "met" Anne. Our cast even had the unique experience of meeting a survivor who was a friend of Margot's and who knew Anne in school.[220] That was an honor, it was very informative, and it was also a little scary and confusing. I'm still not really sure why, but I think about it now and again. I feel deeply connected to Anne and feel an odd sense of disassociated grief that comes from knowing that I portrayed a *real* person whom I will never get to know for real. I'll never really know if she would approve. But what are we *but* storytellers, and what are our lives *but* stories to be told? I think she would understand that and be happy. Maybe even a little amused.

PART VI

Words from Cara

Every moment we have choices—to be kind, to be cruel, to laugh, to connect, to grow, to have hope, to feel hopeless, to live in fear or in love. The choice is ours. No matter what our personal challenge, we must never give up.

—Cara Wilson-Granat, "Welcome," https://www. wordsfromcara.com/

AFTERWORD BY CARA WILSON-GRANAT

"If the end of the world would be imminent,
I still would plant a tree today."

THOSE ARE THE words that my beloved mentor, Otto Frank, expressed to me when I had given up all hope for the world in the Sixties.[221] During that time, there was so much tragedy—the assassinations of President Kennedy, Martin Luther King Jr., and Robert Kennedy; the Vietnam War; unfathomable race riots—it was incomprehensible. I expressed to Otto that I would never bring a child into such a cruel world. In response to my hopelessness, Anne Frank's father encouraged me to never give up. A few months after his inspiring words, I received a note saying that two trees had been planted in Israel in my name from Otto Frank.

To this day I still can't believe that this amazing Holocaust survivor who lost his friends and family with him in hiding under Hitler's regime of hate—among them his beloved daughters, Anne and Margot Frank—would be urging me to keep on going and to plant metaphorical seeds of life. Until his death in 1980 at the age of ninety-one, Otto helped an entire world of young people who reached out to him believe in the power of hope and love.

This is also Tim Whittome's focus in many ways. With this ambitious publication, *"Meeting" Anne Frank,* he has shined a light on others—a sampling of an international family—who help us see how, why, and when they "met" this astounding young girl. I am so grateful for this book and especially for its timing. We are facing a world of rampant hatred—growing anti-Semitism and Holocaust denial, with less and less remembering or even knowing who Anne Frank was. I am shocked to learn that more and more schools are no longer including Anne Frank and the Holocaust in their regular curriculum. It is all I can do to try to keep alive Otto's words to me. We must not ever give up hope trusting that love will ultimately triumph over hate.

Thanks to Tim and each of these good people highlighted here, we're able to embrace an entirely new perspective on this magical soul who wanted to "go on living after [her] death" as she so poignantly expressed in her diary. With *"Meeting" Anne Frank*, we see that Anne's wishes have come to fruition in the lives of the people featured in these chapters who have been positively transformed because of all that she was and continues to be.

Who was Anne Frank? One to be worshipped? A saint to be deified? The epitome of flawlessness and perfection? No! Anne Frank was *not* a supreme being, but *rather* a brilliant writer who was complex, sensitive, mercurial. Caught in the cross hairs of extreme bigotry, Anne was a very human being who was wise beyond her young years and whose words reflected an unthinkable reality that she was forced to experience while in hiding from the Nazis. What we all know is that she would inevitably succumb to an even more horrifying and ultimately tragic reality—a senseless denouement she could never have imagined.

Had she survived Bergen-Belsen, would she still "believe in spite of everything, that people are truly good at heart"? Hard to say. Her father did. Otto Frank had every reason to be bitter and hopeless after the war, and yet he was able to gather all his pain and loss into that of love for each and every one of us who needed his guidance and goodness to grow on.

As Anne was most like him, I would like to believe that she, too, would be able to find her footing and plant seeds of hope like her father did. But we'll never really know, will we?

The truth is that there are legions of "Anne Franks" this very minute worldwide—young people of all cultures, religions, and races whose journals, diaries, letters, and poems express their own epic challenges facing hatred, war, prejudice, bigotry, anti-Semitism, and unthinkable cruelties. Possibly encouraged to "write" the wrongs of their fates by all that Anne Frank was able to accomplish during her brief earthly stay, they, too, will be able to make their voices heard and, in many ways, positively alter the trajectory of their lives as well as ours.

As reflected in this unique book, Anne Frank has become the global voice of hope—especially for young people. And though we must never forget her tragic death, we must equally never forget her beautiful life and indomitable spirit now echoed and reflected in those who continue to "meet" her on their various life paths and who are forever changed for the better.

My wish is that generations to come will be able to meet and be transformed by all that Anne Frank was and will forever be. In this way, she will, indeed, go on living. And so will we.

PART VII

Endnotes and Diary References

Open pages from Anne's original red-and-white checkered diary, "The Diary Room," Anne Frank Huis and Museum, Amsterdam © Anne Frank Huis and Museum Collection

ENDNOTES

All references in the text and endnotes to diary dates published in Anne Frank: The Diary of a Young Girl *are taken from an online version of the* Definitive Edition *or D version of Anne's diary as published by Random House/Doubleday in 1991 and 1996, edited by Otto Frank and Mirjam Pressler, and translated into English by Susan Massotty.*

Publishing details for significant works cited throughout the main text and in these endnotes can be found in our bibliography.

Foreword by Joop van Wijk-Voskuijl

[1]   Joop van Wijk and Jeroen De Bruyn, *Anne Frank, the Untold Story: The Hidden Truth about Elli Vossen, the Youngest Helper of the Secret Annex* (Bep Voskuijl Producties BV, 2018).

[2]   *Editor note:* Joop has done much to bring both his mother and grandfather out of the shadows of Anne's time in the Secret Annex. His biography of his mother is an important corrective. Anne speaks of the construction of the "legendary" bookcase in her diary entry for August 21, 1942. Although it had been Mr. Kugler's idea, it was Mr. Voskuijl's carpentry that was responsible for this ingenious way of concealing the entrance to the Secret Annex. There was a hidden latch behind the bookcase that allowed it to be opened from the inside. Only those who knew where it was could open it easily from the outside.

[3]   *Editor note:* Please see Sondra Learn's contribution. Sondra also produced the play. She worked with the original Frances Goodrich and Albert Hackett 1955 adaptation of Anne's diary.

[4]   *Editor note:* Please see Federica Pannocchia's contribution.

[5]   *Editor note:* Cara Wilson-Granat, Ryan Cooper, and Fr. John Neiman each met Otto Frank (together with Fritzi) toward the end of his life, and they will be talking about their experiences later in this work. They each met Miep Gies. Priscilla has also met an extraordinary number of people who were once part of Anne's life.

6   *Editor note:* This is a reference to Fr. John Neiman, whom we will be hearing from later.

Acknowledgments

7   Please see my author website for my *Denied! Failing Cordelia* trilogy published under an alternative author name of Simon Cambridge: https://www.simoncambridge. com. They are also available at Xlibris's bookstore (https://www.xlibris.com/en/ bookstore/bookdetails/540801-denied-failing-cordelia-parental-love-and-parental-state-theft-in-los-angeles-juvenile-dependency-court) and through other online retail stores.

8   Thank you to Barbara Eldridge, the executive secretary of the Anne Frank-Fonds for informing me that while the use of the hyphen as shown here is the legal name for the foundation, the organization now prefers to use the "Anne Frank Fonds" as a "less complicated" version of the legal name. Moving forward, I have respected her wishes in this regard and only used the hyphenated version on the copyright page.

Editor's Preface

9   The published version of Anne's diary is widely known as "The Diary of Anne Frank," but technically, this title refers to both the 1959 film and the play by Frances Goodrich and Albert Hackett that was first performed on Broadway, October 5, 1955. Most English editions of the printed diary refer to it as *Anne Frank: Diary of a Young Girl* or simply as *Diary of a Young Girl* by Anne Frank.

Anne was not responsible for preparing her own diary for publication; it was originally edited and then published by her father, Otto. The first 1947 Dutch edition was published as *Het achterhuis: dagboekbrieven 12 Juni–1 Augustus 1944*. Later editions of Anne's diary have since restored some 30 percent of the content originally cut for personal and other reasons by Otto Frank from the first 1947 Dutch and 1952 English editions. We now have what is regarded as the *Definitive Edition* or D version as edited by Otto Frank *and* Mirjam Pressler and which has been translated into English by Susan Massotty. There will be more on this topic in later endnotes 52 and 53.

Of the three surviving journals in which Anne wrote her original diary, the most famous is the red-and-white (or red, white, and light green according to Melissa Müller's description) checkered diary that she received for her thirteenth birthday on June 12, 1942. This journal or autograph album is beyond any currently known commercial standard of valuation, a quality that it shares with many famous works of art worldwide. One source suggested that Anne's original diary could be worth more than $250 million today.

Interested readers will find that the Anne Frank Huis and Museum online shop in Amsterdam currently has a broad selection of Anne's diary translated into some thirty-three different languages: https://webshop.annefrank.org/en/the-diary/

[10]   Please see Anne's diary entries for April 5, 1944, and May 11, 1944.

[11]   With respect to those who knew Anne from the last seven months of her life, please review *The Last Seven Months of Anne Frank* by Willy Lindwer. In this important work, Mr. Lindwer documents his interviews with those who came across Anne and her family in Kamp Westerbork, Auschwitz-Birkenau, and Bergen-Belsen.

With the notable exceptions of Hannah Pick-Goslar and Bloeme Evers-Emden, who knew Anne and Margot from their school days together, the following (which I have broken down by location and with some overlap) only came to know both girls during the last seven months of their lives:

Kamp Westerbork (August–September, 1944)

Janny Brilleslijper
Rachel van Amerongen-Frankfoorder
Bloeme Evers-Emden
Lenie de Jong-van Naarden
Ronnie Goldstein-van Cleef

Auschwitz-Birkenau (September–October, 1944)

Janny Brilleslijper
Bloeme Evers-Emden
Lenie de Jong-van Naarden
Ronnie Goldstein-van Cleef

Bergen-Belsen (October 1944–February or March, 1945)

Hannah Pick-Goslar
Janny Brilleslijper
Rachel van Amerongen-Frankfoorder

Please bear in mind that some of the above "sightings" were extremely brief and their recollections very limited. Given that Anne and Margot would have been regarded as distressed Dutch teenagers in circumstances that both they *and* those who later tried to recall them had to survive as best they could, it is understandable that some of the recollections would be vague. The interesting details that historians and those eager to know more about famous historical figures want to know would have passed by unnoticed by the interviewees at a time when no one had the foresight to know that both girls would later become famous. It is possible that others may have met Anne and Margot and not recognized either of them due to the Nazis shaving everyone's hair on entry to Auschwitz-Birkenau.

[12]   Both Hannah Goslar and Nanette Blitz (later Nanette Blitz-Konig) have published not just their recollections of Anne as a friend and classmate, but of hearing or seeing her in her final months or weeks at Bergen-Belsen. Hanneli famously threw food and clothes to Anne over the fence that separated two restricted parts of the camp; although they had never been close at school, Nanette was at least able to give Anne a hug during her final months. This is the last recorded knowledge that we have of Anne receiving any affection in her brief life.

Despite publishing several books herself, Jacqueline van Maarsen (Anne's best friend from their school year spent at the Jewish Lyceum) has been very critical of the commercialization and exploitation of Anne's name over the years. She remains skeptical of the claims of those who have argued how well they knew Anne and Margot before they went into hiding.

Eva Schloss, who was not interviewed by Theo Coster for *We All Wore Stars*, did not know Anne that well while her family and the Franks were still living on Merwedeplein; however, she *has* since become famous as the "posthumous stepsister of Anne Frank" after her mother married Otto Frank in 1953. To leave matters there, however, would ignore the fact that she has written two very powerful accounts of her early life, her experiences in hiding and at Auschwitz (including the liberation of the camp on January 27, 1945 and its chaotic aftermath), her struggle to get back to Amsterdam, and her efforts to find herself after the war. Eva's father and brother did not survive the Holocaust. Some regard *Eva's Story* as a continuation of Anne Frank's diary as Anne might have recalled each of the three camps that she was deported to after her arrest on August 4, 1944.

Eva has also talked extensively in interviews about her complicated feelings toward Anne. This one from *The Guardian* newspaper is very revealing: https://www. theguardian.com/lifeandstyle/2013/apr/06/eva-schloss-anne-frank-stepsister

13   For further information about Kamp Westerbork, please review the website resources section of our book. Officially, the camp was known as the *Polizeiliches Judendurchgangslager Westerbork*. This transit camp figures prominently throughout our anthology.

Interestingly, Kamp Westerbork continued to be used after the war. From 1945–1948, it housed former Nazi collaborators; after July 1950, the camp (renamed as *De Schattenberg*) processed Dutch citizens returning from Indonesia after the former Dutch East Indies colony declared their independence (December 27, 1949); from 1951–1971, the *Woonoord Schattenberg* housed thousands of Moluccans—soldiers who had been loyal to the Dutch crown and who had fought Indonesian nationalists. The camp was finally demolished in 1971. The Kamp Westerbork memorial page in our website resources has further information on the camp's complex history.

Joop van Wijk-Voskuijl has kindly supplied us with pictures of what the camp looks like today. As shown in one of Joop's photographs, visitors are able to see a replica of one of the cattle cars that were once used to transport the Jews and others. There could be as many as sixty or seventy crammed into one of these infamous cars with little food supplied for the journey ahead; there would have been one bucket for water and another that would have functioned as a disgusting toilet that would then have been emptied at stops along the way. Former commandant Albert Konrad Gemmeker's house also remains along with a mangled piece of railroad track and some 102,000 memorial stones shaped in a map of the Netherlands when viewed from above. Most of these stones are topped by a Star of David; the memorial is dedicated to those who never came home after being transported from Kamp Westerbork.

14   Our bibliography includes a broad spectrum of mainly pictorial works suitable for children and younger teenagers as well as more scholarly works targeted at older teenagers and adults.

15   I am grateful to Anne Talvaz for both sending me and then translating the following from Dutch into English for us. This supports her view that the situation was more nuanced on Merwedeplein with blame on both sides for the street fights that I was not previously aware even existed between the girls:

> *Met de meiden van het Merwedeplein hadden we weleens ruzie. We waren elkaar vaak aan het pesten. Liepen wij naar school, kwamen die rotmeiden eraan. Je strik uit je haar trekken, of een voet ertussen zetten bij touwtje springen. Daar deed Anne ook aan mee. Maar we speelden ook wel samen met die meiden hoor . . ., balspelen, naar*

het zwembad. (Testimony submitted by Francien van der Veen-Bachra, Vrijheidslaan 57 | Oorlog In Mijn Buurt)

We did fight with the girls from Merwedeplein. We were always bothering each other. As we walked to school, those mean girls would set on us. They'd snatch the bows from our hair or, if one of us tried to turn a handspring, they'd try to trip her up. Anne did it, too. But we also played with those girls, too . . ., ball games, going to the swimming-pool. (Translated into English by Anne Talvaz)

[16]   Please review *Anne Frank: A Portrait in Courage* (first published in 1958 and since republished with a new title of *The Footsteps of Anne Frank*).

[17]   *Anne Frank: The Biography* by Melissa Müller, *The Hidden Life of Otto Frank* by Carol Ann Lee, and *Anne Frank, the Untold Story* by Joop van Wijk and Jeroen de Bruyn each speculate on possible suspects.

Information on the 1948 and 1963 official investigations are also available in the above works and elsewhere. I have also included links to efforts made to find the betrayers in our website resources section.

[18]   Please see our website resources for the Anne Frank Huis and Museum's "take" on the authenticity of Anne's diary and the controversy surrounding it. The Dutch government released their forensic research on the authenticity of the diaries in two published works: *The Diary of Anne Frank: The Critical Edition* and then *The Diary of Anne Frank: The Revised Critical Edition*. Please review our print bibliography for further information respecting the second of these two editions.

[19]   Trying to resolve, and even to enter, the discussion surrounding who owns the copyright to Anne's diary and other works is outside the scope of this work. I have no wish to wade into this subject area as it too contentious. That said, it *is* still a question that has involved a surprising lot of discussion. Some readers might, therefore, be interested in reading through some of the arguments raised on both sides at the following two websites:

The Times of Israel:

https://www.timesofisrael.com/who-owns-the-diary-of-anne-frank/

Communia Association:

https://www.communia-association.org/2016/04/25/anne-frank-term-copyright-protection-time-move-harmonisation-unification/

[20] For further information on the Siege of Malta (1940–1942), please review our website resources.

[21] For further information on the Hunger Winter (1944–1945) and the failure of Operation Market Garden in September 1944, please review our website resources.

[22] Miep Gies was the first to find Anne's famous red-and-white checkered diary and other school or accounting notebooks several days after the arrest of the hiders in the Secret Annex on August 4, 1944. One of Anne's surviving notebooks is black, while the other has a green-and-gold speckled cover. In adding this observation from *Anne Frank: A Photographic Story of a Life*, I am assuming that Kem Knapp Sawyer is referring here to the notebooks that Anne used to extend her diary entries once she had filled her original red-and-white checkered diary/autograph book. I have not seen any of Anne's diaries to confirm this observation.

Bep Voskuijl, who had supplied Anne with the loose and very thin pink-and-blue writing paper that she needed for the revised version of her diary, found what her son, Joop van Wijk-Voskuijl, says amounted to 70 percent of the surviving diary and other stories by Anne. This happened some ten days later according to Joop in his biography of his mother. Willem van Maaren found some additional papers after Miep and Bep's discoveries. He handed these to Bep, who then gave them to Miep for safekeeping.

As a general point here, it is lucky that Miep and Bep were the ones to find Anne's diary and *not* members of the Gestapo or the Dutch NSB (Dutch Nazi Party). Even *without* any real names used, it would not have been hard to discover who had been helping them for twenty-five months.

Meeting the Authors

[23] Please see Helaine's artist website: https://HelaineSawilowsky.com

Editor note: Helaine is extremely prolific and her pictures of Anne Frank that I have seen are really quite stunning and evocative. Our cover pictures for this anthology are a small sampling of her overall work.

[24] www.bepvoskuijl.nl

25   Please see Joop's author website: www.annefranktheuntoldstory.com

A Brief Life

26   Frankfurt am Main had a substantial Jewish community of 30,000 out of a population of approximately 540,000. From the time of her birth until the end of March 1931, Anne lived at Marbachweg 307. The Franks then moved to Ganghoferstrasse 24 until the end of March 1933. Both homes still exist today. They then lived with Otto's mother at 4 Jordanstrasse until July 1933. This house was destroyed after the war. At that point, Otto relocated to Amsterdam to set up Opekta and look for somewhere to live while Anne and Margot moved to be with their maternal grandmother in Aachen close to the Dutch border. Thank you to Ronald Wilfred Jansen in *Anne Frank* for his photographic record of Anne's early homes in Frankfurt (and later). Thank you also to both Melissa Müller and Carol Ann Lee for their biographical accounts of Anne's early life in Frankfurt.

After she got married, Edith Holländer appears to have been known by a variety of married names. Most sources refer to her as "Edith Holländer-Frank," but on the surviving transport list for the last train to Auschwitz-Birkenau from Kamp Westerbork on September 3, 1944, we see Edith referred to as "Edith Frank-Holländer." The Anne Frank Fonds uses this version of Edith's married name. I wish inconsistencies like this didn't exist!

27   Please review our website resources for more information on the rise and fall of the Weimar Republic, including the rise to power of Adolf Hitler in 1932 and 1933.

28   Please review our website resources for more information on the rise of the Nazi party and the spread of Nazism, including a Wikipedia page on the role of Paul von Hindenburg.

29   Please review our website resources for more information on the passage of the 1933 Enabling Act and its implications for Germany.

30   Please review our website resources for more information on the fascinating history of Opekta. Readers are advised, however, that Wikipedia has flagged this page for further editorial or citational review. Opekta is most associated with its Amsterdam address of Singel 400 (1934–1940), before moving to its even more famous address of Prinsengracht 263 in December 1940.

During the war, Otto Frank was forced to reorganize the company. His subsidiary company, Pectacon, which made herbs and spices for sausages and which was the expertise of Mr. van Pels, was absorbed by the new Gies & Co. in May 1941. Opekta seems to have survived throughout the war since its "Aryan" ownership by Pomosin-Werke in Germany could be proved. Melissa Müller goes into this in some detail in *Anne Frank: The Biography*. Other sources seem to think that Opekta was absorbed into Gies & Co. and readers are invited to research this topic for themselves.

During the war as well, businessmen from Germany would visit Opekta's office at Prinsengracht 263, with Anne relating one such occasion on April 1, 1943, when she, Otto, and Margot listened in on the discussions taking place in the private office below the Secret Annex. Anne fell asleep during the proceedings, while Otto found it difficult to concentrate given the hard floor.

Otto's relationship with Opekta continues to fascinate me. We know from her diary entry for March 4, 1943, that Anne did not think that it was very glamorous to be making pectin and thought that her father should have been making sweets (candy in American) instead. For his part, Otto seems to have felt that he needed to do something to continue to make money for his family both before and during the war.

After the war, Otto Frank returned to work for Opekta at Prinsengracht 263 but later handed it over to Johannes Kleiman. Melissa Müller documents continued legal disputes regarding who should own Opekta Amsterdam after the war before noting how "Opekta was sold in 1982 and dissolved in the mid-nineties for lack of profitability." It is interesting that the company that was so linked to Otto Frank's name should have continued for so long.

Opekta's former premises on Prinsengracht are now, of course, the location of the Anne Frank Huis and Museum.

[31]   Readers may be interested in the following websites from AmsterdamStay, Wikipedia, and *The Times of Israel* regarding some of the important history of the *Rivierenbuurt:*

> https://www.amsterdamstay.com/rivierenbuurt-amsterdam
>
> https://en.wikipedia.org/wiki/Rivierenbuurt_(Amsterdam)
>
> https://www.timesofisrael.com/in-anne-franks-childhood-neighborhood-the-buildings-do-not-forget/

The following City of Amsterdam page has the following information that is relevant to our story of Anne:

From the 1930s, more and more Jewish residents, including Jewish-German refugees, settled in the area. By 1940, there were around 17,000 Jews in this part of the city (40% of the total), including Anne Frank and her family. Only 4,000 of them survived the war. (https://www.amsterdam.nl/en/districts/zuid/rivierenbuurt/)

32   Gert-Jan Jimmink, the current owner of the bookstore where it is likely Anne saw the famous red-and-white checkered autograph album that quickly became her diary, sponsored the commissioning of a special statue of Anne outside her former Merwedeplein home. This was unveiled on July 9, 2005.

33   I was excited to find a link to the interior of Anne's home on the following Google Arts and Culture website:

https://artsandculture.google.com/story/8QXhXqyM_oYkjQ

The above is part of a current exhibition on Merwedeplein at the Anne Frank Huis and Museum in Amsterdam:

https://www.annefrank.org/en/museum/inside-museum/the-other-home-of-the-frank-family/

https://artsandculture.google.com/exhibit/anne-frank's-family-home/2AJCtLmxVrkeKA

Readers may also like to know that the historian Rian Verhoeven runs a bookable Anne Frank walking tour of Merwedeplein and the surrounding *Rivierenbuurt:* https://www.annefrankwalkingtour.com/

34   Readers as interested as I am in learning more about the 6e Montessorischool that Anne attended on Niersstraat between 1934 and 1941, and more about the underlying Montessori educational principles that inspired her time there, can consult the school's website. I have included a link in our website resources.

The school was extremely close (about one-third of a mile) to where Anne lived on Merwedeplein and well within walking or biking distance of her home. Ernst Schnabel in chapter 3 of *The Footsteps of Anne Frank* also has some fascinating stories to relate of Anne's time at the school as he managed to interview several of her teachers who knew her well. The kindergarten was on the lower level of the school with the rest of Anne's time in grades one through six being spent upstairs. Anne seems to have loved being at this school.

I did find a picture on Wikipedia of Margot's elementary school and have included this information in our website resources.

Before being forced to join Anne for the 1941–1942 school year at the Jewish Lyceum, Margot moved to the *Gemeentelijk Lyceum voor Meisjes* (Municipal Lyceum for Girls). According to Melissa Müller in her biography of Anne, Margot stayed at this school for three years. The Gemeentelijk Lyceum voor Meisjes is now the Joke Smit College. While the Jekerschool would have been extremely close and convenient to Merwedeplein for Margot, the Gemeentelijk Lyceum voor Meisjes would have been well over a mile away.

35   I have not been able to find very much information on the Jewish Lyceum on Voormalige Stadstimmertuinen in Amsterdam. I have only been able to find the included links in our website resources to a page on the I Amsterdam website as well as to a second link in Dutch. From these websites, we learn that there was already an existing Jewish high school (since 1938) across the road from the Lyceum and that Anne and Margot's school was used for children displaced from their former schools following the proclamation issued by the Germans. The *Joodse Raad* (Jewish Council) in Amsterdam was tasked with finding suitable premises for Jewish children.

As the Jewish Lyceum was just over a mile from their home (according to what I tried to work out on Google Earth) and on the other side of the Amstel river, it would have been less convenient for Anne and Margot to reach than their earliest schools. Ronald Wilfred Jansen in *Anne Frank* suggests that the school was over two miles away and that Anne would have reached it by cycling across the Berlagebrug that spanned the Amstel. This would have been the closest bridge to Merwedeplein. Cycling was banned for Jews in June 1942.

All that remains of its former function as a school, is a commemorative plaque and the strangely bent remnant of a Jewish star above the door. As the dates above the door chillingly suggest, the school had to close quickly in 1943 due to a lack of Jewish pupils to teach. One of my contributors, Priscilla, took some photos of the commemorative plaque and the star for this book.

Surviving children at the school at any given time would use coded signs to indicate whether a missing child had gone into hiding or had become a victim of one of the Nazi roundups that took place throughout 1942 and 1943. With respect to this point, readers may also like to read Bloeme Evers-Emden's interesting account of her time at the school in *The Last Seven Months of Anne Frank*. Bloeme not only knew both Anne and Margot from their time at the Jewish Lyceum, but she was also one of the last pupils to remain at the school. More information about her life can be found on Wikipedia: https://en.wikipedia.org/wiki/Bloeme_Evers-Emden

For our immediate purposes here, we need to recognize that the Jewish Lyceum offered Anne a quite different education to that of her former 6e Montessorischool with less of the "free flowing" and uninhibited style common to Montessori principles. From the tone of her early diary entries and despite the ugly circumstances that gave rise to her being there, Anne seems to have been very happy at the school. Less is known about Margot's feelings.

[36]   For readers interested in learning more about the similarities and differences between Dutch and German, I did find the following websites that might help us to understand why Edith and Otto (steeped in their native German language) found it harder to learn Dutch than Anne and Margot did. The first is an article written by Conor Clyne (November 17, 2016): http://tsarexperience.com/how-similar-or-different-are-german-and-dutch/. The second was written by Benny Lewis: https://www.fluentin3months.com/dutch-vs-german/

[37]   Although still disturbing, membership in the NSB fortunately peaked at around 100,000 or around 1.5 percent of the total population. That said, the number still seems depressingly high and Otto Frank seems to have managed to meet an awful lot of them. Readers of *The Hidden Life of Otto Frank* by Carol Ann Lee, for example, will meet Anton Ahlers. I included a link to the NSB and to their founder Anton Mussert in our website resources.

[38]   For further information about the history of the Netherlands during the Second World War, please review our website resources. Nor should we forget that Queen Wilhelmina fled with her cabinet to the United Kingdom two days before the Dutch surrender. This move initially divided Dutch opinion with some grateful for the Queen's safety and others resentful that she had "abandoned" her subjects. The Queen continued to speak to the Netherlands from her exile in London via regular Radio Oranje broadcasts. She won hearts and minds by doing so.

[39]   For further information on Operation Market Garden (September 17–25, 1944), please review our website resources.

[40]   Despite these Allied successes in the southern part of the country, Liberation Day in the Netherlands honors the liberation of the entire country on May 5 each year. Kamp Westerbork—where Anne and the other occupants of the Secret Annex were sent after their arrest on August 4, 1944—was not finally liberated until April 12, 1945. Canadian forces found 876 inmates there.

The Dutch were also apparently keen to annex German territory after the war, information that I came upon by accident while looking for something else. As readers will see in our website resources that I consulted for this chapter, I included a page from Wikipedia documenting what would have been an ambitious plan to expand Dutch territory by 30 percent or by as much as 50 percent if it had ever been pursued to its conclusion.

[41] https://en.wikipedia.org/wiki/History_of_the_Jews_in_the_Netherlands

In 1939, there were some 140,000 Jews living throughout the Netherlands with most (nearly 60 percent or nearly 80,000) living in Amsterdam and with some 30,000 having arrived from Germany as refugees. While the Netherlands was only around 1.5 percent Jewish, in Amsterdam the Jews amounted to around 10 percent of the population. According to the above Wikipedia article, German census figures show that there may have been as many as 154,000 Jews in 1941. The Germans referred to those with four Jewish grandparents as "full Jews," to those with only two Jewish grandparents as "half Jews" and to those with only one as "quarter Jews."

Numbers vary for how many transited through the main transit camp of Westerbork to other camps in Germany and elsewhere, but the most reliable and consistent figure that I have found suggests that around 107,000 were transported from Kamp Westerbork and that only 5,000 returned to the Netherlands after the war. This number famously included Anne's father, Otto.

One of the many ironies of the Nazis determined efforts to find a "final solution" to the Jewish question is that they managed to turn many casually observant or nonreligious Jews into strong believers in their Jewish identity and faith. Although Edith Frank and Margot had always been reasonably observant, Otto and Anne were not. Twenty-five months of hiding in the Annex, however, made Anne much more religiously aware than she had been beforehand about her Jewish identity. Anne's growing Jewish self-consciousness (and anger toward those trying to suppress it) can be seen in her diary entries for October 9, 1942, November 19, 1942, April 11, 1944, and May 22, 1944.

By autumn 1943, Amsterdam and most of the Netherlands were believed by the occupying authorities to be largely "free of Jews." According to the Timeline page on the Anne Frank Huis and Museum website:

> On 29 September 1943, a final major raid was held. Approximately
> 10,000 Jews were arrested and taken to Camp Westerbork. There were

now almost no Jews left in Amsterdam. (https://www.annefrank.
org/en/anne-frank/the-timeline/#113)

The last major roundup that took place in Amsterdam on September 29, 1943, also marked the end of the *Joodse Raad* (Jewish Council) which had been the chief liaison between the Jewish population and the occupying Nazis since February 13, 1941. The Jewish Council was even tasked with the humiliating role of compiling the lists of Jews selected for transportation in July 1942. The Council's demise followed on from the fact that their leaders and elders were sent to Kamp Westerbork as part of the last major roundup.

The last train to leave Kamp Westerbork went to Bergen-Belsen on September 13, 1944. There is lingering and understandable resentment in the Netherlands of the complicit role of the Dutch national railway company, Nederlandse Spoorwegen (NS), in transporting prisoners to Westerbork. They would then take the deportation trains forward to the Dutch-German border where German trains would take over the transportation to the labor and extermination camps beyond. According to the Moderate Voice:

> *While 13 years ago [in 2005] NS apologized for its role in the deportations, it has now agreed to set up a commission to investigate how it can make individual reparations to Dutch Holocaust survivors and direct family members of Dutch Jews who were murdered in the concentration camps, calling its involvement 'a black page in the history of our country and our company.'* (https://themoderatevoice.
com/the-last-train-to-auschwitz-revisited-2/)

For further information about the history of the persecution of the Jewish population of the Netherlands during the Second World War, please review our website resources.

[42] Theo Coster in the abovementioned *We All Wore Stars*, Carol Ann Lee in *The Hidden Life of Otto Frank*, the Anne Frank Huis and Museum as part of an "in-depth" website article (there is a link in our website resources), and Melissa Müller in *Anne Frank: The Biography* offer some reasons if readers are interested in looking further into this subject. There is also *Anne Frank and After* by Dick van Galen Last and Rolf Wolfswinkel and Dr. Jacob Presser's seminal work, *Ashes in the Wind: The Destruction of Dutch Jewry*. When I heard recently that *Ashes in the Wind* is a fascinating study, I decided to order the book for my Anne Frank library. Anne discusses some of her concerns for how the Dutch were reacting to their Jewish neighbors in her diary entry for May 22, 1944.

Notwithstanding the above caveats, I still strongly believe that the Dutch suffered greatly during the war and not just during the Hunger Winter of 1944–45. I also acknowledge that many Dutch were sympathetic to their Jewish neighbors and that the more virulent of the collaborators were swiftly dealt with at the end of the Second World War in 1945. As the Dutch still celebrate their liberation every May 5 with a public holiday, I believe that we should maintain our focus on the efforts made by Johan and Bep Voskuijl, Miep and Jan Gies, Victor Kugler, and Johannes Kleiman among others to help the Jewish population during the war—efforts which included a spectacular general strike staged on February 25, 1941—and Dutch efforts to seek out collaborators after it.

[43] Although chiefly centered on Amsterdam, the importance of the February strike cannot be overstated. It was the largest of its kind in occupied Europe to protest the mistreatment of Jews. Please review our website resources for further information.

[44] Reichskommissar Arthur Seyss-Inquart began his tenure with a velvet glove that was soon removed. Unlike other occupied countries that were under military control, the occupational management of the Netherlands was kept in civilian hands.

Seyss-Inquart was an Austrian Nazi and virulently anti-Semitic. After the war, he was tried at Nuremberg, found guilty of crimes against humanity, and executed.

[45] Please review our website resources for more information on the 1935 Nuremberg Laws. I decided to include a timeline website that compares restrictive measures issued in occupied Belgium with those introduced in the occupied Netherlands. Readers will find other sites documenting the incremental measures introduced into the Netherlands. Both Melissa Müller and Carol Ann Lee explore the same topic in their biographies of Anne and Otto and discuss how the introduced measures affected the Frank family. Anne Frank also documents the incrementalism in her famous diary entry for June 20, 1942.

[46] This is a provisional manuscript title with a provisional 2020 publishing date. I added this comment because it is so perfect and captures the essence of Anne's diary perfectly. Federica is one of the contributors to this anthology.

[47] Anne's wishes in this regard have not always satisfied those who have tried to grant her honorary American citizenship by giving her posthumous immigration status. Although this takes note of the fact that Otto had both tried and failed to immigrate to the United States, this was more to protect his family's best interests at a time of existential danger. Despite Anne having been born as a German, I think that it is safe to say that most Dutch are probably more than happy to claim her as

their own and would resent seeing her being given American or any other citizenship. In concluding her long diary entry for April 11, 1944, Anne tells Kitty how much she "loved" the "Dutch," the "country," and the "language." Her "first wish" after the war—even if she would have to "write to the Queen herself"—was to become a full Dutch citizen and to be able to work in the Netherlands.

In terms of Anne's attitude toward the Nazis, she referred to Germans as "monsters" in her diary entry for November 19, 1942. She greatly differed from her father in this regard.

[48]   Please see both *Margot* by Jillian Cantor and *Annelies* by David Gillham.

Ms. Cantor moves her fictional Margot to Philadelphia as she imagines it to be in 1959, while Mr. Gillham has his fictional Anne move to the United States after being miserable in Amsterdam for several years after the Second World War ended. Both girls have successfully avoided death in these works and readers are invited to suspend reality for a better understanding of the experience and worth of the two works. We have to acknowledge that many will not be able to do so.

Personally, I see a certain degree of American guilt in these stories based on the fact that Otto tried so hard to immigrate to America during the war and that the door to immigration was closed after Germany declared war on the United States after Pearl Harbor; thus, the desire to *redirect* reality down a different path that is not rooted in anything truthful beyond what the writer captures of the known personality traits of both sisters. Such a way of thinking does offer a certain degree of creative freedom for writers who decide to take on the task and the results *can* be compelling for those willing to meet the writer halfway or, indeed, to walk on the entirety of the author's journey. The above two books are psychologically authentic.

[49]   Melissa Müller in her biography of Anne has decided to cast some doubt on whether Anne's diary conclusively came from Blankevoort's bookstore around the corner from where the Franks lived on Merwedeplein and mentions a second possibility of Perry's department store on Kalverstraat. This important shopping street in Amsterdam would have been relatively close to Opekta's offices on Prinsengracht. At one point in her diary (October 20, 1942; ver. A), Anne asks Bep Voskuijl to find her another diary from this store. Perry's would have been less convenient if Otto needed to get Anne's present in a hurry in time for her thirteenth birthday; however, by the time that Anne was looking for another diary book in late 1942 after she was close to filling her original, Perry's would have been more convenient for Bep to get to as it was much closer to the Secret Annex.

Blankevoort's is now known as the *Boekhandel Jimmink* and there is a special webpage for Anne: http://www.jimminkboek.nl/pagina46.html#top

As noted in an earlier endnote, Gert-Jan Jimmink, the current owner of this bookstore, commissioned a special statue of Anne to be placed outside her former Merwedeplein home. This was unveiled on July 9, 2005. The idea that Otto might have bought the famous diary from elsewhere is clearly *not* the view of Mr. Jimmink, and I am more than happy to accept this conclusion.

Both Joy Gafa' and Kirsi Lehtola (whom we will be hearing from shortly) have visited the Boekhandel Jimmink as part of their separate trips to Amsterdam.

[50] Please see this important page on the Anne Frank Huis and Museum: https://www.annefrank.org/en/anne-frank/diary/complete-works-anne-frank/

Hannah Goslar believes that Anne was probably writing in other diaries at school long before she received her red-and-white checkered diary, but these have not survived if this was the case. Anne was very secretive about most of her writing in the Secret Annex and, according to Hannah, was just as careful to conceal her efforts at school.

[51] This broadcast took place on March 28, 1944, but was documented by Anne in her diary entry for March 29, 1944.

[52] Laureen Nussbaum, who knew both Anne and Margot from their days in Merwedeplein and who then became friendly with Otto after the war, has since criticized Otto for combining Anne's original and revised entries into one commercial diary. As part of an article published by *The Independent* newspaper in London on May 5, 1995, Ms. Nussbaum is interviewed and notes how the subsequent commercialism of Anne's name has meant that she now "stands as a symbolic figure upon whom the world can heap both its guilt and its commiseration." The full article (complete with other interesting observations) by Angela Lambert can be found here: https://www.independent.co.uk/life-style/anne-frank-after-the-diary-stopped-1618257.html

Laureen feels that the only version of Anne's diary that we should be reading is the author's own revised B copy and nothing of the original A diary. This would, of course, eliminate all of Anne's original writing after March 29, 1944, which is where her revised entries end. A compromise *might* be for editors and publishers to add the forty-eight original dates that follow the end of her revisions as an appendix.

Thanks to the recent *Anne Frank: The Collected Works* edition of her diary, we can now view Anne's original and revised work without the filter of anyone else's subsequent editing. On balance, I do *not* think that it is fair to criticize Otto Frank for decisions that he felt best honored his daughter's intentions to become a famous writer and which also made clear to the world the extent of his own suffering at losing both his daughters and his wife during the Holocaust.

Melissa Müller in an interview with C-SPAN in 1998 is also skeptical about the merits of the *Definitive Edition* and not least because Otto Frank (one of the credited editors) had died eleven years before the D edition was initially published in 1991: https://www.c-span.org/person/?melissamuller

[53] For further reference here, and with thanks to *Anne Frank: The Collected Works* that was published in June 2019, it is possible to make the following observations:

First, Anne's original version A diary comprises three surviving journals. The *first* is the famous red-and-white checkered diary that she received on her thirteenth birthday. Although some have assumed that this is Anne's entire diary, it only contains her diary entries from June 12, 1942, to December 5, 1942, with one entry for May 2, 1943, and another for January 22, 1944, added as in-fill to empty pages. It does also include lots of photos of Anne and Margot with added comments. Her *second* surviving diary begins on December 22, 1943, and ends on April 17, 1944. The *third* surviving original diary begins on April 18, 1944, and ends on August 1, 1944. In all, there are 136 unique dates in Anne's original diary.

Second, Anne's revised diary (version B) comprises ninety-eight unique diary dates, beginning on June 20, 1942 and ending on March 29, 1944. As noted earlier, most of what we read of events in the Secret Annex for 1943 are sourced from this edited version of Anne's diary. According to the Anne Frank Huis and Museum website, Anne began revising her entries on May 20, 1944. At which point and in the time that remained to her in the Secret Annex:

> *Anne worked hard: in those few months, she wrote around 50,000 words, filling more than 215 sheets of paper.* (https://www.annefrank. org/en/anne-frank/diary/complete-works-anne-frank/)

(Outside the scope of *The Collected Works* as this edition only includes the A, the B, and the D editions of Anne's diary, Otto used an edited mix of A and B entries across some 172 diary dates for the first Dutch version C edition in 1947 and the first English edition in 1952.)

Third, the *Definitive Edition* (version D) restored the 30 percent of Anne's diary that had been originally cut by Otto. This latest version now covers diary entries from 184 dates—twelve more than existed in the earlier two versions of the diary. We need to bear in mind, though, that sometimes Anne would write several different entries for the same date. The extra twelve dates obviously account for *some* of the extra 30 percent while the remainder has come from restoring some of the more personal commentary that Otto had decided to cut from the original version C.

Finally, we should note that the helpers, who once went by their pseudonyms of Victor Kraler, Jo Koophuis, Miep and Henk van Santen, Mr. Vossen and his daughter Elli in early editions of her diary now have their real names restored in the *Definitive Edition*. These are now known respectively as Victor Kugler, Johannes Kleiman, Miep and Jan Gies, and Johan and Bep Voskuijl. Only Hermann van Pels, Auguste van Pels, Peter van Pels, and Fritz Pfeffer continue to have their names shielded in the *Definitive Edition* by their respective pseudonyms of Hermann van Daan, Petronella van Daan, Peter van Daan, and Albert Dussel, respectively. Of course, with minimal research, we can know their real identities.

[54]   Although Anne does not mention the source of her inspiration for her "patient" friend in her diary entry for June 20, 1942, Kitty is believed to have been inspired by a character in the "Joop ter Heul" series of novels created by Cissy van Marxveldt, a Dutch writer whom Anne loved. I have tried in vain to find her books available in an English translation. Joop ter Heul's page on Wikipedia is currently in need of so much added revision that I am including a link to her creator instead. According to the writer's page on Wikipedia:

> *Van Marxvelt's [sic] Joop ter Heul novels for teenage girls had a notable influence on the writings of Anne Frank, who addressed her diary letters to an imaginary friend named Kitty. Anne Frank scholars, as well as Anne's friend Kitty Egyedi, are united in their belief that Frank's Kitty was based on a character created by Van Marxveldt: Kitty Francken, a friend of Joop's and a frequent recipient of her letters.* (https://en.wikipedia.org/wiki/Cissy_van_Marxveldt)

[55]   According to the following ThoughtCo. website:

> *In Anne's first, red-and-white-checkered notebook, Anne sometimes wrote to other names such as "Pop," "Phien," "Emmy," "Marianne," "Jetty," "Loutje," "Conny," and "Jackie." These names appeared on entries dating from September 25, 1942, until November 13, 1942.* (https:// www.thoughtco.com/unknown-facts-about-anne-frank-1779478)

There is further information about Kitty and her first appearance in Anne's diary (September 22, 1942) on the Anne Frank Huis and Museum website: https://www. annefrank.org/en/anne-frank/diary/so-who-is-dear-kitty/

56   See Anne's diary entry for June 15, 1942. As a side issue here, but in the recently discovered and now published *Renia's Diary: A Holocaust Journal*, the young polish teenager Renia does exactly the same in *her* opening diary entries when she describes the quirks, personalities, and horrors of her girlfriends at school.

57   Please see Anne's diary entry for March 10, 1943.

58   Given that Anne's diary papers were so obvious for Miep Gies, Bep Voskuijl, and Willem van Maaren to spot amid the chaos when they later searched the Secret Annex for anything personal to the Franks, the van Pels family, and Fritz Pfeffer, it seems somewhat surprising that *no* trace of Margot's diary has ever been found. We only know that she was writing one because Anne tells us so in her diary entry for Wednesday, October 14, 1942.

It is entirely possible that Margot may have destroyed her own work before the arrest or even at the time of the arrest. From what we know of Margot, she would have certainly been sensitive to any possible risk to their helpers should the Nazis have discovered her work. Anne would have known of the risks too, which is why she used pseudonyms for the helpers in her writing and even for herself at one point. Anne once toyed with the idea of calling herself Anne "Aulis" or Anne "Robin" when she was revising her diary. It is only in more recent *Definitive Edition* of her diary that the true names of the helpers can be finally revealed.

Readers may be interested to know that Mazal Alouf-Mizrahi in *The Silent Sister* has offered us a creative imagining of the diary that Margot *might* have written. The writer accentuates "Margot's" faith and develops her desire to move to Palestine with the help of an imaginary boyfriend who may not convince everyone who reads the book!

59   The yellow Star of David was introduced from May 3, 1942, which was not that long before Margot's call-up notice arrived on July 5, 1942.

The Nazis insisted that all Jews over the age of six had to buy four stars each at the cost of four cents per star and then place them visibly on all outer garments. Melissa Müller in her biography of Anne points out that each star was a lurid yellow color to increase their visibility to passersby and, of course, to the patrolling Nazis. Further historical information on the introduction of the yellow star in the Netherlands can be found in our website resources.

[60]   Please see our website resources for additional information on the use made of the Hollandsche Schouwburg (Jewish theater) during the occupation of the Netherlands. According to Ronald Wilfred Jansen in *Anne Frank*, Anne received her school report here on July 3, 1942. Mr. Jansen notes that the Germans then used the building from August 1942 to November 1943 as a depot for Jews prior to their removal to Kamp Westerbork.

[61]   Please refer to our website resources for more information on the ultimate destinations of the cattle car transports from Kamp Westerbork. Most of the transports went to Auschwitz with additional cattle cars dispatched to Sobibór and Bergen-Belsen. I have clearly had to include extensive information on Auschwitz-Birkenau and Bergen-Belsen in our website resources as both are relevant to Anne's story as well as to Margot's. Additional history is offered on some of the other camps (including their operating dates and other reference data) for readers who are interested. Not all of them operated for the entirety of the war.

Outside their deportation to Auschwitz, no one from the Secret Annex ended up transferred to any of the other death camps such as Treblinka or Sobibór.

[62]   As the first trains for Kamp Westerbork did not leave until July 15, 1942, Margot would have had around ten days in which to put together an approved list of belongings that came with her notice to report. Otto decided not to risk any additional precipitate action by the authorities in choosing to go into hiding on July 6.

The Anne Frank Huis and Museum has a sample copy of a typical call-up notice on Margot's page: https://www.annefrank.org/en/anne-frank/main-characters/margot-frank/

[63]   Otto had told Anne that they would need to go into hiding before long but not where. Ironically, Anne would detail this conversation in her last diary entry as a "free" teenager—July 5, 1942.

Please see the following page from the Anne Frank Huis and Museum for further information on the history of Prinsengracht 263 (as a building) and the Secret Annex (including its 1999 reconstructed appearance): https://www.annefrank.org/en/anne-frank/go-in-depth/history-secret-annex/ and https://www.annefrank.org/en/anne-frank/secret-annex/

The Secret Annex is referred to as the "Secret Annexe" with an added "e" in British English.

As per Anne's diary entry for May 11, 1944, *The Secret Annex* was also how she wanted to title her planned book on her life in hiding.

[64] Joop van Wijk-Voskuijl told me recently that his grandfather, Johan, was not included by the Anne Frank Huis and Museum as one of the helpers until 2014 and only after a "ten-year fight." As a reminder, Johan was Opekta's warehouse manager until Summer 1943 but is chiefly honored today for having designed and built the famous revolving bookcase that concealed the door to the Secret Annex. He also made ashtrays for Mr. van Pels and bookends for Otto among other gifts. Anne speaks appreciatively of Johan Voskuijl in her diary entries for August 21, 1942, and June 15, 1943. The Anne Frank Huis and Museum discusses his significant role, and you can read more about Johan on their page as part of our website bibliographical resources.

[65] Melissa Müller references Otto saying:

> "Anne didn't write every day ... but mostly when something particularly upset her and she was able to find relief in writing. ... She therefore made no mention of the many days and weeks that passed in normal family life—we did not live in constant tension."
> (Melissa Müller, *Anne Frank: The Biography*)

It certainly does seem as if the nervous expectation of surviving and having to live day-by-day in cramped circumstances were not fatal attributes in and of themselves. Although it was overpowering at times for Anne, and for everyone else judging by her various diary entries, it is important that no one appears to have broken ranks or tried to run away.

[66] One of Anne's friends, as related by Theo Coster in *We All Wore Stars*, hid in a forest, and at one point a German deserter joined them. Mr. Coster talks about others forced to move because of a lack of money to pay their "rent" to those hiding them.

The Dutch used the word *onderduiker* to apply to anyone who went into hiding during the war. At its peak in 1944, there were 300,000 in hiding. Some 30,000 of these *onderduikers* were Jewish and 12,000 of these were eventually arrested, according to the Anne Frank Huis and Museum website.

Melissa Müller also describes some of the experiences of others in hiding in her biography of Anne.

On balance, I think we can say that while the eight hiding in the Secret Annex on Prinsengracht 263 would have certainly felt cramped, fearful, irritable, and claustrophobic, it was no means an entirely horrible location in which to hide compared to the experiences of others in hiding in the occupied Netherlands.

In selecting the rear annex of his office building, Otto needed to be able to trust his chosen staff to help him and his family with food, other daily necessities, books, and distractions. He also needed a place large enough to keep his family together and with sufficient additional space for the others he agreed to have join them. Unlike other families in hiding who chose to "split their camps" with the parents in one location and their children in another, the Franks believed in remaining together at all costs. This instinct prevailed throughout their time in hiding. They also had the huge advantage, not shared by many others in hiding, of having extremely trustworthy and reliable helpers who were highly unlikely to succumb to the bribes issued by the Nazis to betray those in hiding.

Jews elsewhere in hiding in the Netherlands lived in far worse circumstances than the occupants of the Secret Annex endured for twenty-five months, and they were often at the mercy of nervous, avaricious, or even abusive "helpers." Many had to change locations frequently or provide promissory notes for future payment to their hosts once they ran out of funds. Yet it was not always bad, and other helpers and hiders developed strong relationships that endured once the war ended. It was tough for all Jewish children, but especially for Jewish girls separated from their families and at risk of abuse from their hosts. Each Jewish child's domestic, educational, religious, and social life became extremely unpredictable following the occupation of the Netherlands and the issuance by the authorities of the progressively restrictive proclamations.

From what we know of Anne's personality, delicate health, and love for her father, it is highly unlikely that she would have tolerated being separated from him for any great length of time. I am not sure that Margot would have coped that well either. Melissa Müller mentions the importance of family to Anne several times in her biography and makes it clear that Otto's younger daughter would have been reminded many times of her father's understanding and empathy surrounding this key point. Readers will learn shortly from my own submission for this anthology just how difficult it can be to persuade some children today to absorb the power of this concept.

⁶⁷   The fact that Peter brought along his cat would have upset Anne, who had had to leave her own beloved cat Moortje behind when the Franks left Merwedeplein. This may sound like the least of the many injustices of Anne's story, but anything of a hurtful nature would have taken on a greater importance given the restricted choices available to her in her life. Eventually Mouschi proved herself useful by catching mice and rats. Unfortunately, she also developed fleas and memorably got into a peeing accident that Anne documents in detail in her diary entry for May 10, 1944.

⁶⁸   Dr. Pfeffer, who later died at the Neuengamme concentration camp on December 20, 1944, was married to Charlotte posthumously in 1950. Charlotte Kaletta does not appear to have appreciated the publication of Anne's diary, the Goodrich and Hackett play, or the 1959 film. She complained to the playwrights and eventually broke contact with Otto after he was unable to convince her that Anne was unflattering in her portrayal of *everyone* in the Secret Annex. Based on other sources, Dr. Pfeffer comes across as an interesting and romantic dentist who was clearly very lonely and isolated emotionally in the Secret Annex. It is surprising that Anne was not more sympathetic to this; their sharing the same room and fighting over workspace could not have helped either of them to understand the other.

⁶⁹   The Austrian Karl Josef Silberbauer led the arrest on behalf of the *Sicherheitsdienst* (SD) or security service agency of the SS. It is not confirmed just how many were involved in the arrest but at least three seem to have been present.

There also seems to be some confusion as to whether it was the SD or the Gestapo or a combination of both agencies that arrested everyone in the Secret Annex on August 4, 1944. Victor Kugler, who was forced to lead the police to the Annex at gunpoint, appears to have believed that the Gestapo led the arrest as (by his own account) he whispers these words to Edith Frank.

For what it is worth, Otto Frank also appears to have borne no ill-will toward Silberbauer due to his perceived courtesy in allowing everyone to "take their time" after discovering that Otto had served in the First World War. As a fellow Austrian, Miep Gies quickly decides on the following day to offer Silberbauer money to release everyone, but events had moved on too fast and were no longer in his hands. I feel that it is possible that this strategy *could* have possibly worked given that the Germans had long declared that Netherlands was "free of Jews" and that it would have been embarrassing to them to find that it was not so. According to Otto, Hermann van Pels also tried to bribe Silberbauer.

The above "courtesy" offered by Silberbauer did not extend to the police refraining from ransacking the Secret Annex for jewelry and other valuables. In the chaos,

Otto's briefcase containing Anne's diary and her other stories and papers was emptied and its contents were left scattered on the floor for Miep Gies, Bep Voskuijl, and Willem van Maaren to find over the course of the following days. This hasty dismissal on the part of the SD and the police can be viewed now as somewhat ironic given how valuable Anne's work now is. It would be stretching a point to add that Anne has had the last laugh on the matter, but we can still be thankful that the most valuable of all the personal belongings in the Secret Annex were the ones that the Nazis ignored and left behind; thus, we can enjoy the full measure of Anne's diary, her stories, and the family photograph album. What we do *not* have, of course, is Anne herself.

As noted above, Margot's diary was *not* among the papers left behind. Typically, the Germans and willing Dutch members of the Dutch Nazi Party (NSB) would return later to remove furniture for purposes back in Germany. Abraham Puls, who owned a removal company and who also happened to be a member of the Dutch Nazi Party (NSB), was infamous for working for the Nazis in this regard. Further information about Puls can be found here: http://erijswijk. blogspot.com/2011/02/abraham-puls.html and https://www.joodsamsterdam.nl/ abraham-puls-van-verhuizer-tot-rovershoofdman/

[70]   Anne and her family, the van Pels family, and Dr. Pfeffer were initially taken to the SD headquarters (a converted girls' school) on Euterpestraat in the south of Amsterdam. They were then imprisoned for several days in the *Huis van Bewaring* (House of Detention I) on the Weteringschans in Amsterdam. Readers interested in the history of both facilities can find references in our website resources. The SD headquarters ended up being heavily bombed by the RAF in November 1944. After the war, the "Euterpestraat" was renamed after the Dutch resistance fighter Gerrit van der Veen as the "Gerrit van der Veenstraat." The former SD headquarters has reverted to a school and is now known as the Gerrit van der Veen College: https:// nl.wikipedia.org/wiki/Gerrit_van_der_Veen_College

I should point out that both Johannes Kleiman and Victor Kugler were also arrested with the others on August 4, 1944. They ended up transported to the Polizeiliche Durchgangslager Amersfoort, a Dutch prison. Mr. Kleiman was quickly released at the insistence of the Red Cross for medical reasons with Mr. Kugler later escaping during an RAF raid on a labor convoy that he was assigned to. Readers can find more information on their lives and journeys in our website resources.

For reasons that we can only guess, Miep was not arrested and neither was Bep Voskuijl. It is believed that Miep's Austrian origins (and even looks) may have helped endear her to Karl Silberbauer, as he was also Austrian. Bep Voskuijl had fortunately escaped on Mr. Kleiman's urging.

Investigations into what happened at the time of the arrest in the Secret Annex took place in 1948 and then in 1963. Neither investigation was conclusive.

[71]   Please see *The Last Seven Months of Anne Frank.*

Many sources suggest that the Nazis ran an orderly camp complete with hospitals, cabarets, and comparatively decent food. Although some even helped the elderly and children into the cattle trains prior to departure, it seems likely that they were more terrified of their superiors in Berlin complaining about late trains than they wanted to present any kind of final humane front. Eva Schloss argues that there was nothing inconsistent in the idea of a civilized approach clashing with the more common notion of the brutal response of Nazis. She sees their propensity for unpredictable whims to lie at the heart of both.

Anne Frank and After contains further "ego documentary" insight into life at Kamp Westerbork. Etty Hillesum has also published her *Letters from Westerbork*. Etty's *Letters* have been published in an edition that also includes her *Diary.*

The deportation trains to camps further east ran from July 1942 through to September 1944. Tuesday evenings after the transport train for that week had left were typically the most distracting for the camp inmates as they could relax for a further six days until the next deportation list was read out the following Monday evening. Hasty negotiations and bargaining would take place with the authorities and also between the inmates themselves during those six days.

[72]   I have included a range of interesting information on Albert Gemmeker and his evasion of responsibility as part of our collection of website resources on Kamp Westerbork.

In a chilling observation in *After Auschwitz*, Ms. Schloss tells us that Albert Gemmeker was "a typical Nazi; he combined unfeeling brutality with bursts of 'civilized' humanity, dispensed on a whim."

[73]   There appears to be some minor discrepancy as to the number of transports that left for Auschwitz from Kamp Westerbork. Some of my sources suggest that there were sixty-five, while Melissa Müller in her biography of Anne says that sixty-seven trains out of a 1942–1944 total of 103 left for Auschwitz. Ms. Müller notes that there were "498 men, 442 women, 79 children—1019 names in all on the last transport to Auschwitz." This train was unusual for being rushed out on a Sunday.

Most of those died who were placed on the weekly trains that ended up going to Auschwitz and Sobibór. Those "lucky" enough to go on the fewer transports to Bergen-Belsen and Theresienstadt had the best chances of survival.

[74]   The infamous spur line into the heart of Birkenau remains intact as a memorial to this day both within and just outside the camp. Looking on Google Earth, it is possible to trace some indications of the previous path of the spur line back out to the main line which still runs through the Polish town of Oświęcim. The spur went into operation in May 1944.

The occupants of the Secret Annex would have arrived at Birkenau in the middle of the night and with barking dogs and glaring lights deployed to disorientate everyone. Survivors repeatedly tell of the noise, the dogs held by SS officers in dark uniforms, the lights, the awful selection process, the hair cutting, the delousing, the cold showers, the awful tattooing, the stripped clothes, and the overall disorientation that greeted them for hours on their arrival at Auschwitz-Birkenau.

[75]   For further information on Neuengamme and its history, please review our website resources.

[76]   Anne, Margot, and Mrs. van Pels are believed to have left for Bergen-Belsen on October 28, 1944, but I have also seen early November as a possibility.

[77]   For further information on Mrs. van Pels and the history of the Theresienstadt ghetto, please review our website resources. Readers may also like to read Helga Weiss's diary for a further understanding of what life was like in this former garrison town that quickly became a Jewish ghetto and transit camp under German control during the Second World War. When the Franks were arrested on August 4, 1944, Otto was told that they could have been transported to this marketed "spa town" had they come forward earlier and not become *onderduikers*.

[78]   When I was first writing this, the dates on which Anne and Margot died were unknown with any precision, and so most sources just vaguely say "February or March 1945." Some even come up with misleading, and sadly dramatic, phrases such as "Anne Frank died just weeks before the camp's liberation by the British Army on April 15, 1945."

Accounts that Anne died in Auschwitz are *not* true, as both Hanneli Goslar and Nanette Blitz saw her at Bergen-Belsen. New friends such as Lientje and Janny Brilleslijper also saw the two girls at the camp and later confirmed their deaths to Otto Frank. Otto discovered the names of the Brilleslijper sisters after he had read of his daughters' names on a Red Cross list in Amsterdam on or around July 18, 1945. He then went to visit the Brilleslijpers to verify their preliminary notice of his daughters' deaths to the Red Cross. Anne's death was later confirmed officially by the Dutch Red Cross on May 5, 1954; presumably, Margot's was confirmed at the same time. There are images of Anne's death certificate on the internet.

Any suggestion that the Brilleslijper sisters should have remembered the *actual* dates that Anne and Margot died is unreasonable given the frequency of death at the camp and the merging of chaotic days across the degrading weeks. We must remember that in 1945, Anne and Margot would have been regarded as just two girls whom they barely knew and who had then died as part of a typhus epidemic raging through the camp. Anne and Margot's later historical and literary significance to a wider world eager to know everything about them could not have been anticipated at the time.

As happens a lot with Anne Frank, new works about different aspects of her life in hiding and after her arrest emerge constantly. As I was about to send this book to the publisher for galley proofing, a new book (published only in Dutch so far) by Bas von Benda-Beckmann with important research conducted by Erika Prins—*Na het achterhuis: Anne Frank en de andere onderduikers in de kampen* (After the Annex: Anne Frank and the Other Hiders in the Camps)—has cast a different light on what happened to the hiders after their arrest on August 4, 1944. It is now believed that Anne and Margot may well have died in early February and much earlier than first thought. Please see this important article from the Dutch newspaper *Het Parool*: https://www. parool.nl/kunst-media/zo-verliep-het-laatste-levensjaar-van-anne-frank-b8c1be37/? fbclid=IwAR0z3PrxlPu58DaRnaO_fIQmED1QSritwGwv0cqgIAe0Vgj0hDFgY_ 5U84I

Further details regarding Anne and Margot's last days in Bergen-Belsen (including accounts of collapsed tents, starvation, and the virulent spread of typhus) can be found in *The Last Seven Months of Anne Frank* by Willy Lindwer. Carol Ann Lee in *The Hidden Life of Otto Frank* tells us what had happened to Anne and Margot in Bergen-Belsen based on the testimony of the two Brilleslijper sisters.

Please see our website resources for further information on the history of Bergen-Belsen as a camp. The camp's subsequent infamy is largely because of the awful conditions documented by the British Army when they liberated the camp on April 15, 1945. The frantic efforts to move inmates from camps such as Auschwitz back to Germany led to catastrophic and squalid overcrowding and then to the spread of typhus during the last six or seven months of Bergen-Belsen's existence.

[79]   Hanneli Goslar was held in a special part of Bergen-Belsen along with those deemed worthy of trade with the Allies for high-profile prisoners of their own. This section was kept separated from the parts of Bergen-Belsen that housed Anne, Margot, and Mrs. van Pels. Supposedly, Hanneli had more food in this part of the camp, but this is all relative. She famously managed to throw some to Anne with the second of two attempts being the only one to succeed in reaching her. The first had ended up being "stolen" by another inmate of the camp. Please see Alison Leslie Gold's book, *Memories of Anne Frank*, for more information on Hannah's story as well as Hannah's chapter in *The Last Seven Months of Anne Frank*.

[80]   Please refer to *The Hidden Life of Otto Frank* by Carol Ann Lee's, as well as other print and internet biographies of the Frank family. The Anne Frank Huis and Museum has a useful overview of Otto's life and there is an appropriate link to this in our website resources.

The Legacy of Anne Frank

[81]   According to Otto's page on the Anne Frank Huis and Museum website, we have the following observations made by Otto in a 1968 interview:

> *Otto felt responsible for the atmosphere in the Secret Annex and mediated in the countless larger and smaller arguments. "We had thought that living with my partner's family in our hiding place would make life less monotonous, but we had not foreseen how many problems would arise because of the differences in characters and views."* (Anne Frank Huis and Museum; Otto Frank, 1968)

Anne also discusses the situation in her revised diary entry for October 17, 1943.

[82]   Please refer to endnote 15 for further information on this claim.

[83]   Carol Ann Lee in *Roses from the Earth* mentions that both Miep Gies (as related to Cara Wilson-Granat) and Victor Kugler (as part of what he told the *Holland Herald* in an interview in the 1970s) may have taken photographs of Anne Frank in the Secret Annex; however, as Ms. Lee has been unable to trace any evidence of these photographs, it is better to assume that it is unlikely that we will ever be able to see any intriguing photographic evidence of life in hiding. On the other hand, Ryan Cooper *did* tell me that it is likely that Miep was given Otto Frank's Leica camera for safekeeping; thus, while she *may* have been able to use it to take some photographs, it is *more* likely that she would not have wanted to have risked such incriminating evidence. Always remember that at the time that Anne was still alive, no one would

have had any serious eye on posterity beyond the need to survive. Miep would not have seen herself as a historian.

[84]   Eva Schloss pondered this very point in the preface to her Holocaust memoir, *Eva's Story: A Survivor's Tale by the Stepsister of Anne Frank.* When I first wrote this section, I was not yet aware that Ms. Schloss had written in the preface to this book:

> *In spite of what had happened to me during the war I have no feelings of bitterness or hate, but on the other hand I do not believe in the goodness of man.*
>
> *My posthumous stepsister, Anne Frank, wrote in her diary: 'I still believe that deep down human beings are [truly] good at heart.' I cannot help remembering that she wrote this before she experienced Auschwitz and Belsen.* (Eva Schloss, *Eva's Story*)

In her second work, *After Auschwitz*, Ms. Schloss clarified the issue even further:

> *My experiences revealed that people have a unique capacity for cruelty, brutality and sheer indifference to human suffering. It is easy to say that good and evil exist within each of us but I have seen the unedifying reality of that at close hand, and it has led me to a lifetime of wondering about the human soul.* (Eva Schloss, *After Auschwitz*)

Richard Cohen in a *Washington Post* opinion piece has also taken issue with the phrase and notes:

> *It gets quoted often, and it somehow makes Anne's offstage death not the murder it was but an operatic closing of the eyes, an angelic expiration without pain or degradation.* (https://www.washingtonpost.com/archive/opinions/1997/09/30/anne-franks-book-about-hate/384c7c36-e071-45b9-8d9c-c345d57c0083/)

It is also worth mentioning that in her next diary entry for July 21, 1944, Anne addresses the attempted bomb plot assassination of Adolf Hitler by remarking that "he escaped, unfortunately, with only a few minor burns and scratches." I often refer to this as a way of arguing that Anne's idealism did have a practical limit in extreme cases! Not that this necessarily invalidates her earlier conclusion, merely that idealism *can* have justifiable limits in *extreme* circumstances. The extent to which such limits still apply to the world as it is today is less clear.

The phrase "truly good at heart" was originally translated as "really good at heart" in the first English version of Anne's diary that was translated from the Dutch by Barbara Mooyaart-Doubleday and then published in 1952. Many still refer to Anne's words as such, but throughout this anthology, I have and will continue to be referencing the edition as first published by Doubleday in 1995, published by Puffin Books in 1997, and then reprinted with "previously unpublished material" by Doubleday in 2001.

As a final point here, I would gently remind readers that much of what we honor today as Anne's idealism emanates from what she writes in the forty-eight entries that are part of the *original* A version of her diary that she had yet to review and possibly revise for future publication. In other words, all diary entries written *after* March 29, 1944, are *unrevised* entries. I am not suggesting that Anne *would* have altered anything, only that we do *not* know if she would have left everything as first written. Let us take, for example, Anne's diary entries for March 1944. In version A, there are twenty-five dated entries for this busy month or twenty-four up to the point that she was able to revise her original diary (March 29). In her revised version B, these twenty-four entries for March 1944 had been scaled down to just *nine* diary entries.

On the other hand, the fact that Anne *was* revising her diary for future publication might suggest that she would have had one eye on this possibility as she continued to write her original diary entries. Had Anne's revisions been allowed to catch up with the pace of her original entries, it seems entirely plausible that there *might* have been a merging of tone and content between the two versions or even a merging of the entire two diaries into one ongoing effort.

[85]   See Anne's diary entries for November 27, 1943, December 29, 1943, and January 6, 1944.

[86]   Bep Voskuijl turned twenty-three on July 5, 1942, the day that Margot received her call-up labor notice from the occupying authorities. Although closer in age to Margot, she ended up much closer to Anne. They both had complicated love lives which drew them even closer together. There is a lot of respect for Bep's life throughout this anthology given that she has been unfairly forgotten over the years or overshadowed by the role of Miep. Thankfully, she has a good champion in her son Joop van Wijk-Voskuijl who, of course, has written the foreword to this book.

[87]   Eva Schloss echoes some of Mr. Gillham's imaginary Anne when she writes of herself:

> *Rules and regimentation brought out the rebel in me. I parked at will in the old quarter of Zurich and enraged a policeman by ignoring his commands to move my car. What was the worst thing he could do to me? I had already been in a concentration camp.* (Eva Schloss, *After Auschwitz*)

[88]   Please see Anne's diary entries for December 24, 1943, February 8, 1944, and May 3, 1944. She addresses her need for "fun" in each of these.

[89]   The Holderness family make regular Facebook musical and other videos that are filled with family love and fun. Mat and Savanna Shaw release musical duet videos from their home in Utah and are recognized as much for the father-daughter love that inspires their listening audience as they are for their wonderful singing. Their first album, *Picture This*, was released in October 2020; their second, *Merry Little Christmas*, followed a month later.

Playing Anne (An Interview with Melina Zaccaria)

[90]   *Editor note:* Please review the following archived page from the Theatre Burlington on this production: https://www.theatreburlington.on.ca/the-diary-of-anne-frank/

I was also able to build a suitable catalog reference for this production:

> *The Diary of Anne Frank.* By Frances Goodrich and Albert Hackett. Dir. Sondra Learn. Perf. Melina Zaccaria (Anne), Michael Hannigan (Otto), and Carla Zabek (Edith). Theatre Burlington, Burlington, ON. February 2014.

Federica Pannocchia

[91]   *Editor note:* Please see Federica's website for *Un ponte per Anne Frank* (A Bridge for Anne Frank): www.unponteperannefrank.org

In a message to me, Federica explained a little more about the thinking behind her organization's name:

> *"Anne Frank always shared wonderful messages of hope, love, kindness, respect, inclusion, and tolerance. So it is a 'bridge for' all these ideals since Anne represents all these ideals."*

⁹² *Editor note:* Further information on the Raid on the Ghetto of Rome on October 16, 1943, can be found in our website resources.

⁹³ *Editor note:* This famous saying is from Anne's story "Give!" in *Tales from the Secret Annex.*

Joy Gafa'

⁹⁴ *Editor note:* I agree with Joy here. We do *not* know very much about Peter van Pels's feelings beyond Anne's speculation. It is worth mentioning, though, that while Peter comes across as somewhat dull in the Secret Annex compared to Anne, he certainly rallied around Otto Frank during their time in Auschwitz and became an important source of strength to him.

⁹⁵ *Editor note:* Anne attended her 6e Montessorischool from when she first arrived in Amsterdam in 1934 until she was forced to leave it in 1941 and go with Margot and other Jewish children to the Jewish Lyceum on Voormalige Stadstimmertuinen. Please also see endnotes 34 and 35.

⁹⁶ *Editor note:* As a reminder from my earlier endnote 33, the historian Rian Verhoeven runs a walking tour of Merwedeplein and the surrounding *Rivierenbuurt:* https://www.annefrankwalkingtour.com/

⁹⁷ *Editor note:* The first patent for a ballpoint pen was issued in 1888 to John Loud, an American inventor. From the following Wikipedia article, we learn that RAF pilots used them during the Second World War: https://en.wikipedia.org/wiki/Ballpoint_pen

Tim Whittome

⁹⁸ It does not appear from the program that I still have that we saw the Wendy Kesselman "newly adapted" version of this play. When I saw *The Diary of Anne Frank* recently at the Seattle Children's Theater, I did see the updated version.

⁹⁹ Please see our website resources for further information on the competition for and placement of the Anne Frank saplings in the United States.

¹⁰⁰ At the time, this organization was known as the Washington State Holocaust Research Center: https://holocaustcenterseattle.org/

There is a link to an "Anne Frank Tree" page on this site.

ENDNOTES

Anne mentions the horse chestnut tree directly in only three diary entries (February 23, 1944, April 18, 1944, and May 13, 1944); however, it is clear from some of her other entries on nature that she would have viewed the vastness of the tree at that time as being emblematic of the freedom that she longed for. For the rest of us, the saplings are an important connection to Anne and a visible reminder of the restorative power of nature.

Wikipedia references a speech given by Otto Frank in 1968 in which he recalls how Anne "never took an interest in nature," but that "she longed for it during that time when she felt like a caged bird. She only found consolation in thinking about nature." In *Roses from the Earth* by Carol Ann Lee, we learn how Anne's cousin Buddy Elias also noted that Anne had not been very interested in nature when she was younger and prior to her going into hiding. Ms. Lee references Otto giving an interview in which he explains how his younger daughter was not even interested in touring Amsterdam; however, she *did* like going to the beach at Zandvoort.

With reference to this latter point, Anne includes a supporting picture of herself and Margot in her diary that had been taken earlier on the beach at Zandvoort. Given that Anne says that the picture was taken when Margot was fourteen years old, we can presumably date it to sometime during the summer 1940. Although the Germans had recently invaded and occupied the Netherlands, Jews could still visit the beach this first summer.

Anne's growing interest in nature while in hiding was likely the result of the stress, the loneliness, and the need to focus on something in her life that was under natural and consistent (if seasonably changeable) control. I view the changing chestnut tree as Anne's natural clock, a sad reminder of the world outside, and of something that remained inherently beautiful against the backdrop of Jewish persecution, Nazi atrocities, deportations, and the Allied air raids (accompanied by Nazi antiaircraft fire) that scared Anne beyond measure, and which took her outside her more normal comfort zone.

Readers may be interested to learn that Etty Hillesum's diaries show a similar communing with the natural world. Anne's heightened interest in nature and also her love for pleasant sounds (such as emanated from the bells of the nearby Westertoren) were probably not that unusual given the awful context of the Nazi occupation of the Netherlands and the oppressive reality of having to hide in restricted surroundings. Remember that in the Secret Annex, the outside air could only arrive through cracks in windows that, otherwise, had to remain closed. As noted in the previous chapter of our book, Otto describes how the only "good" part of the later train journey to Kamp Westerbork for Anne was that of being able to see the Dutch countryside flashing by. Such natural feelings invigorated her again within the camp itself, but let's not rhapsodize unduly on either point.

[102] This is an example of the weird connections that those of us with Asperger syndrome often make to understand our world. Simon Rhodes talks more about the Westerkerk church later in this anthology.

[103] Readers may like to read *Second Time Foster Child* by Toni Hoy. In this work, Ms. Hoy compares how she was viewed as one of the "stinking parents" by child-welfare authorities in Illinois with the epithet of "stinking Jews" as used by the Nazis to further their prejudicial agenda. She and I talked briefly over email about the comparisons that could be made between the dehumanizing of parents in child welfare proceedings and the dehumanizing of the Jews by the Nazis. She says that I am one of the few people to corroborate her feelings on the issue which shows both the risk and the rarity inherent to doing so. While Ms. Hoy toned down what she originally wanted to write, I chose *not* to in my *Denied! Failing Cordelia* trilogy.

Pine Delgado

[104] *Editor note:* Please see our website resources for further information relating to the authenticity of Anne's diary.

Sondra Learn

[105] *Editor note:* When I decided to revisit the 1959 *Diary of Anne Frank* movie as part of preparing this anthology, I found it to be more disappointing than I remembered feeling when I first watched it many years ago. Maybe, it is because I now know so much more about Anne than I did and can now see the flaws in the movie and its Hollywood portrayal of Anne. One argument that I have heard is that the audience at the time were sick of learning about the Holocaust and needed a production that was both faithful to the story *and* unaccountably optimistic. As a side note on the production, readers may find Jillian Cantor's depiction of her fictional Margot's reaction to the film in *Margot* to be compelling.

[106] *Editor note:* There are many of these that are worthwhile watching. *Anne Frank: The Whole Story* with Ben Kingsley as Otto and Hannah Taylor Gordon as Anne traces the story of the Franks, the van Pelses, and Fritz Pfeffer before their time in hiding and then beyond their arrest in the Secret Annex. I also really like the television series, *The Diary of Anne Frank* with Iain Glen as Otto and Ellie Kendrick as Anne.

[107] *Editor note:* I did this also with the books that I read. I found most of my girlfriends in the classics written by Jane Austen, George Eliot, and the Brontë sisters. I remarked earlier that I think that Elizabeth Bennet from *Pride and Prejudice* was to Anne as Anne Elliot from *Persuasion* was to Margot. Other suggestive parallels that sprang to mind could be that of comparing Anne to Marianne Dashwood in Jane Austen's *Sense and Sensibility* and Margot to Marianne's older sister Elinor. Let us not run away with some of these associations!

[108] *Editor note:* Please review endnotes 99, 100, and 101, for further information regarding Anne's horse chestnut tree.

[109] *Editor note: The Diary of Anne Frank* was first adapted from Anne's diary in 1955 by Frances Goodrich and Albert Hackett and opened on Broadway on October 5. This decorated husband-and-wife team then wrote the script for the 1959 film directed by George Stevens and starring Millie Perkins as Anne. The original play was then "newly adapted" by Wendy Kesselman in 1997. This is the version that most of us probably see today. Our website resources contain further information from the Anne Frank Fonds in Basel on the various adaptations of Anne's diary.

[110] *Editor note:* Sondra chose to direct the original Goodrich and Hackett 1955 version of *The Diary of Anne Frank.*

Please review the following archived page from the Theatre Burlington on this production: https://www.theatreburlington.on.ca/the-diary-of-anne-frank/

I was also able to build a catalog reference for this production:

> *The Diary of Anne Frank.* By Frances Goodrich and Albert Hackett. Dir. Sondra Learn. Perf. Melina Zaccaria (Anne), Michael Hannigan (Otto), and Carla Zabek (Edith). Theatre Burlington, Burlington, ON. February 2014.

Readers will recall Melina Zaccaria's interview comments about having played Anne Frank in Sondra's production from earlier in this anthology.

[111] *Editor note:* After reading Sondra's piece, I found the poem on the All Poetry website: https://allpoetry.com/poem/3272566-The-Lives-We-Never-Had-by-As-my-last-request

It looks as if this poem is credited to someone called *Heather*, but with no last name included. Although I have decided to retain Heather's layout (which has no punctuation), I have corrected a few typos that she used in the original. It is a beautiful piece and a fitting tribute.

Yvonne Leslie

[112] *Editor note:* As a reminder, the Nuremberg Laws had been promulgated in Germany in 1935. These laws separated the legal identity and standing of Jews from non-Jews and forbade inter-marriages and other contact. Jews were reduced to second-class status with heavy restrictions on almost every activity.

These laws extended to the occupied Netherlands in March 1942. As we have noted before, the Nazis were cunningly incremental in how they approached what they saw as the "Jewish problem." Their ultimate goal was still the total elimination of the Jews as a race and the total crushing and humiliation of Judaism as a religious identity. Please also see our website resources.

[113] *Editor note:* Yes, I totally agree with Yvonne. Most of the wisdom that we now attribute to Anne comes from her many 1944 diary entries when she was fourteen and fifteen years old.

[114] *Editor note:* Please see Anne's diary entry for September 27, 1942, where she contrasts her description of Margot as being "naturally good, kind and clever, perfection itself" with the fact that "I seem to have enough mischief for the two of us."

A little later in her diary entry for October 14, 1942, Anne wonders if her sister believed that she (Anne) could be considered as "ugly"—an argument that engages some fans of the sisters to this day. Margot replies that her sister is "okay" and that she has "nice eyes."

This insecurity continues in an October 30, 1943, diary entry where Anne claims unconvincingly not to be "jealous" or "envious" of Margot. To confuse matters, this diary entry is also oddly attributed by Melissa Müller as November 7, 1942, in accord with what she argues is the order of Anne's revised version B. Situations like this make trying to validate the editorial and publishing integrity of Anne's diary very difficult. When I checked the recent *Collected Works* edition of Anne's diary, I did not find any November 7, 1942, version B date. I also did not see Anne's comments about her sister in her original version A diary entry for November 7, 1942. Unfortunately, and to confuse things even further on this point, Anne's comments about her sister *are* included as part of this November date in the initial version C edition of the diary (Otto's edited version) that was first published in English in 1952.

If the editors of the recently published *Collected Works* are correct—and I have no reason to doubt them—I *did* find the October 30, 1943, entry included as part of their publishing of Anne's revised diary. It is sandwiched between her revised entries for October 29, 1942 and November 9, 1942. It would *appear* that the editors of the *Definitive Edition* of Anne's diary have accepted that Anne must have added the entry to her revised diary with the attributed date of October 30, 1943. How earlier editors of the diary reached their conclusion of November 7, 1942, is unclear to me.

Notwithstanding, I think that we can still conclude that Anne was definitely insecure with respect to how best to answer the question regarding her own attractiveness. Many other young girls both during Anne's time and since have asked themselves similar questions. On the other hand, Anne had clearly convinced herself by the time that she wrote her first diary entries that she was extremely popular among the boys of her acquaintance.

[115]   *Editor note:* Yvonne is referring here to Helmut ("Hello") Silberberg. Anne introduces him in her diary entry for June 24, 1942. Much of what we love and miss about Anne can be found in these early diary entries.

[116]   *Editor note:* Please see Anne's diary entry for June 20, 1942, where she sets out her reasons for writing and for her choice of *Kitty* as her pen friend.

[117]   *Editor note:* Both Melissa Müller in her biography of Anne and Jacqueline van Maarsen in her first book about her friendship with Anne convey the impression that Anne was very happy at the Jewish Lyceum. Although we have no diary entries documenting her time on a daily basis at the Montessorischool with which to compare her two school experiences, Anne does convey in her diary for her time at the Jewish Lyceum as much contentment as was possible given the darkening circumstances. The famous story about the teacher, Mr. Keesing, giving Anne an essay assignment with the title of "'Quack, Quack, Quack,' Said Mistress Chatterback" tells us a lot about her and how she must have been regarded at the school. Anne relates the story in her diary entry for June 21, 1942. This said, the school picture that we have of Anne from that school year shows us a very thoughtful and worried young girl of twelve.

[118]   *Editor note:* Those who went into hiding were known as *onderduikers*. No one knew whether other children and teachers had been rounded up or had decided to hide after their absence was noted in the school. The Jewish Lyceum closed in 1943 for lack of pupils. Please see our website resources and endnote 66, for further information on the experiences of Jews in hiding.

[119] *Editor note:* I could not agree more with Yvonne on all her above points. In chapters 8–11 of Melissa Müller's *Anne Frank: The Biography*, she presents us with an extremely compelling overview of the pressures on Anne's early adolescence in the extraordinary circumstances of being trapped, confined, and surrounded primarily by her parents and other adults.

[120] *Editor note:* As Yvonne does here, I too appreciate Edith, and I feel that Anne unfairly maligns her mother in her diary. Edith Frank did everything she could for her daughters, and we can see this selfless parenting on display when she was with Anne and Margot at Birkenau. Edith starved herself to feed her two daughters, and if this is *not* the essence of motherhood, then I do not know what is.

I do not suspect Otto Frank of pursuing tactics commensurate with what is now known in certain legal and therapeutic circles as "parental alienation." In other words, I do *not* think he intentionally tried to drive a wedge between Anne and her mother. He viewed himself more as a peacemaker but allowed himself to understand his younger daughter in ways that Edith could not. Anne, in common with other girls of her age both at the time and since, ardently sought the approval and validation of her father in everything. This said, it must have hurt Edith that Anne always chose to seek comfort during air raids from her father and not from her mother.

[121] *Editor note:* Anne discusses this in her diary entry for January 6, 1944.

[122] *Editor note:* Although Anne never changes her opinion entirely during their time in hiding, she does show *some* understanding for her "tender and affectionate" mother in her diary entry for January 2, 1944, and she blames their "sad circumstances" for her mother being both "nervous and irritable" as well as "often short" with her.

[123] Editor note: Rootje (Rosa) de Winter saw Anne and Margot and their mother extensively in Auschwitz and also informed Otto of his wife's death on January 6, 1945.

[124] *Editor note:* Although there is no obvious proof, it is possible that Anne was not being entirely honest in her diary entries when she criticizes her mother so ruthlessly or that she was merely going through a "phase" as her father believed. Then again, it is possible to argue how the urgent pragmatism of having to survive at Auschwitz may have made for "strange bedfellows," as Shakespeare suggests for two of his characters in *The Tempest*.

Contrary to the evidence of Anne's diary, it is worth mentioning that Bloeme Evers-Emden later told Willy Lindwer that she saw little evidence of any discord between Edith and Anne while they were at Birkenau.

One could also argue both that the choices in Birkenau were sufficiently limited to the extent that Anne and her mother needed to reconcile *and* that she may have exaggerated some of her earlier disdain for literary effect. Anne is justly famous for her gregariousness and generous warmth of feeling and in the traumatic circumstances of being arrested, transported, and then confined to a concentration camp such as Auschwitz-Birkenau, it seems likely that the underlying love she truly felt for her mother was allowed to come to the fore. Also, Otto was in a different part of the sprawling camp complex. From how Yvonne expresses herself in her next speculative point, I think that she and I would probably agree on the real strength of Anne's relationship with her mother.

[125] *Editor note:* Theo Coster wondered this in *We All Wore Stars*, and reports how their former classmate, Hannah Goslar, asked their primary school teacher, Mrs. Kuperus, whether she saw anything of literary promise in Anne at their old 6e Montessorischool. Based on her response, which I included as an epigraph in my introductory chapter, Mrs. Kuperus would agree with Yvonne here that the circumstances of Anne being in hiding would have certainly matured her much faster than would have happened if she had had a more normal adolescence. This should not surprise us in all honesty.

[126] *Editor note:* Please see Anne's diary entries for March 20 and 22, 1944.

[127] *Editor note:* Anne describes "more or less" what she wrote to her father in her diary entry for May 5, 1944. As I intimated in my own piece, many a parent has received a similar hurtful letter (tweet, message or email) in their time. Would Anne have decided to "publish" this letter *had* she reached this date in her own revisions and been able to publish her own work? This also dovetails with what I was saying earlier regarding how the diary we read today is drawn from editorial assumptions made with respect to how best to edit and merge the original A and revised B versions that Anne has left us with.

[128] *Editor note:* Anne relates her first tentative and then lengthier kisses with Peter in her diary entries for April 16 and 28, 1944.

[129] *Editor note:* Anne uses the German word *Knutscherei* to convey what has been translated as "necking" in her diary entry for May 5, 1944.

[130] *Editor note:* Please see Anne's diary entries for April 28, 1944, and July 15, 1944.

[131] *Editor note:* Please see Anne's diary entry for May 2, 1944.

[132] *Editor note:* Much attention has been given to this. As part of a March 28, 1944, radio broadcast on Radio Oranje (which was based in London during the Second World War and referred to by Anne in her diary entry for March 29), a cabinet member of the Dutch government in exile, Gerrit Bolkestein, announced to the Dutch that all diaries and other journals should be preserved as living testimony of the Nazi occupation and as vital wartime documentation. Anne was inspired to revise her original diary entries. According to the Anne Frank Huis and Museum, Anne did not begin the revision of her diary until May 20, 1944, which is interesting as it would indicate that it either took time to find Anne the paper that she needed or that she possibly lost interest in the idea for a while. It would seem *likelier* that she just needed the time to collect her thoughts, that it was more important for her to continue writing "original" entries, and that the loose paper that she would have needed was indeed scarce.

[133] *Editor note:* Anne famously discusses her parents' complex marriage in her diary entry for February 8, 1944. Anne intuitively sensed that her father did not care for his wife on any romantic level. Readers can now read four added paragraphs (across five original pages) from this date that were unknown until 1998. They had previously been concealed or suppressed by Otto for many decades but with the permission of the Anne Frank Fonds in Basel, they have now finally been included in the recent *Collected Works* edition of Anne's diary.

[134] *Editor note:* Anne wrote about the presence of "two Annes" in her diary entry for April 28, 1944. She wonders whether Peter was aware of this.

[135] *Editor note:* This is probably Anne's most famous quote and comes from her diary entry for July 15, 1944. While I could not agree more with Yvonne on this point, I do recognize just how difficult it is for many of Anne's more ardent fans to talk about this issue given that it is often cited as the foundational core of her revered idealism and legacy. I referred to Eva Schloss's view on this earlier (endnote 84).

Simon Rhodes

[136] *Editor note:* Based on the evidence of Anne's diary (such as in her long diary entry for April 11, 1944), an awful lot of people rattled at this bookcase without being able to open it or the door behind. As a reminder, the bookcase was designed and built

by the then warehouse foreman, Johan Voskuijl. He was Bep Voskuijl's father and Joop van Wijk-Voskuijl's grandfather.

[137] *Editor note:* It seems likely that Simon may have seen a 1999 reconstruction of the Secret Annex. My understanding is that the rooms are now largely empty, and that Otto wished for things to remain this way. Height markings on the wall remind us how Anne and Margot grew during their time in hiding. Elsewhere, Anne's pictures from magazines of members of the British and Dutch royal families and various movie stars are also protected on the wall of Anne and Dr. Pfeffer's bedroom. We need to remind ourselves that the Germans typically cleared out homes they raided and then sent any valuable or useful stuff back to Germany to be sold for their war effort. See my earlier reference to Abraham Puls on this depressing topic (endnote 69).

[138] *Editor note:* The bells of the Westertoren chimed quarterly and provided Anne with a reassuring and familiar way of marking the progress of time while she was in the Secret Annex. The Westerkerk was built between 1620 and 1631, but its accompanying tower (the Westertoren) was not completed until 1638. The bells were cast in 1658.

Anne references the Westertoren bells in her diary entries for July 11, 1942, March 25, 1943, and August 10, 1943. In the last of these, Anne is upset that the Germans have removed the bells so that they could be melted down to raise money for their war effort. Anne expresses her hope that they might be replaced with some cheaper material. As Simon goes on to say, Anne saw both the horse chestnut tree and the Westertoren as evidence of the freer world outside that she longed to rejoin.

How hard it must have been that the air from the outside chiefly only appeared through cracks in windows! Anne could *sense* the life that existed outside the Annex, but she could not actually *live* it.

For a brief history of the Westerkerk, please review the following website: https://www.amsterdam.info/westerkerk/history/

I also found this interesting website, Dutch Amsterdam, that *finally* allowed me to unravel the important difference between the Wester*kerk* as the *church* and the Wester*toren* as comprising the *tower* and *bells*: https://www.dutchamsterdam.nl/167-westerkerk-amsterdam#Westerkerk_and_Westertoren

[139] *Editor note:* Simon makes some very interesting points here, and this paragraph was one of the many that my contributors wrote for this anthology that had me thinking more deeply about the subject matter.

Kirsi Lehtola

[140] *Editor note:* I am sure that Kirsi is referring here to the 1959 movie as directed by George Stevens.

[141] *Editor note:* Sadly, there are plenty of websites mentioned in our website resources that are dedicated to the layout of Auschwitz-Birkenau and to displaying grim pictures of its many infamous buildings and entrances.

When I first decided to pursue this project, I was not sure whether I wanted contributions that included visits to Auschwitz unless the contributing writer had visited the site as part of following in Anne's footsteps. Kirsi has more than fulfilled my expectations in this regard and we should be grateful to her that she felt able to take this journey.

[142] *Editor note:* This is confirmed by others such as Carol Ann Lee in *Roses from the Earth*. Anne, Margot, and their mother were sent to Block 29 in Birkenau (Auschwitz II). Birkenau was both the main women's camp at Auschwitz *and* the location of the more infamous of the gas chambers. My earlier endnote 74 contains additional information on the infamous railway spur line that led directly into Birkenau. Again, please see our website resources for further information on the infamous history of Auschwitz-Birkenau.

Priscilla Smits

[143] *Editor note:* This is an approximate English-translated reference to Anne's relief at being able to write in her diary entry for March 16, 1944. She also talks extensively about the power of writing in her diary entry for April 5, 1944.

[144] *Editor note:* Priscilla is referring to Anne's short stories and vignettes that we can now read in her *Tales from the Secret Annex* as first published by Doubleday in 1984 and then in occasionally updated English translations since then. My own copy was translated into English by Susan Massotty and is also included in *Anne Frank: The Collected Works*.

[145] *Editor note:* The adventures of Joop ter Heul were among some of Anne's favorite stories. As noted earlier (endnote 54), Anne's choice of "Kitty" as her diary friend, was probably inspired by the fictional Joop's friend Kitty Francken.

[146] *Editor note:* As noted earlier, many of Anne's friends have published their own recollections of the Franks, their own childhoods, their wartime experiences, and their lives after the war. Miep Gies has also written about her life and her time helping to provide for the occupants of the Secret Annex. Bep Voskuijl's life has been addressed by her son Joop van Wijk-Voskuijl. Please see our bibliography.

[147] *Editor note:* I think that Priscilla is referring here to the first 1947 Dutch edition of *Het achterhuis*. I can imagine that it is expensive to buy. When I was writing this, I discovered several copies on Abebooks with one listed as high as $17,500: https://www.abebooks.com/book-search/title/het-achterhuis/first-edition/

The Anne Frank Huis and Museum says that the first Dutch edition of Anne's diary had a print run of just over 3,000 copies:

> *After the first edition (3,036 copies), the second edition (6,830) followed in December 1947 and the third edition (10,500 copies) in February 1948. (https://www.annefrank.org/en/anne-frank/diary/publication-diary/)*

[148] *Editor note:* The ceremony for the unveiling of the statue to Anne on Merwedeplein took place on July 9, 2005; this story was covered earlier in endnotes 32 and 49.

[149] *Editor note:* At first, I thought that Priscilla must have been referring here to the 1955 play (*The Diary of Anne Frank*). In fact, there *is* a recent 2014 play called *Anne* by Leon de Winter and Jessica Durlacher and I was able to discover more about it on the Anne Frank Fonds website:

> *Finally, in 2014, almost 60 years after the first dramatization, Anne by Leon de Winter and Jessica Durlacher brought a completely new play to the stage. The play is embedded in a framework plot: after the war, Anne Frank tells a publisher about her Diary and takes the audience back to the year 1942 when she is given the notebook for her 13th birthday. While the role of Otto is shifted slightly into the background, the complexity of the relationship between mother and daughter is given more emphasis in the version by de Winter and Durlacher. The story also goes beyond the Diary. The audience is witness to the raid on the secret annex and watches as the eight*

people in hiding are led away. The story of Anne and Margot Frank's suffering ends with their death in the Bergen-Belsen concentration camp. (https://www.annefrank.ch/en/diary/adaptations)

I then confirmed with Priscilla that this was the play that she did in fact see. Priscilla has included some pictures for this anthology of her meeting Hannah Goslar, Jacqueline van Maarsen, and Nanette Blitz-Konig before and after the performance. Despite my best efforts, I cannot find any English translation of the play, while the Dutch version appears to be out-of-print. This looks like an interesting adaptation.

[150] *Editor note:* Both Jacqueline van Maarsen and Nanette Blitz-Konig have written Holocaust memoirs. Readers interested in their journeys can find their books listed in our bibliography.

[151] *Editor note:* Bernhard ("Buddy") Elias was the son of Otto's sister Helene, or Leni and the first cousin of both Anne and Margot. Like Anne, Buddy was a passionate ice skater. He later had a stage and television acting career and listings for his work can be found on IMDb and on his Wikipedia page. He became an honorary president of the Anne Frank Fonds in 1996 and remained in that position until his death in 2015.

There is a lot more about Buddy's interesting life and career on the Anne Frank Fonds website: https://www.annefrank.ch/en/family/buddy-elias

[152] *Editor note:* Buddy died on March 16, 2015. He was almost ninety years old.

[153] *Editor note:* Please see our bibliography and Joop's author website (https://annefranktheuntoldstory.com/) for further information on *Anne Frank, the Untold Story.*

[154] *Editor note:* The book that Priscilla is referring to is *Anne Frank Remembered* by Miep Gies and Alison Leslie Gold.

[155] *Editor note:* Miep Gies died on January 11, 2010, a month before her 101st birthday.

[156] *Editor note:* This brief film is quite stunning, but it was not intentional as it was caught by accident by a wedding photographer covering a wedding party. Nevertheless, it is hauntingly beautiful and the only known moving film of Anne to exist. She looks as animated and curious as we imagine her to be. I will not, however, provide a direct link to this film because of possible copyright restrictions in place.

Interested readers can find the clip on the internet; it was also unveiled as part of the *Anne Frank Remembered* documentary that is widely available on DVD and Blu-ray.

[157]   *Editor note:* Please refer to our website resources for further information on Anne's 6e Montessorischool as well as my earlier endnote 34.

[158]   *Editor note:* Priscilla kindly went to the site of the Jewish Lyceum on Voormalige Stadstimmertuinen in Amsterdam and took some photographs on my behalf for this book. The crooked Jewish star is a haunting reminder of the oppression of the Jews during the Nazi occupation. As the sign implies, the school was only open for a few years from 1941–1943 as there were not enough Jewish children left to educate after that date. Please also see endnote 35.

Fr. John Neiman

[159]   *Editor note:* Please see our bibliography, our website resources, and plenty of my other endnotes for further information on this important subject.

[160]   Birsfelden is a suburb of Basel and amazingly close to the Swiss border with Germany. In fact, it is a mere stone's throw away with the Swiss-German border running down the middle of the River Rhine. This is testimony to the fact that Otto appears to have always viewed himself as a proud *German* however much he despised the *Nazism* that had corrupted his native country's soul.

[161]   *Editor note:* Otto said much the same thing to Cara Wilson-Granat. Although understandable from Otto's point of view, the persistence of many of his correspondents, including Father John, Ryan Cooper, and Cara, clearly fulfilled a desire to "connect" as E. M. Forster once noted in *Howards End*. Cara feels this to be important to this day. The urge to write can sometimes be overwhelming (as my fellow writers and I can attest to), and I think that it must have surely touched Otto on some level that he had persistent correspondents wanting to know more about his two daughters.

[162]   *Editor note:* A *Kapo* had a horrible position in the camp of being an SS-assigned prisoner empowered to supervise other prisoners and to do the Nazis' bidding. As related to Willy Lindwer in *The Last Seven Months of Anne Frank*, Rachel van Amerongen-Frankfoorder identifies a *Kapo* (Hanka) in Birkenau who might have been as young as sixteen or seventeen years old.

[163]   *Editor note:* Peter van Pels seems to have "flourished" emotionally at Auschwitz as he became a source of mature strength to Otto in ways that would have surely

delighted and surprised Anne had she been able to hear about them. According to Melissa Müller, Peter worked in the camp post office. This sounds absurd when you think about how one could even have existed. I think we can reliably assume that it was *not* for the benefit of the prisoners but only for the SS.

164   *Editor note:* Melissa Müller thinks that he may have died earlier than this but that his death was not recorded until May 5. This date, of course, has also become the day that the Dutch have chosen to celebrate their liberation from Nazi occupation each year. I have provided a link to Mauthausen in our website resources. I learned recently that Mauthausen had a mobile gas chamber which was fortunately rare for German concentration camps outside Poland.

165   *Editor note:* Otto returned to Amsterdam having journeyed via Odessa on the Black Sea and Marseille in France. One must remember that fighting and Allied bombing remained a disrupting factor in significant parts of Europe through to the chaotic end of the Second World War in May 1945. Trains and other modes of transportation as well as postal communication would have been scarce and subject to continuous disruption as other Allied needs took over. We also need to be aware that Otto was not strong, that he was starving, and that he had many health issues to contend with before he could return home in any fit state.

166   *Editor note:* Otto Frank ended up living with the Gies family for seven years, his former home on the Merwedeplein having long since been taken over by another family.

167   *Editor note:* I have seen the date of July 18, or July 19, 1945, in both *Anne Frank: The Biography* by Melissa Müller and *The Hidden Life of Otto Frank* by Carol Ann Lee. Lientje and Janny Brilleslijper confirmed their deaths to Otto having seen both girls in Bergen-Belsen.

168   *Editor note:* Readers interested in learning more about Fritzi's story and her relationship with her daughter can follow what Eva has to say in her two books, *Eva's Story* and *After Auschwitz*. In *Eva's Story*, there are several contributory chapters written by Fritzi that are interlaced with chapters documenting her daughter's experiences both before and during the war. Otto and Fritzi could at least talk to each other about their shared trauma in Auschwitz, which would have been of some comfort to both.

169   *Editor note:* Otto donated Anne's diary and other papers to the Dutch government (the Netherlands National Institute for War Documentation as it then was; it is now

the NIOD Institute for War, Holocaust and Genocide Studies) as part of his will in 1980. Anne's diaries must have been extremely exciting for Father John to see.

[170]   *Editor note:* Readers interested in learning more about the B'nai B'rith Jewish organization can consult the following: https://www.bnaibrith.org/los-angeles.html

[171]   *Editor note:* I could not find much information on this organization (although others here have mentioned it) except from a page on Wikipedia devoted to the American Gathering of Jewish Holocaust Survivors: https://en.wikipedia.org/wiki/American_Gathering_of_Jewish_Holocaust_Survivors_and_their_Descendants

[172]   *Editor note:* This famous quote is from Anne's diary entry for April 5, 1944.

Ryan Cooper

[173]   *Editor note:* I found several useful websites documenting the experiences of Jehovah's Witnesses during the Holocaust. This first one is from the United States Holocaust Memorial Museum:

> https://encyclopedia.ushmm.org/content/en/article/nazi-persecution-of-jehovahs-witnesses

A second resource is from Wikipedia:

> https://en.wikipedia.org/wiki/Persecution_of_Jehovah%27s_Witnesses_in_Nazi_Germany

[174]   *Editor note:* Readers interested in learning more about the Jehovah's Witnesses as a religious organization may like to review their official website: https://www.jw.org/en/.

[175]   *Editor note:* This is an interesting contrast to how Otto Frank seemed keen to stop others from further writing to him. I have not seen the letter, but I am sure that Otto will have been intrigued to learn about Ryan's past as a Jehovah's Witness. Otto would have been familiar with what happened to non-Jews (including Witnesses) during the Holocaust.

[176]   *Editor note:* As referred to earlier, readers can consult *The Hidden Life of Otto Frank* by Carol Ann Lee if they wish to learn more about Otto's life. Ryan has also published his own work on his rewarding friendship with Otto. *We Never Said*

Goodbye: Memories of Otto Frank was published by Amphion Publishing in early February 2021, and is currently available on Amazon.com.

[177] *Editor note:* We should be grateful, I think, that the original was kept in a safe location! Anne's diary and other papers are now with the Dutch government or on display at the Anne Frank Huis and Museum in Amsterdam. Her original plaid red-and-white checkered diary is on display in the museum's Diary Room along with rotating loose pages from her revised B diary, two separate school notebooks of her "favorite quotations," and her "tales." Joy earlier mentioned seeing the red-and-white checkered diary at the Anne Frank Museum as one of the highlights of her visit to Amsterdam.

[178] *Editor note:* Melissa Müller in her biography of Anne suggests that even the train journey to Kamp Westerbork would have seemed a relief to her after being cooped up for twenty-five months. As was mentioned earlier, Otto remembers how Anne was glued to the window, looking at all the passing scenes. At Kamp Westerbork itself, family members may have worked in different locations during the day, but they could get together briefly at night. I would hesitate to argue that Kamp Westerbork was great, but it was probably bearable compared to the other camps … and providing you could avoid the cattle cars.

[179] *Editor note:* Rootje (Rosa) de Winter is an important source of information for what would later happen to Edith Frank in Birkenau and would have the difficult task of informing Otto that his wife had died in delirious circumstances on January 6, 1945. Carol Ann Lee would later be allowed to see Otto's diary that he started to write on his journey home as part of her research for *The Hidden Life of Otto Frank*. She records his reaction to this news. Considering what would happen in the years ahead regarding the publishing of his daughter's diary, we should take note of what Otto has to say here about Anne's "specialness":

> *Told of Edith's death on January 6, 1945, in the hospital, from weakness without suffering. Children October to Sudentenland [sic], very brave, especially Anne, miss special Anne.* (Otto Frank, *Diary*; Carol Ann Lee, *The Hidden Life of Otto Frank*)

[180] *Editor note:* Please see Anne's diary entry for May 2, 1943, where she describes the "attitude of the Annex residents toward the war."

[181] *Editor note:* My understanding is that writers and artists (chosen on a competitive basis) now use the former home of the Franks on Merwedeplein as a creative space for their endeavors.

[182]   *Editor note:* Melissa Müller researched quite a lot of interesting information on Hello Silberberg for her biography of Anne. As she so often does in her biography, Ms. Müller will suddenly disappear down a side road at unexpected, but always interesting, moments. Much of what she decides to tell us about Hello's life during the war (including his eventual liberation in Brussels on September 3, 1944) is interwoven into her account of Anne and her family being loaded onto the final train to Auschwitz from Westerbork. Both events happened on the same day and make for a heartbreaking contrast given what ultimately happened to the two of them. Brussels, Kamp Westerbork, and the two friends were just 168 miles apart at the time.

Colleen Snyman

[183]   *Editor note:* I have seen many aggrieved posters in Facebook groups about Anne Frank suggesting that her diary was considered inappropriate for them at a certain age. At least one male complained that Anne's diary was seen as not at all suitable for boys at *any* age. He attributed this to Anne's famous self-awareness of her personal development as a teenager. Colleen's account here of being too young at almost nine years old is the first time that I have learned of *girls* at this age being recommended against reading Anne's diary. Today, Anne's readership among young teenage girls is extremely high given the resonance of her self-awareness with their own. I cannot comment on how teenage boys are likely to read the same entries, but it must be hard for them to avoid Anne's diary given that *Diary of a Young Girl* is often a prescribed Holocaust book for teenagers to read in high school.

For what it is worth, there are "younger" versions of Anne's diary in publication and, of course, one can still find Otto's edited C version of the diary, with some of the more personal passages removed. In our bibliography, I have included an edition of Anne's diary with lots of graphics that are suitable for younger readers.

[184]   *Editor note:* Anne talks excitedly about the North African campaign in 1942 and the invasion of Italy in 1943 in her diary entries for November 5, 1942, November 9, 1942, July 16, 1943, and September 10, 1943.

I have links to key battles in the North Africa, El-Alamein, Sicily, and Italian campaigns in our website resources.

[185]   *Editor note:* This segregation takes place in Orthodox Judaism. I found one page on Gender Separation in Judaism on Wikipedia: https://en.wikipedia.org/wiki/Gender_separation_in_Judaism

A further interesting website would be this one run by Chabad.org: https://www.chabad.org/library/article_cdo/aid/160962/jewish/Separation-in-the-Synagogue.htm

[186] *Editor note:* Please see Anne's diary entry for June 14, 1942.

[187] *Editor note:* Please see Anne's diary entry for June 6, 1944.

[188] *Editor note:* As noted earlier, Melissa Müller covers the psychological impact of Anne's twenty-five months spent in hiding and the last seven months of her life very well in chapters 8–11 of *Anne Frank: The Biography*. This dovetails nicely with my comment about Anne Brontë's view of poetry in *Agnes Grey* earlier in this anthology—namely, that Anne Frank's diary entries form a collective body of "pillars of witness" to what she was feeling and the events going on around her at the time.

Amanda Tomkins

[189] *Editor note:* Anyone who tries to imagine how Anne Frank would have processed her experiences at Kamp Westerbork, Auschwitz-Birkenau, Bergen-Belsen is to be commended for their courage. When I was editing this anthology, a book by Beth Jacobs was brought to my attention—*Paper Sky* is an imagining of how Anne might have tried to continue writing her diary on scraps of paper and cardboard while she was at Kamp Westerbork. Ms. Jacobs then continues to explore this theme by having Anne mentally compose her diary as a series of dreams or nightmares while at Auschwitz and Bergen-Belsen. I found this work to be extremely creative and have added further publishing details to our bibliography. I especially appreciated the effective creativity of the "kitty kitty kitty kitty" sequence to mimic the traumatic rhythm of the transport train from Westerbork to Auschwitz.

What first drew me to asking Amanda to join me in this project was her decision to write to *Lieve Kitty* as Anne might have written to her from Bergen-Belsen and then to add the letter to a Anne Frank group posting on Facebook. I just *knew* that I had to invite her to join me on this project. Both Amanda and Beth Jacobs have captured Anne's style and what would have been the reality of her experiences in each of the above camps.

[190] *Editor note: Krätze* is scabies, and I imagine that Anne, who hated fleas, would have detested this.

[191] *Editor note:* "Anne" is referring here to the scabies block or barrack.

[192] *Editor note:* The *Appellplatz* (Appell) was the daily roll call that the Nazis used to maintain repressive order in the camps.

Anne and Margot were both selected at the end of October or early November 1944 for transportation into Germany (Bergen-Belsen).

[193] *Editor note:* According to Melissa Müller, the camp was four miles away from the railway station. This would not have been an easy walk (march) for Anne and Margot in their condition. We have established that while Bergen-Belsen was technically not a death camp with gas chambers on site, the conditions became so bad in the months leading up to the camp's liberation as to make the distinction somewhat moot.

[194] *Editor note:* As established earlier, Hanneli Goslar was in a more accommodating part of the camp for prisoners hoping to be exchanged for important German prisoners. Hannah would have been more than surprised to see Anne as she believed her friend had escaped to Switzerland. I am sure that Anne in her turn would have been both excited and sad to see her earliest friend in Amsterdam.

[195] *Editor note:* The tattoo numbers for Anne and Margot are both unknown but according to both Melissa Müller in her biography of Anne and the Anne Frank Holocaust website, they probably ranged between A-25060 and A-25271: https://annefrankholocaust1.weebly.com/diary-and-tattoo-id-number.html

Recent research sponsored by the Anne Frank Huis and Museum and conducted by Erika Prins has cast some doubt on this wide span of numbers. She believes that Anne, Margot, and Edith Frank were tattooed with numbers between A-25109 and A-25116. Ms. Prins was able to work this out by knowing that the deportees were grouped by the first letter of their surname and then eliminating those—usually survivors—whose numbers were known for sure. With thanks to Anne Talvaz for sending me the following title in Dutch of Ms. Prins work:

Onderzoeksverslag naar het verblijf van de acht onderduikers uit het achterhuis in de kampen.

Erika Prins has also uploaded her research to the internet:

https://hethistorischbedrijf.nl/app/uploads/2017/10/2018-02-23-Onderzoeksverslag-voor-website-.pdf

Writing as Anne, Amanda has provided us with a random tattoo number here, but her dramatic point remains the same. During the time of my daughter's case in Los

Angeles, I was identified by a case number and defined by a letter on a file. Such anonymous and demonizing "branding" always made me think of the tattooing of Jewish prisoners in Auschwitz.

Anne Talvaz

[196]   *Editor note:* I have found *Anne Frank and After* (part of a Dutch Holocaust Literature in Historical Perspective published by the Amsterdam University Press) to offer a very strong perspective on the absence of enough or adequate words surrounding any attempt to understand the Holocaust.

[197]   *Editor note:* Anne is referring here to how she is reading Anne Frank's diary. Anne (Frank) adds the comment with an accompanying photograph of herself to her original red-and-white checkered diary. She dates the comment as October 10, 1942.

[198]   *Editor note:* Anne talks with uninhibited abandon about her classmates in her diary entry for June 15, 1942.

[199]   Anne uses the following two illustrative entries from Anne Frank's diary for June 13, 1944 (mocking Mrs. van Daan for what she sees as her unaware *self-referential* complaints about Anne's alleged "stupidity," "pushiness," and the "shortness" of her dresses) and July 21, 1944 (mocking Hitler's new rule for German soldiers being able to shoot their superiors for any sign of treason).

[200]   *Editor note:* Anne describes herself as a "bundle of contradictions" in her diary entry for July 21, 1944, before explaining herself further in her next and final diary entry (August 1, 1944). Interestingly, Bob Dylan, in his recently released "I Contain Multitudes," refers in one of the song's lines to his affinity for Anne Frank. In a post on a Bob Dylan Facebook group page, I alluded to Anne describing herself as a "bundle of contradictions" to support my argument that Dylan views himself in much the same way. I included Dylan's comments about Anne in a recent interview with *The New York Times* as an earlier epigraph.

[201]   *Editor note:* Anne is referring here to Miep Gies and to "Elli Vossen" (now known to us as Bep Voskuijl).

[202]   *Editor note:* Anne may not have been aware that Otto and Fritzi wrote back to everyone who wrote to them.

203 *Editor note:* Ernst Schnabel's book *The Footsteps of Anne Frank* (as it is now named in a reprint edition after being known as *Anne Frank: A Portrait in Courage* when it was first published in 1958) is a big favorite of most of us writing for this book.

204 *Editor note:* Otto Frank died in Birsfelden, Switzerland, on August 19, 1980, and Victor Kugler in Toronto, Canada, on December 14, 1981.

205 *Editor note:* Bep Voskuijl died May 6, 1983. Further details on Bep's role as a helper and her life both before and after the war can be found in *Anne Frank, the Untold Story* by Joop van Wijk and Jeroen De Bruyn. Please see our bibliography for publishing details on *The Revised Critical Edition* and *Anne Frank Remembered* by Miep Gies and Alison Leslie Gold.

206 *Editor note:* Jacqueline (Jacque) van Maarsen has written two important books about her friendship with Anne. Her first book, *My Name is Anne, She Said, Anne Frank*, looks at their brief and truncated friendship in 1941 and 1942. Carol Ann Lee has adapted this book for younger readers. Jacque's second book, *Inheriting Anne Frank*, explores her feelings surrounding her angry dispute with Eva Schloss over claims that the latter knew Anne well when both were living on Merwedeplein. Jacque believes that the public and the Anne Frank Foundation in Amsterdam were being misled with widely disseminated claims of Eva being a "childhood chum" of Anne. As I have yet to read of Eva's direct response to this controversy, I would be loath to take any final position on the matter. I am sensitive, however, to Jacque's argument that Anne's name and legacy do *not* end up being exploited commercially; indeed, this is an issue that anyone wanting to write about Anne her family will likely have to address and resolve at some point in their publishing journey. I know that some of us have talked about it for this anthology and I am sure it will become even more of a discussion point once this book is published.

207 *Editor note:* *The Attic: The Hiding of Anne Frank* stars Lisa Jacobs as Anne and is based on *Anne Frank Remembered* by Miep Gies. It was released as a television movie in 1988. *The Diary of Anne Frank* with Melissa Gilbert as Anne was released as a television movie in 1980 and is based on the Albert Hackett and Frances Goodrich play *The Diary of Anne Frank*.

208 *Editor note:* As noted earlier, Oase (or Oasis in English) was one of the approved Jewish ice-cream parlors that Anne could visit when she was still free. Elsewhere on Anne Talvaz's journey through Anne's various former haunts in the Rivierenbuurt (River District), we must note that Google Earth *Street View* does not offer us a flattering view of the graffiti situation at the Montessorischool Anne Frank.

As I noted earlier (endnotes 33 and 96) there is an official walking tour of the Rivierenbuurt: https://www.annefrankwalkingtour.com/

[209] *Editor note:* When Anne was alive, this bookstore was known as Blankevoort's. It is now the Boekhandel Jimmink.

[210] *Editor note:* Anne made me aware as I was reviewing her story that there is a new book (currently in Dutch) by Rian Verhoeven about the inhabitants of Merwedeplein during the war. This may be in connection with the current exhibition at the Anne Frank Huis and Museum. From this book, we learn that there were Dutch fascists (members of the NSB) living in this otherwise very Jewish part of Amsterdam and that some of them tormented or attacked Jews on the street. In consequence, there was also retaliation against these same NSB members. Anne feels that this makes for an alarming contrast with how Anne Frank portrays her neighborhood in her diary. Likewise, she feels that Otto and Edith would have been painfully aware of the situation and understandably fearful for both Anne and Margot going to and from their respective schools in the neighborhood and playing with their friends.

[211] *Editor note:* Anne is referring here to both Hannah Pick-Goslar and Jacqueline van Maarsen. They are both still alive and in their nineties.

[212] *Editor note:* Anne is now properly memorialized not just on the Merwedeplein but also in places across the world. Trees (including the aforementioned saplings raised from Anne's favorite horse chestnut tree) and plentiful statues have been dedicated to her, including the one in Merwedeplein that was commissioned and then unveiled in 2005 by Gert-Jan Jimmink, the new owner of the former Blankevoort's bookstore. There is also a *Stolpersteine* (memorial plaque) dedicated to the memory of Anne and her family outside Merwedeplein 37. As part of her story for this anthology, Joy Gafa' earlier included two pictures of this special *Stolpersteine*.

Playing Anne (An Interview with Miranda Antoinette Troutt)

[213] *Editor note:* Please review the following website for further information on the production of the *Diary of Anne Frank* (performed April 4–May 19, 2019) at the Seattle Children's Theatre: https://www.sct.org/onstage/productions/the-diary-of-anne-frank/

As I did with Melina Zaccaria's performance as Anne in *The Diary of Anne Frank* in Burlington, Ontario, I was also able to build a catalog reference for this production:

> *The Diary of Anne Frank.* By Frances Goodrich and Albert Hackett; newly adpated by Wendy Kesselman. Dir. Janet Allen. Perf.

Miranda Antoinette Troutt (Anne), Ryan Artzberger (Otto), and Betsy Schwartz (Edith). Indiana Repertory Theatre, Indianapolis, IN; Seattle Children's Theatre (Charlotte Martin Theatre), Seattle, WA. January–February, 2019; April–May, 2019.

[214] *Editor note:* Please review the following website for further information on the production of the *Diary of Anne Frank* (performed January 25–February 24, 2019) at the Indiana Repertory Theatre: https://www.irtlive.com/plays-and-events/2018-2019/the-diary-of-anne-frank

[215] *Editor note:* Miranda is referring here to the original Frances Goodrich and Albert Hackett adaptation that was first performed as the *Diary of Anne Frank* on Broadway, October 5, 1955.

[216] *Editor note:* As we have seen, Seattle has one of the horse chestnut saplings situated about three hundred feet from Seattle Children's Theatre.

[217] *Editor note:* I have confirmed with Miranda that there were no new revelations regarding Margot's diary.

[218] *Editor note:* Yes, Anne certainly hoped, and at times even expected, to survive her life in hiding and the mood in the Secret Annex noticeably improved after D-Day on June 6, 1944.

We also need to be aware that the twenty-five months that Anne spent in hiding is only a known fact in hindsight and clearly such a length of time would not have seemed possible to her or anyone else in the Secret Annex during the earliest days. They lived day by day and week by week. Anne relates in her diary entry for May 2, 1943 that Mr. van Pels believed that the war would be over "by the end of 1943." Anne discusses her hopes for "liberation" in her diary entries for May 3, 1944, May 22, 1944, June 6, 1944, and June 23, 1944.

After hearing about the Allies' invasion of northern France on June 6, 1944 (D-Day), Anne and Margot fully expected to be back at school by September or October. Anne makes her feelings clear in her diary entries for June 6, 1944 and July 21, 1944. Two months before D-Day in her diary entry for April 5, 1944, Anne had declared that she felt she had missed too much formal schooling to feel she *could* go back unless the war was over by September. D-Day greatly changed this mood.

[219] *Editor note:* I attended one of these talks during which I heard a teenager on the panel declaiming, "I love being Jewish!" The energy with which she expressed this to

the audience resonated with me, and she conveyed it with such heart. She conveyed not only what it means to be Jewish, but also what it means to be a member of a race that has spent so much of its long existence expending energy on trying to survive and thrive against a backdrop of persecution and misunderstanding. I thought about dedicating this book to her but have been unable to find her name.

[220] *Editor note:* This "survivor" was probably Laureen Nussbaum as she lives in Washington state. Miranda informed me that this "sounds right."

Afterword by Cara Wilson-Granat

[221] *Editor note:* Please see Cara's own memoir, *Strength from Tragedy* in our bibliography.

Please also see Cara's website www.wordsfromcara.com for more information.

DIARY REFERENCES: *ANNE FRANK: THE DIARY OF A YOUNG GIRL*

The following are the dates from Anne's published diary that have been referenced in our anthology. Readers will find that the dates correspond to those published in the online Definitive Edition *or D version of the text as published by Random House/Doubleday.*

1942	1943	1944
June 14, 1942	March 4, 1943	January 2, 1944
June 15, 1942	March 10, 1943	January 6, 1944
June 20, 1942	March 25, 1943	January 22, 1944
June 21, 1942	April 1, 1943	January 28, 1944
June 24, 1942	May 2, 1943	February 8, 1944
July 5, 1942	June 15, 1943	March 16, 1944
July 10, 1942	July 16, 1943	March 28, 1944
July 11, 1942	July 23, 1943	March 29, 1944
August 21, 1942	August 5, 1943	April 5, 1944
September 22, 1942	August 9, 1943	April 11, 1944
September 27, 1942	August 10, 1943	April 15, 1944
October 9, 1942	September 10, 1943	April 18, 1944
October 10, 1942	September 16, 1943	April 21, 1944
October 14, 1942	October 17, 1943	April 28, 1944
October 20, 1942	October 30, 1943	May 3, 1944
October 29, 1942	November 8, 1943	May 5, 1944
November 2, 1942	November 27, 1943	May 8, 1944
November 5, 1942	December 24, 1943	May 11, 1944
November 7, 1942	December 29, 1943	May 13, 1944
November 9, 1942		May 22, 1944
November 17, 1942		May 26, 1944

1942	1943	1944
November 19, 1942		June 6, 1944
December 22, 1942		June 13, 1944
		June 23, 1944
		July 5, 1944
		July 15, 1944
		July 21, 1944
		August 1, 1944

PART VIII

Bibliography, Website Resources, and Index

Priscilla Smits's Anne Frank book collection © Priscilla Smits

BIBLIOGRAPHY

Some differences exist in the accounts and viewpoints of some of the details of Anne's final seven months. Perhaps the exact historical facts are less important than a record of what Anne and these women—who approached the limits of human endurance—went through.

—Willy Lindwer, *The Last Seven Months of Anne Frank* (1988; 1991)

THERE IS CLEARLY a wealth of online, dramatic, film, and other biographical information regarding Anne Frank; just as importantly, this wealth covers the needs and expectations of a vast age range; moreover, new works are emerging all the time with this humble anthology being among them for 2021.

As we review the following works in our bibliography, we need to remember that Anne's story resonates not just with younger children and idealistic teenagers, but also with older adults. Although some of the latter may be more leery of Anne's perceived idealism than younger readers and searchers, they can certainly identify with her story on other levels. The works that have been published reflect a wide span of likely interests; thus, we have books targeted at young children who will probably be looking for pictorially rewarding studies of someone they know to be meaningful and famous, at teenagers eager to know about both Anne's life and the contextual horrors of the Holocaust, and at adults who may appreciate both pictorial works targeted at younger readers as well as those full of scholarly analysis.

Many books about Anne that I have seen are hybrid efforts that include both plenty of iconic photographs of her and the neighborhoods that she lived in as well as informative and scholarly text. I am hopeful that the present work is also a hybrid of interesting pictures associated with our personal journeys as well as informative text designed to aid readers as they experience Anne's world through our eyes. I am acutely conscious of the fact that there is probably no perfect or definitive book about Anne, and what works perfectly for one reader will not work for another. Because this bright fifteen year old is understandably surrounded by a public armed with protective blankets of warm emotion, we often see this reflected in overly subjective commentary about Anne and her family.

Hardly any work relating specifically to Anne Frank is not a favorite in some capacity and this is often despite any factual inconsistencies that may be obvious in the sources available and to which I have already referred with some degree of exasperation it has to be said. In many respects, these errors barely matter because of how Anne speaks to us despite them and because of the strength of her broader message of emotional and physical endurance in the face of extreme danger. It is needless quibbling to fixate on such matters given the overall tragic arc of her story.

Readers looking for reliable, well-researched, but also very readable overviews of Anne's life (and the lives of the rest of her family) should find Melissa Müller's biography among the best available. Carol Ann Lee's *The Hidden Life of Otto Frank* is also highly recommended. *Anne Frank: A Complete Illustrated Biography* is also worth seeking; *The Footsteps of Anne Frank* by Ernst Schnabel is much loved by many, as is Miep Gies's memoir, *Anne Frank Remembered*. I have obviously been quietly recommending other books by the frequency with which I have mentioned them throughout the endnotes!

As mentioned throughout, several of Anne's surviving former school friends and classmates such as Hanneli (Hannah) Pick-Goslar, Jacqueline van Maarsen, and Nanette Blitz-Konig, have been keen over the years to share details of their friendship with her. With the added testimony of some of the helpers, we can learn more about everyone's experiences as Jews, as hiders, and as helpers during and after the Second World War. We have a greater understanding of just how difficult life was in the occupied Netherlands. *Anne Frank, the Untold Story* by Joop van Wijk-Voskuijl is recommended as further valuable insight into the life of his mother who helped provide the occupants of the Secret Annex with support throughout their time in hiding.

Anne's own life *and* literary ambitions were both cruelly curtailed which leaves us with the legacy of a young teenager as a fascinating flower in the bud and with unfulfilled literary promises. As I review most of the available literature, we can see this mixture of hope and curtailment in the beautiful photographs that remain of Anne, in the vivid promise of her writing, and in the way that each subsequent writer drawn to her story tries to connect the important pictorial, literary, and historical threads. There is a longing for a different ending and not just for Anne, but also for Margot, for Edith, for all their friends, and for everyone else caught up in the chaos and madness.

Although at one time I was going to, in the end I decided *not* to separate pictorial works aimed at younger children from those aimed at older teenagers and adults as such decisions end up being highly arbitrary; moreover, such decisions can end up unfairly setting aside the advanced reading ability and likely interest of some younger children and the fact that many adults can also appreciate those works that have been targeted at younger readers. Although I have generally found that works with lots of pictures of Anne and of places associated with her life are among the more suitable for younger readers, I should also point out that these are often the very ones that I love the best! Anne's life lends itself to both the pictorial and the scholarly because of the influence she merits through both the iconic pictures taken by her father and the literary power of her words.

*   *   *

There are many documentary, film, television, and theatrical productions that cover Anne's life and times. Most take her diary and time in the Secret Annex as their starting and ending points. *Anne Frank: The Whole Story* with Hannah Taylor Gordon as a marvelous Anne takes her story beyond the narrower dramatic and film coverage of other versions. It is extremely powerful in its portrayal of the lives of the Franks, the van Pelses, and Dr. Fritz Pfeffer both *before* their time in the Secret Annex and then *after* their arrest. My contributors and I generally speak highly of this production and have no issue with recommending it although it is extremely hard to find on DVD for a reasonable price.

Anne Frank Remembered is a great documentary about Anne's life and times and contains some great vintage footage. We usually recommend this film, and it is available on DVD. It also includes the only known moving footage of an animated Anne at an open window of her apartment on Merwedeplein.

Wendy Kesselman has written a great "newly adapted" version of the original Frances Goodrich and Albert Hackett 1955 play, *The Diary of Anne Frank*. Priscilla mentioned earlier in this anthology how she watched an even newer adaptation called *Anne* written by Leon de Winter and Jessica Durlacher.

Each theatrical performance, documentary, and cinematic production of Anne Frank's life can, unfortunately, only be as complete and tragic as her life was short and prematurely curtailed. While most dramatic and film productions choose to rely mainly on Anne's diary as their source material, when documentaries and films do branch out and attempt to look at her life before and after she went into hiding, then we have more of a complete view of what is known. Both the aforementioned *Anne Frank: The Whole Story* and *Anne Frank Remembered* make compelling efforts to address this question.

Sadly, this comprehensive approach only reveals just how incomplete Anne's life really was in all its various facets. If we add to what we know of her life from her diary by also looking at her schools, her life on Merwedeplein, and at her many friendships, then we see even more of what was tragically lost by removing the centrality of her diary as a historical Holocaust document. Anne thus becomes achingly normal, a lively child, a difficult teenager, a challenging daughter to one of her parents and a loving daughter to the other, and a promising writer. This is all fascinating, but we miss her even more.

*   *   *

I added a separate fiction section after deciding that fictional portrayals of Anne and Margot merited appropriate separation from nonfiction works. Four have been mentioned in this anthology—*Annelies, Paper Sky, Margot,* and *The Silent Sister. Annelies* and *Margot* imagine how Anne and Margot might have responded to a postwar world had they survived Bergen-Belsen. There is no "alive" Margot in *Annelies* and there is no "alive" Anne in *Margot* which is interesting in that it keeps the focus squarely on the one "alive" sister while using the other as a lost creative reference point.

Though *Paper Sky* and *The Silent Sister* are both fictional, each is rooted in the reality that both girls did die. Beth Jacobs in *Paper Sky* has Anne able to continue writing her diary on scraps of paper at Kamp Westerbork and in her mind at Birkenau. Mazal Alouf-Mizrahi in *The Silent Sister* has Margot writing a diary that has never been found in reality.

While each of these above works has its creative merits, collectively, and as part of what seems to be a larger genre than I first realized, some readers will undoubtedly find some of these efforts to border on the blasphemous or the distasteful. After all, the two girls died, and their ultimate destiny cannot now be changed. When I addressed this question to the Anne Frank Fonds in Basel, the organization felt that while it was powerless to influence or censor the books in a free society, it could review the works for any copyright violations arising from their publication.

In the end, liking or rejecting these works will be a matter of personal taste. While I appreciated each of them from a creative perspective, I sometimes feel that the genre risks substituting fictional wishful thinking for known cruel reality and then merging the two in the minds of some—especially, for those not otherwise familiar with the true trajectory of Anne and Margot's story. This was the primary concern of the Anne Frank Huis and Museum.

* * *

I have included several "bookazine" efforts about Anne. These special standalone publications usually center on anniversaries associated with famous and historical events and individuals. The Civil War, Civil Rights, the Second World War, President Kennedy, and, of course, Anne Frank spring to mind as examples.

What could have been Anne's ninetieth birthday on June 12, 2019, was widely celebrated in a number of well-illustrated bookazines. These can still be found through online stores. Both her life and the betrayal of all the occupants of the Secret Annex appear to be of equal interest to the writers.

*   *   *

Our website resources in the following separate section are extensive and collated by subject or theme. They should each be current as of early 2021.

Two excellent starting points for journeying through further information on Anne and her legacy are the websites for the Anne Frank Huis and Museum and the Anne Frank Fonds. Each has a wealth of information regarding Anne's life and times, the publishing history and adaptations of her diary, the lives of those who were helpers to the occupants of the Secret Annex, the infamous arrest on August 4, 1944, and the subsequent fates of everyone involved in the seven months following.

I have referenced these and other websites extensively in this anthology both in my introductory chapters and in my editorial commentary on the submissions of my several writers. Readers are advised that websites spring up like mushrooms and are generally only as good and useful as they are vigorously edited for errors and maintained for currency based on changing facts and information. Websites can also disappear or become deactivated but this is an unlikely fate for most of the ones included here.

Although I have relied heavily on Wikipedia, I must warn readers that each entry in this online encyclopedia can be variously edited by the motivated and serious, the needlessly provocative, the frivolous, and

"MEETING" ANNE FRANK: AN ANTHOLOGY

the divisive. While I have not seen any evidence of malicious vandalism in the Wikipedia entries included in this anthology, readers should still be aware of the potential for some "editors" to want to make their mark by contaminating an article with a trail of false or provocative information. This is especially so with subjects as inconceivable as the Holocaust and as prejudicially driven as anti-Semitism.

I have done my best throughout to cross-reference website information for their factual consistency. As noted earlier, though, this anthology is *not* being positioned in the Anneverse as a work of completely original research, but, instead, as one reliant where necessary on reliable secondary resources. Throughout, our motivation has been to provide readers with a stimulating and contextual understanding of Anne Frank's journey.

Given the monumental scale of the Holocaust, I would suggest that accurate documented information on the number of Jews who lived in the Netherlands, who went into hiding, who were then betrayed, arrested, and deported to concentration camps from the Netherlands, who then died or were lucky enough to survive, must be necessarily approximate. Although we know that the Nazis were obsessed with keeping meticulous, obscenely detailed, and probably reliable records of the 107,000 who were sent to Kamp Westerbork in the Netherlands and then transported further to camps such as Auschwitz-Birkenau and Sobibór, we also know that those who were sent immediately to their deaths on arrival were *not* documented regarding their eventual fates.

Nevertheless, our included websites *should* still serve as useful starting points for readers who wish to delve more deeply into topics raised throughout this anthology. Readers can be reasonably assured of the targeted accuracy of an official website for a legitimate and well-known organization, a museum, a memorial, or a concentration camp. The reader should then be able to follow any relevant hyperlinks to narrower (and more specific) or broader (and less detailed) information. He or she is encouraged to cross-reference what is found for consistency with other online resources.

Pictures of Anne and her family are iconic and readily available on the internet. The ones included in my introductory chapter are each in the public domain through the Anne Frank Huis and Museum Flicker page.

*   *   *

Finally, all the published material, films, documentaries, and plays included in our bibliography should be readily available in public libraries, through physical and online bookstores, or through online streaming services. If *not*, then they *should* be. Only *Anne Frank: The Whole Story* is currently very difficult to find as a reasonably priced DVD. It is available on YouTube, however, for readers who are interested.

Books (Nonfiction/Anne Frank)

Adler, David A., and Karen Ritz. *A Picture Book of Anne Frank.* New York, NY: Holiday House, 1993.

Anne Frank Stichting (House), and Aukje Vergeest. *Anne Frank in the Secret Annex: Who Was Who?* 2nd edition. Amsterdam: Anne Frank Stichting, 2015

Anne Frank Stichting (House). *Anne Frank in the World, 1929–1945.* Translated into English by Steven Arthur Cohen. Fifth revised edition. Amsterdam; Wageningen, NL: Anne Frank Stichting, 1993. Originally published as *O Mundo de Anne Frank, 1929–1945.*

———. *Anne Frank House: A Museum with a Story.* Ed. Anne Frank House, Menno Metselaar, Ruud van der Rol, and Dineke Stam. Translated by Epicycles, Amsterdam, and Lorraine T. Miller. Amsterdam: Anne Frank Stichting, 2001, 2008.

Bloomsbury. *Anne Frank: The Collected Works.* London: Bloomsbury Continuum, 2019.

Cooper, Ryan. *We Never Said Goodbye: Memories of Otto Frank.* Yarmouth Port, MA: Amphion Publishing, 2021.

Coster, Theo. *We All Wore Stars: Memories of Anne Frank from Her Classmates.* New York, NY: Palgrave Macmillan, 2011.

Frank, Anne. *Anne Frank's Tales from the Secret Annex.* Ed. by Gerrold van der Stroom and Susan Massotty. Translated by Susan Massotty. New York, NY: Bantam Books, 2003.

———. *The Diary of a Young Girl: The Definitive Edition.* Ed. Otto H. Frank and Mirjam Pressler. Translated by Susan Massotty. New York, NY: Doubleday, 2001.

Gies, Miep, and Alison Leslie Gold. *Anne Frank Remembered: The Story of the Woman Who Helped to Hide the Frank Family.* Simon & Schuster trade paperback. New York, NY: Simon and Schuster Paperbacks, 2009.

Gold, Alison Leslie. *Memories of Anne Frank: Reflections of a Childhood Friend.* New York, NY: Scholastic Press, 1997.

Jansen, Ronald Wilfred. *Anne Frank* [Back cover title: *Anne Frank 80 Years: Photographic Impressions; A Memorial Tour in Current Images*]. Translated by Patty Snijders. Hoogeveen, NL: RWJ-Publishing, 2011.

Konig, Nanette Blitz. *Holocaust Memoirs of a Bergen-Belsen Survivor & Classmate of Anne Frank.* Amsterdam: Amsterdam Publishers, 2018.

Last, Dick van Galen, and Rolf Wolfswinkel. *Anne Frank and After.* Amsterdam: Amsterdam University Press, 1996.

Lee, Carol Ann. *Anne Frank and the Children of the Holocaust.* New York, NY: Viking, published by Penguin Group, 2006.

————. *Roses from the Earth: The Biography of Anne Frank.* London; New York, NY: Penguin Books, 2000.

————. *The Hidden Life of Otto Frank.* 1st ed. New York, NY: Morrow, 2003.

Lindwer, Willy. *The Last Seven Months of Anne Frank.* Translated by Alison Meersschaert. First Anchor Books. New York, NY: Anchor Books, 1992.

Metselaar, Menno. *Anne Frank: Dreaming, Thinking, Writing.* Translated by Nancy Forest-Flier. Amsterdam: Anne Frank Stichting, 2016.

Metselaar, Menno, and Ruud van der Rol. *Anne Frank: Her Life in Words and Pictures from the Archives of the Anne Frank House.* Translated by Arnold Pomerans. 1st American ed. New York, NY: Roaring Brook Pr, 2009.

Metselaar, Menno, Piet van Ledden, and Huck Scarry. *All about Anne: Anne Frank's Life Story, with Answers to Frequently Asked Questions and Beautiful Drawings.* Amsterdam: Anne Frank Stichting and Second Story Press, 2017.

Müller, Melissa. *Anne Frank: The Biography.* 2nd US ed. New York, NY: Metropolitan Books/Henry Holt and Company, 2013.

Netherlands Institute for War Documentation, with an introduction by Harry Paape, Gerrold van der Stroom, and David Barnouw; a summary of the report by the Netherlands Forensic Institute compiled by H. J. J. Hardy. *The Diary of Anne Frank: The Revised Critical Edition.* Edited by David Barnouw and Gerrold van der Stroom. Translated by Arnold J. Pomerans, B. M. Mooyaart-Doubleday, and Susan Massotty. New York, NY: Doubleday, 2003.

Perricone, Kathleen, with a foreword by Laureen Nussbaum. *Anne Frank: A Complete Illustrated Biography.* Illustrated edition. New York, NY: Centennial Books, 2020.

Pressler, Mirjam, with Gerti Elias. *Treasures from the Attic: The Extraordinary Story of Anne Frank's Family.* Translated from the German by Damion Searls. New York, NY: Doubleday, 2011.

Prose, Francine. *Anne Frank: The Book, the Life, the Afterlife.* 1st ed. New York, NY: Harper, 2009.

Sawyer, Kem Knapp. *Anne Frank: A Photographic Story of Her Life.* 1st American ed. New York, NY: DK Publishing, Inc., 2004.

Schnabel, Ernst, with a new foreword from the Anne Frank House in Amsterdam. *The Footsteps of Anne Frank*. Translated from the German by Richard and Clara Winston. Harpenden, UK: Southbank Publishing, 2014.

Schnabel, Ernst. *Anne Frank: A Portrait in Courage*. Translated from the German by Richard and Clara Winston. 1st American ed. New York, NY: Harcourt, Brace, [1958].

van der Rol, Ruud, and Rian Verhoeven. *Anne Frank*. Translated by Tony Langham and Plym Peters. Amsterdam: Anne Frank Stichting and LRV-info, 1992.

———. *Anne Frank: Beyond the Diary; A Photographic Remembrance*. New York, NY: Puffin Books, 1995.

van Maarsen, Jacqueline, and Carol Ann Lee. *A Friend Called Anne*. Retold for children by Carol Ann Lee. New York, NY: Puffin, a division of Penguin Young Readers Group, 2007.

van Maarsen, Jacqueline. *Inheriting Anne Frank*. Translated from the Dutch by Brian Doyle. London: Arcadia Books, 2009.

———. *My Name Is Anne,* She Said, *Anne Frank*. Chicago, IL: Distributed in the US by Independent Publishers Group, 2007.

van Wijk, Joop, and Jeroen De Bruyn. *Anne Frank, the Untold Story: The Hidden Truth about Elli Vossen, the Youngest Helper of the Secret Annex*. Translated by Tess Stoop. Laag-Soeren, NL: Bep Voskuijl Producties BV, 2018.

———. *Bep Voskuijl, het zwijgen voorbij: een biografie van de jongste helpster van het achterhuis*. Laag-Soeren, NL: Bep Voskuijl Producties BV, 2015; 2018.

von Benda-Beckmann, Bas, and Erika Prins. *Na het achterhuis: Anne Frank en de andere onderduikers in de kampen*. Amsterdam: Querido's Uitgeverij BV, 2020.

Westra, Hans. *Inside Anne Frank's House: An Illustrated Journey through Anne's World*. Woodstock, NY: Overlook Duckworth, 2004.

Wilson-Granat, Cara. *Strength from Tragedy: Anne Frank's Father Shares His Wisdom with an American Teen*. Middletown, DE: August Words Publishing, 2015.

Woodward, Kay. *The Life of Anne Frank*. Buffalo, NY: Firefly Books, 2020.

Books (Nonfiction/Holocaust Memoirs)

Afori Publishing. *Letters from the Ledermanns*. Translated by Catherine Yekimov, Inge R., and Lizze Vrijsen. [United States]: CreateSpace Publishing, 2016; 2017.

Hillesum, Etty, with a foreword by Eva Hoffman; introduction and notes by Jan G. Gaarlandt. *An Interrupted Life: The Diaries, 1941–1943; And Letters from Westerbork*. Translated from the Dutch by Arnold J. Pomerans. First Holt paperbacks edition. New York, NY: Henry Holt and Company, 1996.

Schloss, Eva, and Evelyn Julia Kent. *Eva's Story: A Holocaust Survivor's Tale by the Stepsister of Anne Frank*. Reprint edition. Grand Rapids, MI: Eerdmans Books for Young Readers, 2019.

Schloss, Eva, and Karen Bartlett. *After Auschwitz: A Story of Heartbreak and Survival by the Stepsister of Anne Frank*. Paperback reissue (2019). London, UK: Hodder & Stoughton, 2013.

Spiegel, Renia, and preface, afterword, and notes by Elizabeth Bellak with Sarah Durand; foreword by Deborah E. Lipstadt. *Renia's Diary: A Holocaust journal*. Translated by Anna Blasiak and Marta Dziurosz. New York, NY: St. Martin's Press, 2019.

Weiss, Helga, with an introduction by Francine Prose. *Helga's Diary: A Young Girl's Account of Life in a Concentration Camp*. Translated by Neil Bermel. New York, NY: W. W. Norton & Company, 2013.

Wiesel, Elie. *Night*. Translated from the French by Marion Wiesel. Commemorative edition. New York, NY: Hill and Wang, a division of Farrar, Straus and Giroux, 2017.

Documentaries, Films, and Plays

Blair, Jon. *Anne Frank Remembered*. Directed by Jon Blair. Performed by Kenneth Branagh and Glenn Close. Produced by Jon Blair. Columbia TriStar Home Entertainment, 2004. DVD.

Ellis, Kirk, and Melissa Müller. *Anne Frank: The Whole Story*. Directed by Robert Dornhelm. Performed by Hannah Taylor Gordon, et al. Milk & Honey Pictures; Dorothy Pictures; Touchstone Television. American Broadcasting Company (ABC); Walt Disney Home Video, 2001. DVD.

Frank, Anne, Miep Gies, and Alison Leslie Gold. *The Attic: The Hiding of Anne Frank*. Directed by John Erman. Performed by Paul Scofield, Mary Steenburgen, and Lisa Jacobs. Produced by David Cunliffe. 1988. Film.

Goodrich, Frances, Albert Hackett, and newly adapted by Wendy Kesselman. *The Diary of Anne Frank*. Definitive ed. New York, NY: Dramatists Play Service Inc., 2016. Play.

————. *The Diary of Anne Frank*. Directed by Janet Allen. Performed by Miranda Antoinette Troutt, Ryan Artzberger, and Betsy Schwartz. Seattle Children's Theatre (Charlotte Martin Theatre), Indianapolis, IN; Seattle, WA. 2019.

Goodrich, Frances, and Albert Hackett. *The Diary of Anne Frank (Motion picture: 1959)*. Directed by George Stevens. Performed by Millie Perkins, et al. Produced by George Stevens. 20th Century Fox Home Entertainment, 2004. DVD.

————. *The Diary of Anne Frank*. Directed by Sari Ketter. Performed by Lucy DeVito, et al. Intiman Theater, Seattle. May 2008.

————. *The Diary of Anne Frank*. Directed by Sondra Learn. Performed by Melina Zaccaria, Michael Hannigan, and Carla Zabek. Theatre Burlington, Burlington, ON. February 2014.

Goodrich, Frances, Anne Frank, and Albert Hackett. *The Diary of Anne Frank*. Directed by Boris Sagal. Performed by Melissa Gilbert, Maximilian Schell, and Joan Plowright. Produced by Raymond Katz. 1980. Film.

Moggach, Deborah. *The Diary of Anne Frank*. Directed by Jon Jones. Performed by Iain Glen, Tamsin Greig, and Ellie Kendrick. Prod. Elinor Day. IMG Entertainment, 2008. DVD.

Pannocchia, Federica. *Il Nostro Nome è Anna*. Directed by Mattia Mura. Performed by Ludovica Nasti. Produced by Sergio Martinelli and Sara Martinelli. n.d. DVD.

Fiction (Anne Frank and Margot Frank)

Alouf-Mizrahi, Mazal. *The Silent Sister: The Diary of Margot Frank*. Bloomington, IN: AuthorHouse, 2011.

Cantor, Jillian. *Margot*. New York, NY: Riverhead Books, 2013.

Gillham, David R. *Annelies*. New York, NY: Viking, an imprint of Penguin Random House, 2019.

Jacobs, Beth. *Paper Sky: What Happened after Anne Frank's Diary Ended*. CreateSpace Independent Publishing Platform, 2012.

Magazine Publications ("Bookazines")

Centennial Entertainment. *Anne Frank 75 Years Later: Who Betrayed Her*. New York, NY: Centennial Media, 2019.

Centennial Entertainment. *Anne Frank 75 Years Later: Her Untold Story*. New York, NY: Centennial Media, 2020.

Centennial Entertainment. *Anne Frank 75 Years Later: The Untold Story of her Sister Margot*. New York, NY: Centennial Media, 2020.

Time Inc. Books with an introduction by President Bill Clinton. *Anne Frank: Her Life and Legacy; The Diary at 70*. New York, NY: Life Books, 2017.

WEBSITE RESOURCES

Many of the websites that are included in our website resources regarding Auschwitz-Birkenau, Bergen-Belsen, and the other Nazi concentration camps referenced in this work contain imagery and information that are not suitable for younger readers and sensitive teenagers or adults. This caution applies less to the informational trail provided by the main Anne Frank Huis and Museum *website in Amsterdam or to the footsteps through Anne's world provided by the* Anne Frank Fonds *in Basel. I would consider both websites to be safe for all but the youngest and most sensitive of children. My contributors and I believe that Anne's life and world will always need to be explored in an exploratory, safe, and informed manner while anti-Semitism and ignorance surrounding the horrors of the Holocaust remain.*

Anne and Margot's Friends

United States Holocaust Memorial Museum

https://encyclopedia.ushmm.org/content/en/id-card/barbara-ledermann

Wikipedia

https://en.wikipedia.org/wiki/Hanneli_Goslar
https://en.wikipedia.org/wiki/Jacqueline_van_Maarsen
https://en.wikipedia.org/wiki/Laureen_Nussbaum
https://en.wikipedia.org/wiki/Nanette_Blitz_Konig
https://en.wikipedia.org/wiki/Sanne_Ledermann

Anne and Margot's Schools, Amsterdam

Primary Schools

6e Montessorischool Anne Frank (Anne Frank)

https://www.annefrank-montessori.nl/english-info/
https://www.annefrank-montessori.nl/geschiedenis/anne-frank/

Jekerschool (Margot Frank)

https://en.wikipedia.org/wiki/File:Jeker_School_Amsterdam_-_Elementry_School_of_Margot_Frank,_Barbara_Ledermann,_Sanne_Ledermann,_Eva_Schloss.png

Secondary Schools

Het Gemeentelijk Lyceum Voor Meisjes (Margot Frank)

https://onh.nl/verhaal/het-gemeentelijk-lyceum-voor-meisjes
https://www.translatetheweb.com/?from=nl&to=en&ref=SERP&dl=en&rr=UC&a=https%3a%2f%2fonh.nl%2fverhaal%2fhet-gemeentelijk-lyceum-voor-meisjes#

Jewish Lyceum (Anne and Margot Frank)

https://nl.wikipedia.org/wiki/Joods_Lyceum_(Amsterdam)
https://www.iamsterdam.com/en/amsterdam-qr/centrum-oost-de-plantage/joodse-hbs-en-joods-lyceum

Anne Frank Biographical Web Resources

Anne Frank Diary Reference (Website Administered by Suzanne Morine)

https://web.archive.org/web/20141219232042/http://www.annefrankdiaryreference.eu.pn/index.html

Anne Frank Fonds (Foundation), Basel

https://www.annefrank.ch/en/family/anne-frank

Anne Frank Huis and Museum, Amsterdam

https://www.annefrank.org/en/anne-frank/main-characters/anne-frank/
https://www.annefrank.org/en/anne-frank/the-timeline/entire-timeline/

Wikipedia

https://en.wikipedia.org/wiki/Anne_Frank
https://en.wikipedia.org/wiki/List_of_people_associated_with_Anne_Frank

Anne Frank Center for Mutual Respect, USA

https://www.annefrank.com/

Anne Frank Diary, Adaptations, and Publishing History

Anne Frank Huis and Museum, Amsterdam

https://webshop.annefrank.org/en/the-diary/
https://www.annefrank.org/en/anne-frank/diary/
https://www.annefrank.org/en/anne-frank/diary/complete-works-anne-frank/
https://www.annefrank.org/en/anne-frank/diary/publication-diary/
https://www.annefrank.org/en/anne-frank/diary/so-who-is-dear-kitty/
https://www.annefrank.org/en/anne-frank/go-in-depth/two-versions-annes-diary/

The Anne Frank Fonds (Foundation), Basel, Switzerland

https://www.annefrank.ch/en/diary/adaptations
https://www.annefrank.ch/en/diary/publications

Wikipedia

https://en.wikipedia.org/wiki/The_Diary_of_a_Young_Girl

Anne Frank Fonds (Foundation), Basel

https://www.annefrank.ch/en

Anne Frank Huis and Museum, Amsterdam

https://www.annefrank.org/en/

Anne Frank Sapling Project

Anne Frank Center for Mutual Respect

https://e7bcbdf8-accf-4e54-9ae9-d1f8b0f11c1d.filesusr.com/
ugd/7279dd_4df6fd91487744ca89b9efe2a11f505b.pdf?index=true
https://www.annefrank.com/sapling-project

The New York Times

https://cityroom.blogs.nytimes.com/2009/04/16/anne-franks
-tree-in-new-york-soil/
https://www.nytimes.com/2009/10/16/nyregion/16anne.html

Washington State Holocaust Center for Humanity

https://holocaustcenterseattle.org/visit/anne-frank-tree

Wikipedia

https://en.wikipedia.org/wiki/Anne_Frank_tree

Anne Frank Trust, London

https://annefrank.org.uk/

Auschwitz–Birkenau Extermination Camp (Poland)

Auschwitz-Birkenau Memorial and Museum

http://auschwitz.org/en/
http://auschwitz.org/en/history/auschwitz-ii/the-construction-of-the-camp

Encyclopaedia Britannica

https://www.britannica.com/topic/Why-wasnt-Auschwitz-bombed-717594

The Guardian

https://www.theguardian.com/world/2009/sep/09/auschwitz-allied-bomb-second-world-war

Jewish Virtual Library

https://www.jewishvirtuallibrary.org/history-and-overview-of-auschwitz-birkenau.

Miscellaneous

https://www.bing.com/images/search?q=Auschwitz+II+Birkenau+Map&FORM=RESTAB

United States Holocaust Memorial Museum

https://encyclopedia.ushmm.org/content/en/article/auschwitz
https://www.ushmm.org/information/exhibitions/online-exhibitions/special-focus/liberation-of-auschwitz
https://encyclopedia.ushmm.org/content/en/article/auschwitz-key-dates

Wikipedia

https://en.wikipedia.org/wiki/Auschwitz_concentration_camp
https://en.wikipedia.org/wiki/Auschwitz-Birkenau_State_Museum

Authenticity of Anne's Diary

Anne Frank Huis and Museum, Amsterdam

https://www.annefrank.org/en/anne-frank/go-in-depth/authenticity-diary-anne-frank/

Bergen-Belsen Concentration Camp (Germany)

Holocaust Research Project

http://www.holocaustresearchproject.org/othercamps/bbelsen.html

United States Holocaust Memorial Museum

https://encyclopedia.ushmm.org/content/en/article/bergen-belsen

Wikipedia

https://en.wikipedia.org/wiki/Bergen-Belsen_concentration_camp

Betrayal and Arrest of Anne Frank and the Hiders in the Secret Annex

Anne Frank Huis and Museum, Amsterdam

https://www.annefrank.org/en/anne-frank/go-in-depth/was-anne-frank-betrayed/

Cold Case Diary

https://www.coldcasediary.com/

Wikipedia

https://en.wikipedia.org/wiki/Karl_Silberbauer
https://nl.wikipedia.org/wiki/Gerrit_van_der_Veenstraat
https://nl.wikipedia.org/wiki/Huis_van_Bewaring_I_(Weteringschans)

World History Project

https://worldhistoryproject.org/1944/8/7/anne-frank-and-her-family-are-transported-to-westerbork-concentration-camp

Fall of the Weimar Republic in Germany and the Rise of Nazism

Wikipedia

https://en.wikipedia.org/wiki/Enabling_Act_of_1933
https://en.wikipedia.org/wiki/Nazi_Party
https://en.wikipedia.org/wiki/Nazism
https://en.wikipedia.org/wiki/Paul_von_Hindenburg
https://en.wikipedia.org/wiki/Sicherheitsdienst
https://en.wikipedia.org/wiki/Weimar_Republic

Hiding and Deportation of Jews in the Netherlands during World War Two

Anne Frank Huis and Museum, Amsterdam

https://www.annefrank.org/en/anne-frank/go-in-depth/how-unique-was-secret-annex-people-hiding-occupied-netherlands/
https://www.annefrank.org/en/anne-frank/the-timeline/#113

Holocaust Education and Archive Research Team or HEART (part of the Holocaust Research Project)

http://www.holocaustresearchproject.org/nazioccupation/holland/netherdeports.html

Kamp Westerbork Memorial

https://kampwesterbork.nl/en/the-persecution-of-the-jews/deportation

The Moderate Voice

https://themoderatevoice.com/the-last-train-to-auschwitz-revisited-2/

Wikipedia

https://en.wikipedia.org/wiki/Dutch_resistance

Kamp Westerbork, Drenthe Province, The Netherlands

Holocaust Education and Archive Research Team or HEART (part of the Holocaust Research Project)

http://www.holocaustresearchproject.org/othercamps/westerbork.html

The Holocaust—Lest We Forget

http://www.holocaust-lestweforget.com/albert-konrad-gemmeker.html

Kamp Westerbork Memorial

https://kampwesterbork.nl/en/
https://kampwesterbork.nl/en/museum
https://kampwesterbork.nl/en/the-persecution-of-the-jews/deportation

Moderate Voice

https://themoderatevoice.com/the-last-train-to-auschwitz-revisited-2/

Traces of War

https://www.tracesofwar.com/articles/2613/Gemmeker-Albert.htm

Wikipedia

https://en.wikipedia.org/wiki/Westerbork_transit_camp

Margot Frank Biographical Web Resources

Anne Frank Fonds (Foundation), Basel, Switzerland

https://www.annefrank.ch/en/family/margot-frank

The Anne Frank Huis and Museum, Amsterdam

https://www.annefrank.org/en/anne-frank/main-characters/margot-frank/

Wikipedia

https://en.wikipedia.org/wiki/Margot_Frank

Miscellaneous Resources

Cara Wilson-Granat
    Words from Cara

    https://www.wordsfromcara.com/

Facebook Groups
    Anne Frank Book Collectors' Club

    https://www.facebook.com/groups/annefrankbookclub/

    Remembering Anne Frank

    https://www.facebook.com/groups/RememberingAnneFrank

Federica Pannocchia
    Un ponte per Anne Frank (A Bridge for Anne Frank)
    www.unponteperannefrank.org

Helaine Sawilowsky

https://HelaineSawilowsky.com

Nazi Concentration Camps in the Second World War

Mauthausen Memorial

https://www.mauthausen-memorial.org/en/History/The-Mauthausen-Concentration-Camp-19381945

Wikipedia

https://en.wikipedia.org/wiki/Appellplatz
https://en.wikipedia.org/wiki/Kapo_(concentration_camp)
https://en.wikipedia.org/wiki/List_of_Nazi_concentration_camps
https://en.wikipedia.org/wiki/Neuengamme_concentration_camp#Well-known_inmates
https://en.wikipedia.org/wiki/Theresienstadt_Ghetto

Nazi Persecution of the Jews (Germany)

Wikipedia

https://en.wikipedia.org/wiki/Nuremberg_Laws
https://en.wikipedia.org/wiki/The_Holocaust

The Netherlands during the World War Two (1940–1945) and Liberation (May 5, 1945)

NIOD Institute for War, Holocaust and Genocide Studies

https://www.niod.nl/en

Wikipedia

https://en.wikipedia.org/wiki/Anton_Mussert

https://en.wikipedia.org/wiki/Arthur_Seyss-Inquart
https://en.wikipedia.org/wiki/Dutch_annexation_of_German_
territory_after_the_Second_World_War
https://en.wikipedia.org/wiki/Dutch_famine_of_1944–45
https://en.wikipedia.org/wiki/February_strike
https://en.wikipedia.org/wiki/National_Socialist_Movement_in_the_
Netherlands
https://en.wikipedia.org/wiki/Netherlands_in_World_War_II
https://en.wikipedia.org/wiki/NIOD_Institute_for_War,_Holocaust_
and_Genocide_Studies
https://en.wikipedia.org/wiki/Wilhelmina_of_the_Netherlands

Opekta

Wikipedia

https://en.wikipedia.org/wiki/Opekta

Otto and Edith Frank

Anne Frank Foundation, Basel

https://www.annefrank.ch/en/family/edith-frank-hollaender
https://www.annefrank.ch/en/family/otto-frank

The Anne Frank Huis and Museum, Amsterdam

https://www.annefrank.org/en/anne-frank/main-characters/
edith-frank/
https://www.annefrank.org/en/anne-frank/main-characters/otto-frank/

Wikipedia

https://en.wikipedia.org/wiki/Edith_Frank
https://en.wikipedia.org/wiki/Otto_Frank

Persecution of the Jews in the Netherlands during World War Two

Anne Frank Huis and Museum, Amsterdam

https://www.annefrank.org/en/anne-frank/go-in-depth/
netherlands-greatest-number-jewish-victims-western-europe/
https://www.annefrank.org/en/anne-frank/the-timeline/#126

The Ellen Land Weber

http://ellenlandweber.com/rescuers/book/Strobos/Conditions.Holland.
html

Facing History and Ourselves

https://www.facinghistory.org/resource-library/text/anti-jewish-
measures-netherlands-and-belgium-between-1940-and-1944

Geni

https://www.geni.com/projects/Holocaust-in-the-Netherlands/18628

Kamp Westerbork Memorial

https://kampwesterbork.nl/en/the-persecution-of-the-jews/
timeline-of-the-persecution-of-the-jews

Montreal Holocaust Memorial Centre

https://www.ilholocaustmuseum.org/wp-content/uploads/2016/06/
Netherlands-Holocaust-History.pdf
https://erijswijk.blogspot.com/2012/02/jews-star.html

United States Holocaust Memorial Museum

https://encyclopedia.ushmm.org/content/en/article/the-netherlands

Wikipedia

https://en.wikipedia.org/wiki/History_of_the_Jews_in_the_
Netherlands
https://en.wikipedia.org/wiki/History_of_the_Jews_in_the_
Netherlands#The_Holocaust
https://en.wikipedia.org/wiki/Hollandsche_Schouwburg

Second World War Resources

United States Holocaust Memorial Museum

https://www.ushmm.org/

Wikipedia

https://en.wikipedia.org/wiki/Allied_invasion_of_Sicily
https://en.wikipedia.org/wiki/Italian_campaign_(World_War_II)
https://en.wikipedia.org/wiki/North_African_campaign
https://en.wikipedia.org/wiki/Operation_Market_Garden
https://en.wikipedia.org/wiki/Raid_of_the_Ghetto_of_Rome
https://en.wikipedia.org/wiki/Second_Battle_of_El_Alamein
https://en.wikipedia.org/wiki/Siege_of_Malta_%28World_War_II%29
https://en.wikipedia.org/wiki/The_Holocaust
https://en.wikipedia.org/wiki/Timeline_of_the_surrender_of_Axis_
forces_at_the_end_of_World_War_II

Secret Annex Helpers

Anne Frank Huis and Museum, Amsterdam

https://www.annefrank.org/en/anne-frank/main-characters/
bep-voskuijl/
https://www.annefrank.org/en/anne-frank/main-characters/jan-gies/
https://www.annefrank.org/en/anne-frank/main-characters/
johan-voskuijl/

https://www.annefrank.org/en/anne-frank/main-characters/johannes-kleiman/
https://www.annefrank.org/en/anne-frank/main-characters/miep-gies/
https://www.annefrank.org/en/anne-frank/main-characters/victor-kugler/

Joop van Wijk-Voskuijl (Bep Voskuijl)

www.annefranktheuntoldstory.com
www.bepvoskuijl.com
https://www.facebook.com/profile.php?id=100009179969779

Wikipedia

https://en.wikipedia.org/wiki/Bep_Voskuijl
https://en.wikipedia.org/wiki/Jan_Gies
https://en.wikipedia.org/wiki/Johannes_Hendrik_Voskuijl
https://en.wikipedia.org/wiki/Johannes_Kleiman
https://en.wikipedia.org/wiki/Miep_Gies
https://en.wikipedia.org/wiki/Victor_Kugler

Secret Annex Residents (The van Pels family and Dr. Fritz Pfeffer)

Anne Frank Huis and Museum, Amsterdam

https://www.annefrank.org/en/anne-frank/main-characters/auguste-van-pels/
https://www.annefrank.org/en/anne-frank/main-characters/fritz-pfeffer/
https://www.annefrank.org/en/anne-frank/main-characters/hermann-van-pels/
https://www.annefrank.org/en/anne-frank/main-characters/peter-van-pels/

Wikipedia

https://en.wikipedia.org/wiki/Fritz_Pfeffer

INDEX

relationship with Margot, 49, 114,
178, 181, 183, 246, 273n41,
297n114
revises her diary (May 1944), 105,
237, 278n49, 301n132.
*See also under Anne Frank: The Diary
of a Young Girl*
Frank, Edith Holländer, 8, 13–15, 21,
43, 45, 49, 74, 76, 91, 96–97,
100, 151, 180–81, 184, 201, 205,
236, 268n26, 272n26, 273n41,
299n120, 315n210
arrest (August 4, 1944), 20, 46,
78, 95, 113, 151, 181, 186,
201, 244, 267n22, 280n58,
284n69, 285n70, 295n106
death at Auschwitz (January 6,
1944), 80, 101, 202, 214
Frank, Fritzi, xvi, xxviii, 34–35, 201–
6, 212–16, 261n5, 307n168,
313n202
Frank, Margot, vii, xxxiv, xxxvii, 12–15,
17, 21, 45–46, 49, 52, 69–70,
75–76, 84–87, 91, 95, 100, 102,
105–6, 114, 126, 178–79, 181,
183, 185, 193–94, 198, 201,
229, 231, 236, 243, 246, 252,
255, 271n42, 272n36, 273n41,
280n58, 280n59, 287n76,
289n79, 291n86, 293n95,
296n107, 297n114, 299n120,
302n137, 303n142, 305n149,
312n192, 312n193, 312n195,
315n210, 316n217, 316n218
arrest (August 4, 1944), 78, 95,
113, 244, 267n22, 280n58,
284n69, 295n106
at Auschwitz-Birkenau, 14, 51–52,
101, 116, 190, 214, 227–30,
248–49, 287n78, 290n84,
299n124, 311n189

at Bergen-Belsen, xxxvii, 12, 14, 19,
52, 80, 84–86, 97, 99, 102,
116, 152, 200, 227–28, 230,
249, 256, 287n76, 289n79,
305n149, 311n189, 312n192,
312n192, 312n193
birth (February 16, 1926), 15, 44
call-up notice, 126, 179, 280n59,
291n86
death (February or March, 1945),
xxxvii, 84, 287n78
early education (Jekerschool, 1934–
1938), 46, 271n34
forced to go to the Jewish Lyceum
(1941–1942), xxxiv, 12, 46, 68,
194, 271n34, 271n35, 272n35,
293n95, 298n117, 298n117
secondary education (Gemeentelijk
Lyceum voor Meisjes, 1938–
1941), xxxiv, 271n34
writes her own diary in the Secret
Annex, 69, 114, 198, 246,
280n58, 285n69, 316n217
Frank, Otto, vi–viii, xxviii, 8, 13, 15,
20–21, 23, 34–35, 38, 43–46,
49, 66, 71–74, 76, 78, 87–88,
91, 93, 100, 102, 108, 115, 122,
140–43, 154–56, 160, 162, 179,
184, 192, 200–206, 211–16,
234, 236–37, 246–47, 255–56,
261n5, 264n12, 268n30, 272n36,
272n37, 273n41, 275n47, 276n49,
282n64, 283n66, 284n65,
284n69, 289n81, 289n83, 293n94,
294n101, 299n120, 300n124,
301n133, 304n149, 306n160,
306n161, 306n163, 307n165,
307n166, 307n168, 307n169,
308n175, 308n176, 310n183,
313n202, 314n204, 315n210

death (August 19, 1980), 88, 205, 215, 236–37, 244, 255, 314n204

edits and publishes Anne's diary (version C), 66, 97, 106, 117, 133, 155–56, 213, 278n53, 297n114, 301n133, 310n183

learns about his daughters' deaths (July 1945), 102, 202

love for photography, 46, 96, 289n83

marries Edith Holländer (May 12, 1925), 15, 44

marries Elfriede Geiringer (November 10, 1953), 206, 264n12

survives Auschwitz (January 27, 1945), 87, 273n41

visits by authors to, xvii–xviii, xxviii, 8, 34–35, 201–5, 212–14, 255, 261n5

Frank-Holländer, Edith. *See* Frank, Edith Holländer

Frankfurt am Main, 43, 268n26

G

Gafa,' Joy, xviii, 27–30, 125–33, 277n49, 277n49

Geiringer, Elfriede. *See* Frank, Fritzi

Gemeentelijk Lyceum voor Meisjes (Municipal Lyceum for Girls), xxxiv, 271n34

Germany, 44–45, 50–52, 178, 268n29, 269n30, 276n48

Enabling Act (1933), 44, 268n29

Gerrit van der Veen College, 157, 285n70

Gestapo, 151, 246, 284n69

Gies, Miep, xviii, 22, 34, 73, 75, 92, 182, 193, 198, 202, 204, 206, 269n30, 275n42, 279n53, 289n83, 305n155, 307n166, 314n207

Anne Frank's diaries and writings rescued by, 106, 267n22, 280n58, 285n69, 313n201

attempts to ransom the hiders of the Secret Annex, 284n69

visits by authors to, 34–35, 213, 261n5

Gies & Co., 269n30

Gillham, David, 99, 116, 248

Gold, Alison Leslie, 289n79

Goldstein-van Cleef, Ronnie, 79, 263n11

Goodrich, Frances, 143, 245, 262n9, 284n68, 296n116, 296n110, 314n207, 315n213, 316n215

Goslar, Hannah ("Hanneli"; also "Lies" in editions of *Anne Frank: The Diary of a Young Girl*), xxxiii, 9, 20, 55, 72, 85, 90, 98, 192–93, 228, 230, 289n79, 300n125, 312n194, 315n211

Goslar, Hanneli. *See* Goslar, Hannah ("Hanneli")

H

Hackett, Albert, 143, 245, 262n9, 284n68, 296n109, 296n110, 314n207, 316n215

Het achterhuis (Frank), xxxv, 3, 65, 138, 156, 262n9, 304n147

Hidden Life of Otto Frank, The (Lee), 140, 155, 266n17, 272n37, 274n42, 288n78, 289n80, 307n167, 308n176, 309n179

Hillesum, Etty, 103, 286n71

Hitler, Adolf, 44, 119, 127, 139, 177, 211, 255, 290n84, 313n199

Holländer-Frank, Edith. *See* Frank, Edith Holländer

Hollandsche Schouwburg (Jewish Theater, Amsterdam), 71, 157, 281n60

M

N

O

P